First World War
and Army of Occupation
War Diary
France, Belgium and Germany

38 DIVISION
Headquarters, Branches and Services
Royal Army Veterinary Corps
Assistant Director Veterinary Services
22 April 1914 - 5 April 1919

WO95/2544/3

The Naval & Military Press Ltd
www.nmarchive.com
Published in association with The National Archives

Published by

The Naval & Military Press Ltd

Unit 10 Ridgewood Industrial Park,

Uckfield, East Sussex,

TN22 5QE England

Tel: +44 (0) 1825 749494

www.naval-military-press.com

www.nmarchive.com

This diary has been reprinted in facsimile from the original. Any imperfections are inevitably reproduced and the quality may fall short of modern type and cartographic standards.

© Crown Copyright
Images reproduced by permission of The National Archives, London, England, 2015.

Contents

Document type	Place/Title	Date From	Date To
Heading	WO95/2544/3 Assistant Director Veterinary Services		
Heading	38th Division Asst Dir. Very Services Dec 1915-Apr 1919		
Heading	A.D.M.S. 38th Div Vol 1 Div Vol 1 Dec 15 Apr 19		
Heading	War Diary Of A.D.V.S. 38th. Division. From 1st. December 1915 To 31st. December 1915 (Volume I)		
War Diary	Winchester	01/12/1915	02/12/1915
War Diary	Sthmpton	02/12/1915	02/12/1915
War Diary	Havre	03/12/1915	04/12/1915
War Diary	Aire	05/12/1915	05/12/1915
War Diary	Rqt'oire	06/12/1915	20/12/1915
War Diary	St. Venant	21/12/1915	31/12/1915
Heading	A.D.V.S. 38th Div. Vol. 2 Jan 16		
War Diary	War Diary Of A.D.V.S., 38th Division From 1st. January 1916 To 31st January 1916 (Volume II)		
War Diary	St. Venant	01/01/1916	24/01/1916
War Diary	Lestrem	25/01/1916	31/01/1916
Heading	A.D.V.S. 38th Div Vol 3		
Heading	D.A.G., G.H.Q., 3rd. Echelon Base.	29/02/1916	29/02/1916
Heading	War Diary Of A.D.V.S. 38th. Division. From 1st. February 1916. To 29th February 1916. (Volume III)		
War Diary	Lestrem	01/02/1916	18/02/1916
War Diary	Locon	19/02/1916	29/02/1916
Heading	War Diary Of A.D.V.S. 38th. Division. From. 1st. March 1916 To 31st. March 1916 (Volume IV.)		
War Diary	Locon	01/03/1916	31/03/1916
Heading	War Diary Of A.D.V.S. 38th (Welsh) Division. From 1st. April 1916. To 30th April 1916 (Volume V.)		
War Diary	Locon	01/04/1916	10/04/1916
War Diary	La Gorgue	22/04/1914	30/04/1914
Heading	War Diary Of A.D.V.S. 38th. (Welsh) Division. From 1st. May 1916. To 31st. May 1916. (Volume) VI.		
War Diary	La Gorgue	01/05/1916	31/05/1916
Heading	War Diary Of A.D.V.S. 38th. (Welsh) Division. From 1st. June 1916. To 30th. June 1916. (Volume VII).		
War Diary	La Gorgue	01/06/1916	12/06/1916
War Diary	St. Venant	13/06/1916	15/06/1916
War Diary	St. Michel	16/06/1916	26/06/1916
War Diary	Le Mellard	27/06/1916	30/06/1916
Heading	War Diary Of A.D.V.S. 38th. (Welsh) Division From 1st. July 1916 To 31st. July 1916 (Volume VIII.)		
War Diary	Le Meillard	01/07/1916	01/07/1916
War Diary	Rumempre	02/07/1916	02/07/1916
War Diary	Lealvillers	03/07/1916	03/07/1916
War Diary	Treux	04/07/1916	05/07/1916
War Diary	Morlancourt	10/07/1916	11/07/1916
War Diary	Treux	12/07/1916	12/07/1916
War Diary	Pont-Remy	13/07/1916	15/07/1916
War Diary	Couin	16/07/1916	29/07/1916
War Diary	Bus	30/07/1916	31/07/1916

Miscellaneous	General Staff, 38th. Division.	01/09/1916	01/09/1916
Heading	War Diary Of A.D.V.S. 38th. (Welsh) Division. From 1st. August 1916 To 31st. August 1916. (Volume IX.)		
War Diary	Esquelbecq	01/08/1916	21/08/1916
War Diary	St Sixte	22/08/1916	31/08/1916
Heading	War Diary Of A.D.V.S. 38th. (Welsh) Division From 1st. September 1916. To 30th. September 1916. (Volume X)		
War Diary	St. Sixte	01/09/1916	29/09/1916
War Diary	War Diary Of A.D.V.S. 38th. (Welsh) Division From 1st. October 1916. To 31st October 1916. (Volume XI)		
War Diary	St. Sixte	01/10/1916	31/10/1916
Heading	War Diary Of A.D.V.S. 38th. (Welsh) Division From 1st. November 1916. To 30th November 1916 (Volume XII)		
War Diary	St Sixte	01/11/1916	30/11/1916
War Diary	War Diary Of A.D.V.S. 38th. (Welsh) Division From 1st. December 1916. To 31st. December 1916. (Volume XIII)		
War Diary	St. Sixte	01/12/1916	14/12/1916
War Diary	Esquelbecq	15/12/1916	31/12/1916
Heading	War Diary Of A.D.V.S. 38th. (Welsh) Division From 1st. January 1917. To 31st. January 1917. (Volume XIV)		
War Diary	Esquelbecq	01/01/1917	11/01/1917
War Diary	St. Sixte	22/01/1917	31/01/1917
Heading	War Diary Of A.D.V.S. 38th. (Welsh) Division From 1st. February 1917. To 28th. February 1917. (Volume XV.)		
War Diary	St Sixte	01/02/1917	28/02/1917
Heading	War Diary Of A.D.V.S. 38th (Welsh) Division From 1st March 1917. To 31st. March 1917. (Volume XVI)		
War Diary	St Sixte	01/03/1917	31/03/1917
War Diary	War Diary Of A.D.V.S. 38th. (Welsh) Division From 1st. April 1917. To 30th. April 1917. (Volume XVII.)		
War Diary	St. Sixte	01/04/1917	30/04/1917
Heading	War Diary Of A.D.V.S. 38th. (Welsh) Division. From 1st. May 1917. To 31st. May 1917. (Volume XVIII)		
War Diary	St. Sixte.	01/05/1917	31/05/1917
Heading	War Diary Of A.D.V.S. 38th. (Welsh) Division. From 1st. June 1917. To 30th. June 1917. (Volume XIX)		
War Diary	St Sixte	01/06/1917	07/06/1917
Operation(al) Order(s)	33rd. Infantry Brigade No. G. 934	10/02/1918	10/02/1918
War Diary	Vox Vrie Camp	14/06/1917	16/06/1917
War Diary	Vox Vrie Farm.	17/06/1917	28/06/1917
War Diary	Fontes	30/06/1917	30/06/1917
Heading	War Diary Of D.A.D.V.S. 38th. (Welsh) Division. From 1st. July 1917. To 31st. July 1917. (Volume XX.)		
War Diary	Fontes	01/07/1917	20/07/1917
War Diary	Proven	21/07/1917	21/07/1917
War Diary	Dragon Camp.	23/07/1917	31/07/1917
Heading	War Diary Of D.A.D.V.S. 38th. (Welsh) Division. From 1st. August 1917. To 31 August 1917. (Volume XXI)		
War Diary	Dragon Camp	01/08/1917	06/08/1917
War Diary	Proven	07/08/1917	19/08/1917

War Diary	Dragon Camp	30/08/1917	31/08/1917
War Diary	War Diary Of D.A.D.V.S. 38th. (Welsh) Division. From 1st. September 1917 To 30th. September 1917. (Volume XXII).		
War Diary	Dragon Camp	01/09/1917	11/09/1917
War Diary	Proven	12/09/1917	13/09/1917
War Diary	Estaires	14/09/1917	17/09/1917
War Diary	Croix Du Bac	18/09/1917	30/09/1917
Heading	War Diary Of D.A.D.V.S. 38th (Welsh) Division. From 1st October 1917. To 31st October 1917 (Volume XXIII)		
War Diary	Croix Du Bac	01/10/1917	31/10/1917
Heading	War Diary Of D.A.D.V.S. 38th. (Welsh) Division. From 1st. November 1917. To 30th. November 1917. (Volume XXIV).		
War Diary	Croix Du Bac	01/11/1917	30/11/1917
Heading	War Diary Of D.A.D.V.S. 38th. (Welsh) Division. From 1st. December 1917. To 31st. December 1917. (Volume XXV.)		
War Diary	Croix Du Bac	01/12/1917	31/12/1917
Heading	War Diary. Of D.A.D.V.S. 38th (Welsh) Division. From 1st. January 1918. To 31st. January 1918. (Volume XXVI.)		
War Diary	Croix Du Bac	01/01/1918	15/01/1918
War Diary	Merville	16/01/1918	31/01/1918
Heading	War Diary Of D.A.D.V.S. 38th. (Welsh) Division. From 1st. February 1918. To 28th. February 1918. (Volume XXVII)		
War Diary	Merville	01/02/1918	15/02/1918
Heading	War Diary Of D.A.D.V.S. 38th. (Welsh) Division. From 1st. March 1918. To 31st. March 1918. (Volume XXVIII)		
War Diary	Steenwerck	01/03/1918	31/03/1918
War Diary	War Diary Of D.A.D.V.S. 38th (Welsh) Division. From 1st. April 1918. To 30th. April 1918. (Volume XXIX)		
War Diary	Merville	01/04/1918	02/04/1918
War Diary	Toutencourt	03/04/1918	12/04/1918
War Diary	Contay	13/04/1918	30/04/1918
Heading	War Diary Of D.A.D.V.S. 38th. (Welsh) Division. From 1st. May 1918. To 31st. May 1918. (Volume XXX)		
War Diary	Contay	01/05/1918	06/05/1918
War Diary	Toutencourt	07/05/1918	30/05/1918
War Diary	Herissart	30/05/1918	31/05/1918
Heading	War Diary Of D.A.D.V.S. 38th. (Welsh) Division. From 1st. June 1918. To 30th. June 1918. (Volume XXXI)		
War Diary	Herissart	01/06/1918	05/06/1918
War Diary	Lealvillers	06/06/1918	30/06/1918
Heading	War Diary Of D.A.D.V.S. 38th. (Welsh) Division. From 1st. July 1918. To 31st. July 1918. (Volume XXXII)		
War Diary	Lealvillers	01/07/1918	31/07/1918
Heading	War Diary Of D.A.D.V.S. 38th. (Welsh) Division. From 1st. August 1918. To 31st. August 1918. (Volume XXXIII).		
War Diary	Lealvillers	01/08/1918	25/08/1918
War Diary	Headauville	26/08/1918	26/08/1918
War Diary	Bouzincourt	27/08/1918	27/08/1918

War Diary	W.12.a	28/08/1918	28/08/1918
War Diary	W.12.a.central sheet 57D.	29/08/1918	31/08/1918
Heading	War Diary Of D.A.D.V.S. 38th (Welsh) Division. From 1st. September 1918. To 30th September 1918. (Volume XXXIV)		
War Diary	Ancre	01/09/1918	02/09/1918
War Diary	A.15.a.2.4. Sheet. 57.a.	03/09/1918	04/09/1918
War Diary	S.14.c.3.7 Sheet 57.c.	05/09/1918	09/09/1918
War Diary	Le Transloy	10/09/1918	12/09/1918
War Diary	Rocquigny	13/09/1918	14/09/1918
War Diary	V.1.k.8.8	15/09/1918	30/09/1918
Heading	War Diary Of D.A.D.V.S. 38th (Welsh) Division. From 1st. October 1918. To 31st. October 1918. (Volume XXXV)		
War Diary	V.1.b.8.8. Sheet 57c.	01/10/1918	02/10/1918
War Diary	Sorel-Le-Grand	03/10/1918	08/10/1918
War Diary	X.18.c.9.5. Sheet 57c	09/10/1918	12/10/1918
War Diary	Bertry	13/10/1918	22/10/1918
War Diary	Troisvilles	25/10/1918	26/10/1918
War Diary	K.17.c.1.1	27/10/1918	31/10/1918
Heading	War Diary Of D.A.D.V.S. 38th. (Welsh) Division. From 1st November 1918. To 38th. November 1918. (Volume XXXVI)		
War Diary	Montay	01/11/1918	05/11/1918
War Diary	Wagonville	07/11/1918	07/11/1918
War Diary	Englefontaine	08/11/1918	08/11/1918
War Diary	Locquignol	09/11/1918	10/11/1918
War Diary	Awlnoye	11/11/1918	30/11/1918
Heading	War Diary Of D.A.D.V.S. 38th. (Welsh) Division. From 1st. December 1918. To 31st. December. 1918. (Volume XXXII)		
War Diary	Aulnoye	01/12/1918	11/12/1918
War Diary	Berlaimont	12/12/1918	21/12/1918
Heading	War Diary Of D.A.D.V.S. 38th. (Welsh) Division. From 1st. January 1919. To 31st. January 1919. (Volume XXXVIII)		
War Diary	Neuvilly	01/01/1919	01/01/1919
War Diary	Masnieres	02/01/1919	02/01/1919
War Diary	Malancourt	03/01/1919	03/01/1919
War Diary	Meaulte	04/01/1919	04/01/1919
War Diary	Lahoussoye	05/01/1919	15/01/1919
War Diary	Querrieu	16/01/1919	31/01/1919
Heading	War Diary Of D.A.D.V.S. 38th. (Welsh) Division. From 1st. February 1919. To 28th. February 1919. (Volume XXXIX)		
War Diary	Querrieu	01/02/1919	28/02/1919
Heading	War Diary Of D.A.D.V.S. 38th (Welsh) Division From 1st March, 1919 To 31st March, 1919 (Volume XL)		
War Diary	Querrieu	01/03/1919	30/03/1919
Heading	War Diary Of D.A.D.V.S. 38th (Welsh) Division From 1st April, 1919 To 5th April, 1919. (Volume XLI)		
War Diary	Querrieu	01/04/1919	05/04/1919

60165/2544/3

Assistant Director Nutrition Services

38TH DIVISION

ASST DIR. VETY SERVICES

DEC 1915 – APR 1919

A.S.V.S. 3965tri-
Vol I

8cbl/161

Dec 15
ap 19

CONFIDENTIAL

WAR DIARY

OF

A. D. V. S.   38th. DIVISION.

FROM 1st. DECEMBER 1915 To 31st. DECEMBER 1915

(VOLUME I.)

INTELLIGENCE SUMMARY
of
A.D.V.S., 38th. Division.

Place	Date	
Winchester.	1/12/15.	Received orders to prepare to proceed overseas.
''	2/12/15.	Marched out of Camp with Div. Hd. Qrs. 10th. 13th. &14th Welsh Regts. Tsp. of 15th. Welsh Regt, 114th. Inf. Bd. Hd Qrs. and 2 Cos. of Div. Train.
Sthmpton		Arrived Southampton at 3.30.P.M., all horses embarked by 6.30.P.M, without accident.
Havré	3/12/15.	Arrived outside Havre about 5.A.M., got alongside of Wharf at 8.A.M. Disembarked all animals by 12.15.P.M. without accident, although Slings and Derrick had to be resorted to in five or six cases as several animals would not leave the bottom deck. Proceeded to Rest Camp and remained there until midnight, at which time we left and marched to Point 3.
''	4/12/15.	Completed entraining by 2.30.A.M.
Aire	5/12/15.	Arrived at Aire at 6.30.A.M. and proceeded by road to Roquetoire and got into our billets. Arranged to hire Forge for shoeing Horses of Hd.Qrs. at F.2 per day including Coal.
Rqt!oire.	6/12/15.	Visited the Units of the Div. which had arrived previous to us, and arranged for Veterinary attendance.
''	7/12/15.	Arranged for Office, and occupied in Office routine. The 49th. M.V.S. attached to this Div. arrived and I arranged Billets for them.
''	8/12/15.	Called on AD.D.V.S. 1st. Army at Aire and Consulted him about sending in Returns and other matters relating to the routine of my work. Received copy of Standing Orders of 1st. Army (Veterinary) for my guidance.
''	9/12/15.	Office routine.
''	10/12/15.	Prepared Weekly Returns and held conference with V.Os. of the Div.
''	11/12/15.	Received intimation that the 1st. Artillery and 10th. Div. AMM. Coln. had been attached to this Div.

(2)

INTELLIGENCE SUMMARY.
of
A. D. V. S. 38th. Division.

Place	Date	
Rqt'oire	12/12/15	Received visit from D.D.V.S. 1st. Army who informed me that the Lahore Division were moving from there area & were going to evacuate some animals through the 49th. M.V.S., as they were unable to procure trucks.
"	13/12/15	Inspected animals of Divl. Signal Co, at H.Q., & found them improving after there Sea and Railway journey.
"	14/12/15	Visited 2nd. London Bde., Artillery, at Boesinghem & met Lieut. Townsend, A.V.C., Veterinary Officer to the Brigade. Inspected all cases in his sick lines and ordered two to be evacuated.
"	15/12/15	Visited H.Q., London Artillery interviewed C.R.A, & met Lieut. Heaney, A.V.C. Veterinary Officer to the 1/1st. Brigade of London Artillery. Inspected animals in his sick lines and ordered one horse with poll evil to be evacuated. The animals in this Bde., were for the most part in poor condition. Made enquiries re. scale of feeding & was informed that latterly they had not been receiving their full amount, but representations having been made in the proper quarter, they were now receiving their full scale. Received visit from D.D.V.S., 1st Army, who indicated his intention of inspecting the 10th. Divisional Ammunition Column with me. Arranged for inspection to take place the following day. Telephoned Bde/major Headquarters, R.A., London Artillery & arranged to have animals of this Column paraded at 2-15 p.m., the following day.
"	16/12/15	In company with D.D.V.S., 1st. Army, inspected the animals of the 10th. D.A.C., at MOLLINGHEM, Brigadier General, R.A., being present. <u>No. 1 Section.</u> Animals in this Section are in a very

(3)

INTELLIGENCE SUMMARY
of
A. D. V. S.   38th.   Division.

Place	Date.	
Rqt'oire	16/12/15.	Contd. poor condition. Coats are dirty and scurfy, and in some cases patches of skin are bereft of hair, due to rubbing against fixed objects, and biting themselves, to relieve irritation. Probably due to Lice, as many eggs were visible. On enquiry, was informed grooming kit had been burned, prior to the unit becoming attached to this Division, by order of V.O., on account of skin disease. Instructions were given to indent for grooming kit at once. Evacuated nine animals for Debility and eleven animals for suspected Mange and Debility.

No.2 Section. Animals in this Section are somewhat better in condition and cleaner in the coats, although leaving much to be desired. Evacuated seven animals for Debility.

No.3 Section. Animals in this Section are very similar (perhaps a shade better) to those in No.2. Evacuated seven for Debility.

"	17/12/15	Visited 14th. Bn. Welsh Regt., at CRECQUE, inspected Transport animals. Ordered one case of Laminitis to be evacuated. Prepared weekly returns and held conference of V.O's in the Division, including those of the First London Artillery.
"	18/12/15	Received instructions from Divisional Headquarters to prepare to move into another area. Inspected Transport animals of 19th. Pioneer Regt. Found them in fair condition, only one case of Lameness (slight).
"	19/12/15.	Morning occupied in preparing for early departure from this area. Afternoon proceeded to St. Venant, by Motor car to inspect billets, those intended for M.V.S., are not very satisfactory, but as it was

INTELLIGENCE SUMMARY
of
A.D.V.S. 38th. Division.

Place	Date	
Rqt'oire	19/12/15	Contd. dark, I was unable to obtain any better.
"	20/12/15	Departed from Roquetoire at 8-30 a.m., by motor car
St. Venant	"	Arrived at St. Venant at 9-15 a.m.
"	21/12/15	Office Routine and arranging for posting of V.O's to units.
"	22/12/15	With Major General, G.O.C., Division, inspected the 10th. D.A.C., animals show some improvement. Visited MERVILLE and inspected Remounts arriving for Division. *Circular* Issued to Veterinary Officers with Division, re evacuation of animals early, and not leaving them behind as in the case in the recent move.
"	25/12/15	Learned that the 1st. and 4th., Bdes., London Artillery had moved to RINCQUE and GLOMINGHEM. O/c., M.V.S, received instructions to proceed to area recently vacated and collect animals left behind.
"	23/12/15	O.C., M.V.S., reported sick, arranged for M.O., to visit and report, wired D.D.V.S., 1st Army. Office Routine.
"	24/12/15	O.C., M.V.S., resumed duty. Visited St. Floris and Cpalonne and inspected horse standings for animals under treatment or awaiting evacuation. Arranged for these billets to be secured.
"	25/12/15	Xmas Day.
"	26/12/15	Inspected animals of 14th. Bn. Welsh Regt., with V.O., i/c (Lieut. Howard, A.V.C.) Took scrapings from horses suspected to be effected with Mange and submitted same to O.C., Bactl. Labty., for microscopical examination.
"	27/12/15	Received intimation from Lieut. Howard, that he was confined to bed with Diarrhoea. Wired D.D.V.S., 1st Army and requested M.O. to visit and report. Received

INTELLIGENCE SUMMARY
of
A. D. V. S.   38th. Division.

Place	Date	
St. Venant	27/12/15	Contd. Intimation from O.C. Bactl. Labty., that scrapings examined showed no parasite. Inspected all animals in the 119th. Brigade, R.F.A., which arrived yesterday. Found all animals in good condition all well groomed. Shoeing good, especially those of the Brigade Ammunition Column, which were excellent.
"	28/12/15	Visited 120th., 121st., 122nd. Brigades, & 38th. Divl. Ammunition Column, which have been arriving during the past few days from ENGLAND and arranged for Veterinary attendance.
"	29/12/15	Received a report that carcase of horse was lying aboved ground at LE CORBIE, alleged to have been left there by London Artillery. Arranged for M.V.S., to bury same. Office Routine.
"	30/12/15	Made a tour of inspection of animals in sick lines in the 115th. Infantry Brigade, also the 333rd. Co. A.S.C, and 131st. Field Ambulance, with Lieut. Howard, A.V.C., Veterinary Officer i/c.
"	31/12/15	Visited Mobile Veterinary Section. Held conference with Veterinary Officers in this Division and Office Routine.

Acad. 38ᵃ str:
Vol. 2
Va > 16

CONFIDENTIAL

WAR DIARY

OF

A. D. V. S., 38th. DIVISION

FROM

1st. JANUARY 1916

TO

31st. JANUARY 1916

(VOLUME II.)

(1)

INTELLIGENCE SUMMARY
of
A. D. V. S., 38th. Division.

Place	Date	
St. Venant.	1/1/16.	Office Routine. Received visit from D.D.V.S., 1st. Army.
" "	2/1/16.	Inspected Sections No. 1,2, & 3 of the 38th. D.A.C, alsp "C" Batt: 121st. Bde. R.F.A. Animals in good condition, but showing signs of the long sea & rail journey.
" "	3/1/16.	Office Routine.
" "	4/1/16.	Went to LESTREM & LA GORGUE interviewed A.D.V.S., 19th. Divn., at the former & A.D.V.S., Guards Divn., at the latter. Conferred relative to arrangements re Units being transferred to & from the different areas.
" "	5/1/16.	Visited 119th. Bde. R.F.A, inspected all animals, the latter in excellent condition. Sergt. Brady, A.V.C., reported at my office with Lieut. T. Finch, A.V.C, to be examined in his knowledge in animal management, in consequence of complaint from G.O.C, R.A. Found his knowledge in this subject very inadequate. Decided to report the D.D.V.S., on the matter, and recommend his transfer for further training.
" "	6/1/16.	Visited & inspected animals in 120th. Bde. R.F.A.
" "	7/1/16.	Visited D.D.V.S., 1st. Army, & consulted him with reference to various matters in connection with the Division. Held conference of V.O's in afternoon.
" "	8/1/16.	Visited 121st. Bde. B.A.C., by request of Lieut. Finch, A.V.C, & examined a horse suspected of Glanders. Found perforation of Septum Nasi. Injected ~~1 c.c. Mallein subtaneous~~. 1 c.c. Subtaneously.
" "	9/1/16.	Visited 121st. Bde. B.A.C, & examined horse injected with Mallein the day previously, found no reaction whatever. Visited D.D.V.S, 1st. Army, & arranged with him to examine a horse referred to on the following day. Held enquiry on charge

(2)

INTELLIGENCE SUMMARY

of

A. D. V. S., 38th. Division.

Place	Date	
St. Venant.	9/1/16.	of Sergt. Stickland, A.V.C, for neglect of duty, preferred by Lieut. W. Tully Christie, A.V.C. Finding Sergt. Stickland, A.V.C, guilty of carelessness in missing his train when in charge of a conducting party to ABBEVILLE & failing to deliver his descriptive roll, remanded pending enquiry from No. 22, Vety. Hospital, relative to the truth of otherwise of statements made by Sergt. Stickland, A.V.C, in reference to the latter.
"	" 10/1/16.	Visited 121st. Bde. B.A.C, with D.D.V.S, 1st. Army, examined horse under suspicion, decided to destroy & make post mortem. Post mortem revealed an absence of Nodules in the Lungs or any other legions of Glanders, except the aforementioned perforation of the Septum Nasi, which in my opinion was a traumatic lesion.
"	" 11/1/16.	Met D.D.V.S., 1st. Army, by appointment & proceeded to 49th. Mobile Vety. Section, where the method of Palprebal testing was demonstrated to all V.O's in the Division by the D.D.V.S, 1st. Army.
"	" 12/1/16.	Visited MERVILLE & attended conference with Supply Officer, at the office of A.A.Q.M.G., XI Corps, in reference to feeding of animals. Office Routine.
"	" 13/1/16.	Visited & inspected animals 16th. Bn. Welch Regt, 11th. Bn. S.W.B, 151st. Field Co. R.E., which had been tested the previous day. No reactions. Also visited 131st. Field Ambulance.
"	" 14/1/16.	Visited M.V.S., and CALONNE, collecting station. Conference of Divisional Vety. Officers in afternoon, Office Routine.
"	" 15/1/16.	Visited LESTREM & LOCON, with A.D.V.S., 19th. Divn, also 30th. M.V.S., made arrangements for movement into this area.

(3)

INTELLIGENCE SUMMARY
of
A. D. V. S., 38th. Division.

Place	Date	
St. Venant	16/1/16.	Visited 49th. M.V.S., in morning. Office routine in afternoon. Pte. Goodwin, A.V.C., 49th. M.V.S., paraded, & charged with disobedience & insolence to an N.C.O, found guilty & awarded 7 days C.B. and forfeit 7 days pay.
"	" 17/1/16.	Inpsected H.Q., horses, prescribed for 6, with injuries. Orderly room at 3 o'clock at my office Sergt. Stickland, A.V.C., was paraded for sentence in connection with the charge for neglect of duty, which was remanded pending enquiries from No. 22, Vety. Hospital. Award reduce to rank of Tempy. Corporal.
"	" 18/1/16.	Office Routine in the morning. Received visit from A.D.V.S., 19th. Division, and together visited 49th. M.V.S.
"	" 19/1/16.	Visited the 330th. Co. A.S.C., 129th. & 130th Field Amb, & 124th. Field Co. R.E., made an inspection of animals with Lieut. J. Macfarlane, A.V.C., V.O. i/c. Found everything satisfactory.
"	" 20/1/16.	Received intimation from D.D.V.S., 1st. Army, that No. 794 Sergt. Brinning, A.E., A.V.C, had been posted to "C" Batt: Bde. 121st. R.F.A., in lieu of Sergt. Brady, A.V.C, who was instructed to proceed ABBEVILLE for further training. Sent for O/C., 49th. M.V.S., and admonished him in connection with the conduct of his duties.
"	" 21/1/16.	Visited 121st. Bde. R.F.A., and examined a case of Tetanus, with Lieut. T. Finch, A.V.C., also another case, which this Officer was doubtful about in connection the Mallein test. Also visited and examined several cases in the 122nd. Bde. R.F.A, with the V.O.i/c. Lt. Finch, A.V.C. Conference with Veterinary Officers of this Division, in afternoon.

(4)

INTELLIGENCE SUMMARY
of
A.D.V.S., 38th. Division.

Place	Date	
St. Venant.	22/1/16.	Inadvertently got some information concerning O.C., 49th. M.V.S., Sent a message for him to parade at my office at 3 o'clock. At 2 o'clock I received a communication, desiring to be relieved from his Command as O.C., as he found he was unfitted for it. At 3 o'clock he paraded, & explained his reasons, which were that he avoided riding, having lost his nerve in a smash up at Salisbury, expressed his desire to be transferred to a Station Vety. Hospital, where riding was not essential
" "	23/1/16.	Sent memorandum to Major General, Commanding this Division, concerning the scale of food at present being issued to animals. Visited D.D.V.S. 1st. Army, .
" "	24/1/16.	Moved into our new area, occupying billets vacated by the 19th. Division.
LESTREM.	25/1/16.	Notified D.D.V.S., 1st. Army, of change of office and informed him of the 49th. M.V.S., remaining until the 27th. at St. VENANT. Received visit from Lieut. Finch, A.V.C, who desired me to visit & consult with him with reference to an animal in "D" Batt: 122nd. Howitzer Bde. Proceeded with this Officer to CORBIE & examined the animal, my opinion, was no reaction whatever. While there, examined the animals in Battery, found them in excellent condition, shoeing & grooming above the average.
"	26/1/16.	Office Routine.
"	27/1/16.	Acting on instructions from G.O.C., of this Division, visited No. 3 Sec., 17th. Reserve Park & inspected the animals, found the majority of them in very poor condition, very tired & jaded in appearance. Reported the matter fully to the G.O.C., 38th. Divn., sending a copy to the D.D.V.S., 1st. Army.

INTELLIGENCE SUMMARY
of
A. D. V. S., 38th. Division.

Place	Date	
LESTREM	28/1/16.	Re visited No. 3 Sec., 17th. Reserve Park, & arranged for evacuation, 17 animals. Visited M.V.S., at thier new billet in this area, they having arrived the previous day.
"	29/1/16.	Visited, O.C., 49th. M.V.S., Office Routine. Received instructions that Lieut. J. M. Culhane, A.V.C posted for duty to this Division, Lieut. W. Tully Christie, A.V.C., transferred to No. 13, Base Veterinary Hospital, and Lieut. P. Howard, A.V.C., posted as Officer Commanding, 49th. Mobile Vety., Section.
"	30/1/16.	Accompanied by Lieut. Percy Howard, A.V.C., visited 49th. M.V.S., and arranged for Lieut. Howard, A.V.C, to take Command of that Section. Lieut. J. M. Culhane A.V.C., arrived and reported for duty. Posted to the 113th. Infantry Brigade.
"	31/1/16.	Lieut. W. Tully Christie, A.V.C., departed from this Division to join No. 13 Base Veterinary Hospital. Accompanied by D.D.V.S., 1st. Army, inspected No. 3 Section, 17th. Reserve Park.

Major. A.V.C.
A.D.V.S., 38th. Division.

A.D.V.S.
38 D 3
Vol 3.

V405/4

D.A.G.,
  G.H.Q.,
    3rd. Echelon Base.

      I herewith enclose Original War Diary, of
A.D.V.S., 38th. Division, for month ending
February 29th. 1916., Volume 3, please.

                                                        Major. A.V.C.
February 29th. 16.   A.D.V.S., 38th. Division.

C O N F I D E N T I A L

WAR   DIARY

OF

A. D. V. S., 38th. DIVISION.

FROM

1st. F E B R U A R Y   1916.

TO

29th. F E B R U A R Y   1916.

(V O L U M E   III)

(1)

INTELLIGENCE SUMMARY
of
A.D.V.S., 38th. Division.

Place	Date.	
Lestrem.	1/2/1916.	Visited CALONNE, MERVILLE & LA GORGUE in search of stationery gone astray & made enquiries at M.F.O's. Stationery arrived in afternoon by messenger.
"	2/2/1916.	Office Routine. Arranging for Veterinary Officers to take over Veterinary charge of Units billeted in the new area.
"	3/2/1916.	Visited 49th. M.V.S., in morning. Office Routine.
"	4/2/1916.	Conference with Veterinary Officers in afternoon Office Routine.
"	5/2/1916.	Visited and inspected 26th. Battery, 2nd. Heavy Brigade, R.G.A., animals in a good condition. Standings very much in need of renewing. Grooming indifferent. Recommended animals to be clipped trace high, more attention to grooming and standings to be renewed. 1 case Laminitis, 1 case Suspected Mange, 1 very bad Rope Gall. Instructions given to evacuate these animals. Strength of animals 119. Visited 35th. Heavy Batt: strength in animals 181 horses. Animals in a very good condition also standings and shoeing good. Ordered 1 horse with Laminitis to be evacuated and to clip all animals trace high. Visited 2nd. Heavy Bde. Ammunition Column, attached to 26th. Battery, R.G.A. Strength 52. Condition good. Standings and grooming good. Shoeing fair. 2 shoeing smiths sick. Farrier Sergt. working in shoeing forge only. 2 slight cases in sick lines. Brigade Ammunition Column, attached 35th. Heavy Bde., strength 50 horses, all of which were in excellent condition. Standings good, shoeing good.

(2)

INTELLIGENCE SUMMARY
of
A.D.V.S., 38th. Division.

Place	Date.	
Lestrem	5/2/1916.	Contd. Recommended all horses to be clipped trace high. No animals in sick lines. 1st. Siege Batt: Strength 103, 91 in lines and 12 away. Condition fair. Standings fair. 1 case Laminitis ordered to be evacuated. 3 other horses lame N.Y.D. Recommended clipping trace high.
"	6/2/1916.	Visited M.V.S. in morning. Sergt. S. Hart, A.V.C. arrived and posted for duty to 49th. M.V.S. Office Routine.
"	7/2/1916.	Visited 1st. Siege Co., in response to telegram received. Examined horse, disease Grease. Visited 49th. M.V.S.
"	8/2/1916.	Visited B.A.C., 119th. Bde. R.F.A., examined 1 horse suspected Mange. Gave instructions for animal to be evacuated.
"	9/2/1916.	Inspected 119th. Bde. R.F.A., & B.A.C., Sub. Sections "A" Condition fair, standings fair. 1 horse tucked up, recommended this animal to be put out of work and treated generously. Sec. "B" Similar to "A". Sections "C" & "D" similar to "A". 1 Cracked heel in "D" lines, gave instructions for animal to be put out of work. 2 Greys and 2 Bays in sick lines B & C. Visited 49th. M.V.S., and confirmed O.C., decision to destroy horse with Open hock joint. Animal sent to BETHUNE for destruction at Abbatoir, price realised Fr. 130.

(3)

INTELLIGENCE SUMMARY
of
A.D.V.S., 38th. Division.

Place	Date	
Lestrem.	10/2/1916.	Office Routine. Prepared a report to A.A.Q.M.G., 38th. Division, re Ration scale of Animals.
"	11/2/1916.	By appointment, met O.C., 17th. Reserve Park, and accompanied with O.C., 38th. Divl. Train, inspected animals in No. 3 Section, of this Unit. Conference with Veterinary Officers in afternoon.
"	12/2/1916.	Office Routine.
"	13/2/1916.	Visited 13th. Bn. R.W.F., strength 7 L.D., 6 H.D., 12 R., 37 Mules, Total 62. Condition good, standings bad. 16th. Bn. R.W.F., 8 H.D., 5 L.D., 12 R., 38 Mules, condition good, standings bad. 13th. Bn. Welsh Regt., 9 H.D., 5 L.D., 29 Mules, 11 R., Condition good, shoeing good, standings fair. 10th. Bn. Welsh Regt., 9 H.D., 5 L.D., 29 Mules, R 10. Condition good. 15th. Welsh Regt., 9 H.D., 7 L.D., 25 Mules, 11 R, Condition fair, standings bad. 14th. Bn. Welsh Regt., 7 H.D., 4 L.D., 28 Mules 13, R., condition poor, animals feeding off the ground. No Nose bags, signs of neglect. Very unsatisfactory.
"	14/2/1916.	Visited FOSSE and LOCON Mobile Veterinary Section stations. Office Routine.
"	15/2/1916.	Visited Royal Wilts. Yeomanry, examined a horse picked up nail, pared out foot, ordered evacuation. Visited M.V.S.
"	16/2/1916.	Visited Animals in 38th. Division Headquarters and M.M.P. Received visit from A.D.V.S., 35th. Division.
"	17/2/1916.	Office Routine. Visited M.V.S. outpost at LOCON. Ordered new standings to be fixed.

(4)

INTELLIGENCE SUMMARY
of
A.D.V.S., 38th. Division.

Place	Date.	
Lestrem	18/2/1916.	Change of Office from Lestrem to LOCON. Conference with Veterinary Officers in afternoon.
Locon.	19/2/1916.	Office Routine. Inspected animals in Division Headquarters and M.M.P.
"	20/2/1916.	Visited 10th. S.W.B., who have just moved into a new area, and billet. Animals in good condition. Premises left in a filthy condition by outgoing Unit. Visited 11th. Bn. S.W.B., animals not in such good condition. Evacuated Major Dalton's horse, being very lame. Visited 17th. Bn. R.W.F., condition of animals excellent. Very satisfactory. 1 bad kick in forearm. 16th. Bn. Welsh Regt., condition of animals fair. Visited LOCON Mobile Veterinary Section outpost. Received intimation from C.R.A., that 2nd. Indian R.H.A., are now attached to this Division.
"	21/2/1916.	Visited 15th. Bn. Cheshire Regt., 105th., Bde., 35th. Division, horses in good condition. Visited 13th. & 15th. Bn. Welsh Regts., of 38th Division. Prepared distribution for 2nd. Indian R.H.A., and 105th. Infantry Bde., to Veterinary Officers.
"	22/2/1916.	Visited M.V.S., in morning. Held enquiry re case Pte. Strudwick, A.V.C., for refusing to obey an order given by a superior Officer. To be tried by Court Martial.
"	23/2/1916.	Office Routine.

(5)

INTELLIGENCE SUMMARY
of
A.D.V.S., 38th. Division.

Place	Date.

Locon.   24/2/1916.   Visited B.A.C., 122nd. Howitzer Bde., condition fair, standings fair. 5 cases P.U.N. Visited "A" Battery 122n.d Howitzer Bde., condition a little better. Visited Sec. 3., 38th. D.A.C., standings very bad, and also horses are hard worked and long hours. Condition fair. Visited Headquarters, D.A.C., standings good, condition good, ordered to be evacuated 2. Sec. 2., D.A.C., standings very bad, condition fair. Sec. 1. D.A.C., condition good, standings bad. Ordered to be evacuated 2. Visited 49th. M.V.S., inspected float horse, which met with an accident with motor car. Wound near hind quarter, very deep, 15 inches long. Severing the triceps muscles. Fearfl it will have to be destroyed. Forwarded a report to A.A. & Q.M.G., in connection therewith.

"   25/2/1916. F.G. Court Martial on Bte. Strudwick, A.V.C., awarded 56 days, No. 1 Field punishment. Conference with Veterinary Officers in afternoon.

"   26/2/1916. Office Routine.

"   27/2/1916. Visited 49th. Mobile Veterinary Section. Office Routine.

"   28/2/1916. Visited "D" Battery, 119th. Bde. R.F.A., strength 128 horses, condition excellent. Standings and shelter all that could be desired. 4 slight cases in sick lines. Visited B.A.C., 121st. Bde., condition excellent. 1 horse suspected with Mange. Had just been clipped. Directed, that the animal should be washed and evacuated.

INTELLIGENCE SUMMARY
of
A.D.V.S., 38th. Division.

Place	Date	
Locon.	28/2/1916.	Contd. Visited "C" Battery, 121st. Bde. R.F.A., animals in good condition, standings and shelter excellent. Recommended clipping trace high. "B" Battery, 121st. Bde. R.F.A., condition, standings and shelter not so good. 2 or 3 cases suspicious cases of skin disease. Gave instructions for isolation, clipping and washing pending further inspection. 3 bad cases of kicks. B.A.C., 119th. Bde., R.F.A., Animals, standings and shelter excellent. This Column showed signs of very careful management. Everything *excellent* and all that could be desired.
"	29/2/1916.	Visited 49th. Mobile Veterinary Section, and inspected animals prior to their evacuation. Office Routine.

Major. A.V.C.
A.D.V.S., 38th. Division.

ADVS 38D3 Vol 4

CONFIDENTIAL

WAR DIARY

OF

A. D. V. S. 38th DIVISION.

FROM

1st. MARCH 1918

TO

31st. MARCH 1918

(VOLUME IV.)

-:-:-:-:-:-:-

[signature]
MAJOR,
A.D.V.S. 38th (WELSH) DIVISION.

(1)

INTELLIGENCE SUMMARY
of
A. D. V. S. 38th. Division.

Place	Date	
LOCON.	1/3/1916.	Inspected 120th. Bde. R.F.A. B.A.C; Condition good, standings fair. 3 or 4 cases in sick lines of little importance. This unit shows careful management in the care of animals, harness, feeding etc. Inspected 129th. Field Amb; standings fair, animals only in fair condition. Recommended that they should be clipped trace high, no animals in sick lines. Also inspected 131st. Field Amb; condition good, standings fair, no animals in sick lines. Visited and inspected X. Battery, R.H.A; temporarily attached to this Division. Strength 240 horses and 10 mules. Condition of animals excellent. Standings deplorable. Inspected 204th. Co. R.E. 35th. Divn; most of the animals out working. 2 bad cases of picked up nails in sick lines. Ordered evacuation. Inspected 123rd. Co. R.E; standings excellent, 4 or 5 cases suspected skin disease took scrapings, gave instructions for animals to be clipped and washed with mild solution of disinfectant.
"	2/3/1916.	Visited and inspected B.Battery, 120th. Bde. R.F.A, standings good, condition excellent. 5 cases of Lice, ordered clipping and washing with a mild solution of disinfectant. Inspected D.Battery, 120th. Bde. R.F.A, condition good, with the exception of 1, which as ordered to be evacuated; Debility. Visited M.V.S.
"	3/3/1916.	Visited A.D.V.S. 35th. Division in reference to

(2)

INTELLIGENCE SUMMARY
of
A. D. V. S. 38th. Division.

Place	Date	
LOGON	3/3/1916.	304th. Co. R.E. which is at present is located in our area. Conference of Veterinary Officers.
"	4/3/1916.	Visited collecting station M.V.S. Office Routine.
"	5/3/1916.	At the request of Lieut. J. Culhane, A.V.C. V.O. i/c visited the 114th. Inf. Bde. H. Qrs; & examined horse suspected with skin disease. Diagnosed Lice, gave necessary instructions for washing and clipping. Visited 19th. Pioneer Bn; and inspected 1 mule and 1 horse suspected with skin disease, gave instructions for their evacuation.
"	6/3/1916.	In consequence of a report from the G.O.C. R.A; a horse was lying on a farm with a broken leg, instructed Lieut. J. Macfarlane, A.V.C; to proceed to the place & examine, destroy if necessary, and report. Report received the animal belonged to 33rd. Division, leg not broken, but suffering acoute pain, from a punctured wound in the shoulder which had become septic. Notified A.D.V.S. 33rd. Divn.. Received a reply from C.R.A. in answer to enquiries made by me in reference to Sergt. Yallop, A.V.C; to the effect that the aforesaid Sergt: had been tried by F.G.C.M. for disobeying an order given by his superior Officer & found guilty, penalty awarded 6 months imprisonment with hard labour & to revert to the ranks, which was commuted by the G.O.C. R.A, to 3 months Field punishment No. 1 and to revert to the ranks. Issued instructions to O.C. 49th. M.V.S. to transfer his section from place at present located, to LOGON from the 7th. instant.

INTELLIGENCE SUMMARY
of
A. D. V. S. 38th. Division.

Place.	Date
LOCON	7/3/1916.	48th. M.V.S. moved into new billets at LOCON. Office Routine.
"	8/3/1916.	In compliance with a circular received from D.D.V.S. First Army, called on the Mairie, LOCON, and informed him that as far as practicable in cases of illness of animals belonging to the Civil Population arrangements would be made for their treatment when called upon, also informed him that meat inspection and sanitation would be carried out where possible by the Veterinary Officers of this Division.
"	9/3/1916.	Inspected the 19th. Pioneer Bn; and found many animals scratching and biting in a suspicious manner. Addressed a memorandum to the A.A. & Q.M.G 38th. Division, asking if anything could be done to obtain a Stewart Clipping Machine and thus enable this Unit to clip all their animals (68 in number) and have them washed with a weak solution of disinfectant. I pointed out the urgency of this matter & the altogether inadequate provision of clipping machines for a Battalion with such a large number of animals, provided by War Est'ment.
"	10/3/1916.	Inspected meat in slaughter house at LOCON. Conference of Veterinary Officers.
"	11/3/1916.	Accompanied by Lieut. Macfarlane A.V.C. V.O. i/c of the 330th. Co. A.S.C, inspected this Unit. Total strength 264, condition excellent, well groomed & well shod, evidence of care in stable management. Clipping of animals proceeding, standings bad, new ones in course of construction, percentage of

INTELLIGENCE SUMMARY
of
A.D.V.S. 38th. Division.

Place	Date	
LOGON	11/3/1916.	animals in sick lines high, principally from punctured wounds, kicks and picked up nails. Also inspected animals sent from the 10th. Division to this Unit, very poor miserable specimens.
"	12/3/1916.	Visited and inspected 157th. Bde. R.A.C. & 35th. D.A.C. 35th. Division, but found that a Vety. Officer of that Division in charge, therefore I did not proceed with the inspection. Inspected 16th. Bn. R.W.F; in consequence of memorandum received from G.O.C. 113th. Infantry Bde. Found the hoofs of animals in many instances much too long. Animals crowded into buildings, altogether unsuitable, no ventilation, atmosphere VITIATED and offensive. Sent Memorandum to G.O.C. 113th. Infantry Bde. drawing his attention to these matters and making certain recommendations for his consideration and communication to Commanding Officers of Battalions in his Brigade.
"	13/3/1916.	Visited 176th. Tunnelling Co, at GORRE, found Unit had left the area, leaving 1 horse behind with P.U.N., evacuated same. L/Sergt. G. Murray, A.V.C. reported for duty with 120th. Bde. R.F.A.
"	14/3/1916.	Visited 49th. M.V.S, and examined 2 animals which arrived in a very poor condition, ordered destruction for both. Received notification that 5 horses belonging to 121st. Bde. R.A.C. were drowned in the canal LA BASSEE.
"	15/3/1916.	Received visit from D.D.V.S. First Army, who inspected 49th. M.V.S, and billets. Received a reply from A.A. & Q.M.G, with memorandum from XIth. Corps

(5)

INTELLIGENCE SUMMARY
of
A.D.V.S. 38th. Division.

Place	Date	
LOCON	15/3/1916.	declining to supply Stewart Clipping machine for 19th. Pioneer Bn. Forwarded the correspondence to D.D.V.S. First Army.
"	16/3/1916.	Inspected 13th. Bn. Welsh Regt, at GORRE, animals in good condition, standings good, recommended clipping, was informed that clipping machines had been indented for on 3rd. Feby. and had not yet been received. Made representations to D.A.D.O.S. to hasten. Inspected the 15th. Bn. Welsh Regt, animals not so good in condition found one eating his food off the ground. 1 case of Laminitis evacuated. Inspected 14th. Bn. Welsh Regt, condition good, standings good, 1 case of Grease in sick lines, to be evacuated. Inspected 151st. Co. R.E, animals in good condition except 3, these were doing very hard work, carting materials to the trenches, recommended extra diet.
"	17/3/1916.	Issued circular to all Vety. Officers in reference to evacuation of animals, when disease is so far advanced as to render the destruction the only course open, and reminding them of their duty to evacuate all cases which are likely to prove serious as soon as possible after the occurence. Conference of Vety. Officers.
"	18/3/1916.	Visited 129th. Field Amb; and inspected 21 animals remainder being at work. Animals mostly poor in condition, feet neglected, hair too long, coats ragged and bare patches from rubbing. Lice present. Itching badly

INTELLIGENCE SUMMARY
of
A.D.V.S. 38th. Division.

Place	Date	
LOCON	18/3/1916.	ventilated, dirty and unsuitable. Forwarded report to A.D.M.S. 38th. Divn, with recommendations concerning these matters.
"	19/3/1916.	Inspected animals No. 3 Section 17th. Reserve Park; standings bad, no bricks, shoeing good, condition fair, many animals still unfit, although recommended to do so on the 17th. January 1916.
"	20/3/1916.	Office Routine.
"	21/3/1916.	Visited 35th. Heavy Battery. R.G.A; Investigated cases of Colic. 3 animals were dead, two having recovered. Enquired into the watering and feeding, proceeded to BETHUNE and arranged for floats to come and remove the animals to Knackery for post mortem examinations. Made post mortem examinations on one, which arrived at dusk. Found contents of stomach fluid, large quantity of undigested food in the large Colon, congested mucous patches in the large bowels. Death due to Asphyxia, ~~from~~ to Flatulent Colic.
"	22/3/1916.	Visited Knackery at BETHUNE and made P.M. exam. on the other two animals, found similar conditions existing.
"	23/3/1916.	Forwarded Memorandum to O.C. 2nd. Heavy Bde. R.G.A, in reference to this outbreak of Colic with recommendations for future ~~drinking~~ guidance
"	24/3/1916.	Office Routine. Conference of Vety. Officers.
"	25/3/1916.	Office Routine. Visited 48th. M.V.S, and inspected the animals under treatment and for evacuation.
"	26/3/1916.	Office Routine. Visited 48th. M.V.S,. Issued circular to Vety. Officers in reference to Colic

(7)

INTELLIGENCE SUMMARY
of
A.D.V.S. 38th. Division.

Place.	Date	
LOCON	26/3/1916.	and its sequelea and drawing their attention to the necessity of their being present as frequently as possible when the animals in their Units are being watered and fed, as Colic is due as a rule to irregularities occuring during these operations.
"	27/3/1916.	Inspected 35th. Heavy Batty; R.G.A, animals looking well, shoeing good, grooming good.
"	28/3/1916.	Inspected 26th. Heavy Baty; R.G.A, condition of animals excellent, shoeing good, grooming good. Also inspected 26th. Ammunition Column, animals condition good, except one, special diet ordered for this one. Inspected 1st. Siege Batty; R.G.A, animals good in condition, standings good, evacuated 3 horses, (1 suspected skin disease, 1 Lame kick, 1 Shiverer.) Inspected 2nd. London Batty; horses is fair condition, animals feeding off the ground, reasons given short of nose bags.
"	29/3/1916.	Visited XIth. Corps H.Qrs; inspected H.Qr. animals also those of Sections Signal Co. Animals excellent in condition.
"	30/3/1916.	Visited 38th. Divisional Mounted Troops, inspected animals in accordance with instructions from D.D.V.S. First Army, in consequence of their leaving this area to join the First Cavalry Divn. for training. Evacuated 16, majority Lame, and kicks, 1 Roarer, 1 Dropped sole. Sent 6 to M.V.S. for treatment.
"	31/3/1916.	Office Routine. Conference of Vety. Officers.

MAJOR,
A.D.V.S. 38th (WELSH) DIVISION.

CONFIDENTIAL.

WAR DIARY.

OF

A. D. V. S.   38th. (Welsh) Division.

FROM

1st. APRIL 1916.

TO

30th. APRIL 1916.

(VOLUME V.)

-:-:-:-:-:-:-:-:-

MAJOR.
A.D.V.S. 38th (WELSH) DIVISION.

WAR DIARY or INTELLIGENCE SUMMARY

Army Form C. 2118

(Erase heading not required.)

Instructions regarding War Diaries and Intelligence Summaries are contained in F. S. Regs., Part II and the Staff Manual respectively. Title Pages will be prepared in manuscript.

Place	Date	Hour	Summary of Events and Information	Remarks and references to Appendices
LOCON	1/4/16		Visited 35th D.A.C. 4 soldiers tendons animals in No 2 section sore. Evacuated 1 horse mad 1 mule for debility and lymphatic membrane and 1 horse gutted. Section 3 tendons excellent, shoeings good, cassette 1, cassette with flexor 1, cassette bad cassettes 1. Visited on transit Acutyt section, tendons feet, cassette 1, sore back. Visited A.D.V.S. 39th Division at LESTREM.	
"	2/4/16		Visited 25th Div. H.Q. The 9th Div. trainings good, tendons fair. None of the far mare allowed to good too long. Visited 155th Bn R.F.A. animals feet shoeing regular, attention animals clipping. Visited 16th Br R.F.A. animals in good condition, shoeing fair, animals clipped to assist as rapid improvement. Visited 14th Br R.F.A. tendons excellent, shoeing good, 1 sore tongue (tetanus) stopped, wounds and hocks.	
"	3/4/16		Visited 49th M.I.B. Visited 10th Bn Welsh Regt. Animals in good condition, shoeing good. Clipping fair. Visited 15th Bn Welsh Regt. Animals fair in condition. 1 very bad cassette. Stirrup bar. Visited 14th Bn Welsh animals fair clipping proceeding. New transport officer. Visited 13th Bn Welsh animals in the whole good, clipping proceeding.	
"	4/4/16		Visited 1st Bn L.W.B. animals on the whole fair. Shoeing requires attention. Visited 16th Bn Welsh Regt. Animals condition good. No transport officer at present. Shoeing neglected, feet too long. Lent attention to my mules who narrow clipping.	

1875 Wt. W593/826 1,000,000 4/15 J.B.C. & A. A.D.S.S./Forms/C. 2118.

WAR DIARY or INTELLIGENCE SUMMARY

Army Form C. 2118

(Erase heading not required.)

Instructions regarding War Diaries and Intelligence Summaries are contained in F. S. Regs., Part II. and the Staff Manual respectively. Title Pages will be prepared in manuscript.

Place	Date	Hour	Summary of Events and Information	Remarks and references to Appendices
LOCON	2/4/16	10 AM	Horses shifted to fresh standing. Moved to South and finishing line. Visited 103rd Bn. S&B. Animals fit in condition and turned out over the floor. No foot information can be extracted. Visited 19th Bn. P.H.T. Animals in good condition, showing good record of veterinary management.	
"	3/4/16		Visited "B" Batt. 122nd Heavy Bde. - Tradition fair. Standings good. Shoeing moderate. Feet too long. Shoeing good. Office Routine.	
"	6/4/16		Inspection of animals in 38th Division, by A.D.V.S. First Army.	
"	7/4/16		Continuation of inspection of animals in 38th Division, by A.D.V.S. First Army.	
"	8/4/16		Completion of inspection of animals in 38th Division, by A.D.V.S. First Army.	
"	9/4/16		Office Routine.	
"	10/4/16		Office Routine.	
"	11/4/16		On leave of absence to April 18th, 1916.	
"	15/4/16		Change of Hdqrs. to La Gorgue, on 17-4-16.	
LA GORGUE	19/4/16		Returned to Duties and resumed duty.	
"	20/4/16		Office Routine. Visited 19th Reserve Pk. Animals improving. Standings good. Results 1512 by DGE.	
"	21/4/16		Animals in good condition.	
"			Confirmed Veterinary Officers. Office Routine.	

WAR DIARY
or
INTELLIGENCE SUMMARY

Army Form C. 2118

Place	Date	Hour	Summary of Events and Information	Remarks and references to Appendices
LA GORGUE	22/4/16		Office Routine. Infected animals in 38 Division - 4 Ox.	
"	23/4/16		Visited 38th Bat Signal Co. Hastings intelligent, battalion fast.	
"	24/4/16		Inspected Royal Welsh Yeomanry. 1 horse very hot — in condition — want of attention. Cow growing. Condition fast. Other 2 Coys condition fast. Stampings fast. All animals showing signs insomnia. Harnesses dirty (horses) head Res 16 condition chiefly bone. Visited 19 Army Bus. Horse Co. Shiny good, condition good. Stampings good. Visited 49th M.T.C.	
"	25/4/16		Office Routine.	
"	26/4/16		Visited 15th Bn Welsh Regt. Stampings good, condition fast. Visited 10th Bn Welsh Regt Stampings bad, Sanitation good. 1 animal Lame, shot wound. Horse 10th J.A.B. trimmers in need sanitation, with the exception of one, to be censured for Vice. Stampings good. Visited H.Q. Rich train, condition good. Harness fair. Large amount of cases on sick lines. Principally P.W.N. & Galls. Arranged for that to be sent to MERVILLE for shoes, met with accident R3 121 F. field ambulance.	
"	27/4/16		Visited 10th Bn Welsh Regt. Remounts shoed, Lame, inspected. Horse 13th Bn Welsh Regt animals in stops, placed to be put outside, condition fast, not improving.	

WAR DIARY or INTELLIGENCE SUMMARY

Army Form C. 2118

Place	Date	Hour	Summary of Events and Information	Remarks and references to Appendices
LA GORGUE	27/4/16	10 a.m.	Inspected 14th Bn. Welsh Regt. Lines, men & gun, considerable improvement. Inspected 15th Bn. R.W.F. Animals & condition good. Turnout not efficient and horses flatter in flesh, very unsatisfactory. Men lookings alert & smart.	
"	28/4/16		Saw landings sent 114th Bn S.W.B. bedding good, landings good. 16 Batt. R.W.F. Bedding good, condition of animals good.	
"	29/4/16		Conference of Veterinary Officers. Office routine.	
"	30/4/16		Inspected all sections of 38th D.A.C. Animals in for 2 and 3 horses shows considerable improvement. Casualties & 3 animals for various causes. Office routine. Inspected 445th Co. (Army Troops) R.E. Animals in excellent condition.	

X. M. Baldwin
MAJOR,
A.D.V.S. 38th (WELSH) DIVISION.

CONFIDENTIAL

WAR DIARY

OF

A.D.V.S. 38th. (WELSH) DIVISION.

FROM

1st. MAY 1916.

TO

31st. MAY 1916.

(VOLUME) VI.

-:-:-:-:-:-:-:-:-:-:-:-:-:-:-:-

[signature]
Major. A.V.C.
A.D.V.S. 38th. (Welsh) Division.

WAR DIARY
or
INTELLIGENCE SUMMARY

Army Form C. 2118

Place	Date	Hour	Summary of Events and Information	Remarks and references to Appendices
LA GORGUE	1/5/16		Visited 49th Mobile Vety Section. Office Routine.	
	2/5/16		Visited "F" Battery 120th Bgde R.F.A. Condition of animals excellent, except 2 rather poor and lousy. Harmonical clipping. Shoeings good. Shoeing fair. 1 horse nearly shod and the fore nail of his leg cast. Legs rather lame. Slight heat, fret and cut and molested. Visited "D" Battery 122 Btte. R.F.A. Animals good. Shoeings fast, condition 4 or 5 rather poor, shoeing not good. Feet allowed to grow too long. Visited "L" Battery 120th Bgde. R.F.A. Condition excellent. Small 2 which were rather poor, but receiving special attention. Visited B.A.C. 121st Bde. R.F.A. Animals only fair, one the whole rather poor, seals rough, shoeing bad. Gave instructions for 2 ferry hocks to be stopped. Visited "B" Battery 120th Bde. R.F.A. Animals fat, condition shoeing fair. Standings fair. Visited "D" Bde. R.F.A. Animals met to good. Condition rather poor. Evacuate on for Details. 2 hind and 2 fore weak, gave instructions to see them shod, and make note. Shoeing good. Visited B.A.C. 120th Bde R.F.A. Condition good. Shoeing good. 2 animals evacuated for Details.	
	3/5/16		Visited MDVS 19th Division	
	4/5/16		Visited 49th Mobile Vety Section. Office Routine	
	5/5/16		Visited 10th Fd. Am. S.A.B. Standings dry and good. H.D. horses excellent. Mules very good. Park Mules	

Army Form C. 2118

WAR DIARY
or
INTELLIGENCE SUMMARY
(Erase heading not required.)

Place	Date	Hour	Summary of Events and Information	Remarks and references to Appendices
LA GORGUE	5/5/16	(CONTD)	Conference Veterinary Officers. Office Routine. Lieut F. M. Buchan A.V.C. went on leave today arranged for Vety	
"	6/5/16		car at his units	
"	7/5/16		Attended Conference at A.D.V.S. Attended at D.D.V.S. Zeist Army Office.	
"	8/5/16		Visits 49 Mobile Vety Section. Office Routine	
"	9/5/16		Inspected animals on Division Hd Qrs. & been signed for. Animals in	
			good condition. Standings good. Saw instructions to the 49 M.V.S. to	
			give his new fort with lime weekly and mounted and occasionally.	
"	10/5/16		Visits 1293 Field Amb. Animals condition fair. 1 horse dies since met 50	
			long. Evidence of lameness to numbering in foot feet that animal taken to	
			forge and gave the necessary instructions to Farrier	
"	11/5/16		Office Routine. Visits 49 Mobile Vety Section	
"	12/5/16		Examined report to D.D.V.S. Zeist Army, on Duties and Mess Berne	
			Orderlies. Conference Veterinary Officers	
"	13/5/16		Office Routine. Visits 49th M.V.S.	
"	14/5/16		Lieut F. M. Buchan A.V.C. returned from leave. Office Routine.	
"	15/5/16		Visits "A" Battery 121st R.A. on return from LAMBRES, 1 lieuten fore	
			& other sections inspected. Some horses dangerously poor. Firmenich on	
			Stoppage of work. Debital diet, chaffes hay, crushed oats and a little	
			corrot followed declaration of inquiry. Examined Lame horse, Just shot removed,	

WAR DIARY
INTELLIGENCE SUMMARY

Army Form C. 2118

Instructions regarding War Diaries and Intelligence Summaries are contained in F. S. Regs., Part II. and the Staff Manual respectively. Title Pages will be prepared in manuscript.

(Erase heading not required.)

Place	Date	Hour	Summary of Events and Information	Remarks and references to Appendices
LA GORGUE	15/5/16	(Contd)	Foot inspection. Farrier's report to D.O.V.S. sent repeated matter to A.D. + D.V.S. Inspected "D" Battery 121 Bde. R.F.A. Condition good, shoeing good. Inspected "E" Battery 121 Bde. R.F.A. Condition good with few exceptions.	
	16/5/16		Visited 16th Bn. Welsh Regt. Condition fairly good. Standings in open, and very 2 animals sick. Visited 17th Bn. R.W.F. Animals in good condition. Standings good. Visited 19th Welsh Fld Section.	
	17/5/16		Visited Hd. Qrs 70th Section, 1st Echelon R.A.C. Animals newly debited and classified. Standings good. Animals look well. Appearance of care and attention. Visited No. 1 Section 1st Bridging Train. 30 H.D. + 5 P. All animals looking well. 1 horse very bad head. Acute Laminitis etc. to Mis. Unit and notified him to send the case for treatment to M.V.S.	
	18/5/16		Visited Divn. H Qrs + Signal Co. — Animals in good condition. Standings good. Lieut How Magarian A.V.C. went on leave, arranged for Maj. care of his Unit.	
	19/5/16 20/5/16		Visited by Welsh Vety Section. Office Routine. Conference Veterinary Officers. Corresponded with B.E.F. + Act. A.D.V.S. First Army inspected "B" Battery 121 Bde. R.F.A. 30 animals were picked out and put on separate lines for feeding with authority. 2 evacuated for debility, 1 evacuated by D.R.P. old + worn out	

Army Form C. 2118

WAR DIARY or INTELLIGENCE SUMMARY

(Erase heading not required.)

Place	Date	Hour	Summary of Events and Information	Remarks and references to Appendices
LA GORGUE	21/5/16		Visited 47th Reserve Park at CAUDISCURE (not in this area) in reference to mare received from 6.O.V.S. First Army. The animal had received from Belso prior to my arrival, but was suffering from front, sound & P.U.N. Had feet pared out & gave instructions for further treatment. Left instructions at Vety. attendance was required to commence with one.	
	22/5/16		Inspected "B" Battery 121 Bde. R.F.A. Putting up new shed about from the others for feet animals. Face contaminations to the S.D. Dépôt not effect being passed, with regard to having of grazing land at to obtain green forage in accordance with memo. received from 6.O.V.S. also consultation with S.S.O. 38th Division. Visited "B" Battery 121 Bde. R.F.A. which had just returned from LAMBRES. Animals were fatigue and showed signs of having had harder work but with the exception of 2 or 3 were in fair condition, very different from "A" Batt, on its return from LAMBRES. Visited "E" Batt. 119 Bde. R.F.A. which is proceeding to LAMBRES to-morrow for training purposes. Condition of animals very good. Gave orders for one animal with broken hill not to go.	
	23/5/16		Visited "B" Batt. 119 Bde. — condition of animals good. Shoeings good. Shoeing good: 10 or 5 horses shod. Operate and receiving plenty attention, satisfactory. Visited "D" Batt. 119 Bde. R.F.A. Condition good.	

Army Form C. 2118

WAR DIARY
or
INTELLIGENCE SUMMARY
(Erase heading not required.)

Place	Date	Hour	Summary of Events and Information	Remarks and references to Appendices
LA GORGUE	23/5/16	cont'd	Standings good. Shoeing requires attention, but the long number of animals suffering from thrush and old galls, which indicates picketing lines are not kept clean. Visited "B" Bty. 119 Bde. Condition excellent, with 1 or 2 exceptions. Animals in little over-crowded standings, requiring another standing during dry weather. Visited the Res 119 Bde. Condition only fair. 1 or 2 rated feet in condition recommended more attention in the care of their animals. Sent short to 346 119 Bde B=9.	
	24/5/16		Visited 114th Fld. Machine Gun Co. Just arrived in the country. Animals shod in condition. Shoeing very bad. Feet for long only one had been let to dice animals. 2 men have been sent for training in field shoeing to MSG. 1 case tetanus & 2 cases ringworm. Visited 10 Bn. Welsh Regt. Condition of animals excellent. Shoeing good. Officers charger lame. Visited 14th Bn. Welsh Regt. Condition of animals greatly improved. Shoeing good. Visited 13th Bn. Welsh Regt. Visited 15th Bn. Welsh Regt. Condition very good. Shoeing good. Great improvement. Visited 115 3 Bde. Machine Gun Co. Truly arrived. Animals in rather condition than the other two. Shoeing bad. No sickness.	
	25/5/16		Visited Animals in Recn. Rm. Res. & Recn. Signal Co. Office Routine.	

Army Form C. 2118

WAR DIARY
or
INTELLIGENCE SUMMARY
(Erase heading not required.)

Instructions regarding War Diaries and Intelligence Summaries are contained in F.S. Regs., Part II. and the Staff Manual respectively. Title Pages will be prepared in manuscript.

Place	Date	Hour	Summary of Events and Information	Remarks and references to Appendices
LA GORGUE	26/5/16		Visited 38th Divisional Artillery Details, resulting from breaking up of Brigade Ammunition Columns.	
"	27/5/16		Visited 19th Mobile Vety Section. Found Pow. Section O.a.b. 38th Divt Artillery Details, inspected. Stallions excellent. Animals very good. Animals first to departure to the Base on 28/5/16. Lieut John Maydwell A.V.C. returned from leave.	
	28/5/16		Visited 38th Divn Details and inspected all animals departing to C.P.V.S at 8 a.m.	
	29/5/16		Office Routine. Visited "D" Battery 121 Bde. R.F.A. inspected animals referred to another part of the Diary. Out of 20 animals put aside for special treatment 10 have sufficiently improved to occupy their old positions in the lines. Remainder do not show much improvement.	
	30/5/16		Visited 130th Field Ambulance. Lieut J. Laurie. A.V.C. who is on sick leave. Examined & described 2 cases on sick lines. Animals in good condition except two sick 19th Mobile Vety Section.	
	31/5/16		Visited 130th Field Ambulance. Evacuated sick animal to M.V.S. to be Initial for Scoviette Mange. Office Routine.	

D.D.V.S./Forms/C. 2118.

CONFIDENTIAL

WAR DIARY

OF

A.D.V.S. 38th. (WELSH) DIVISION.

FROM

1st. JUNE 1916.

TO

30th. JUNE 1916.

(VOLUME VII.)

-:-:-:-:-:-:-:-:-:-:-:-:-:-

[signature]
Major. A.V.C.
A.D.V.S. 38th. (Welsh) Division.

Army Form C. 2118.

WAR DIARY
or
INTELLIGENCE SUMMARY.
(Erase heading not required.)

Instructions regarding War Diaries and Intelligence Summaries are contained in F. S. Regs., Part II. and the Staff Manual respectively. Title pages will be prepared in manuscript.

Place	Date	Hour	Summary of Events and Information	Remarks and references to Appendices
LA GORGUE	1/6/16		Visited 130th Field Ambulance — Animals feet in condition. Visits ???? officer ?????.	
"	2/6/16		Visited 131st Field Ambulance — Animals excellent condition. Visits ????? ???? ???. Exercise of animals — 1 case practised want lock (????? ?????? were) ?????? riding officer.	
"	3/6/16		Visited 10th Bn L.A.B. — Harness leather. Harness condition recommended lifting ???? ???? animals. Moves ????????? to the feet. ??????? the ????? ???. Visited 115th ???? the Horses lost in the harness and harness only feet 1 saw horses alias 1½ ????. Seeing that ??????????? lift A.V.C. 38th Division not offered to "A" Battery 121st Bn R.I.A. was arranged to inspect what shall be inspected. Interview M/the Coloner B.B. re visit to ????? ????? ?? ??????.	
"			visit of inspection. Battery 121st Bn 3.F.B. suggested that he should visit all official to observe ??? feeding and watering animals. He wishes have not influence officers to undertake this. Visits G' Battery 131st Bn B.F.B. also Battery commenced found no horses.	

Army Form C. 2118.

Instructions regarding War Diaries and Intelligence Summaries are contained in F. S. Regs., Part II. and the Staff Manual respectively. Title pages will be prepared in manuscript.

WAR DIARY
or
INTELLIGENCE SUMMARY.
(Erase heading not required.)

Place	Date	Hour	Summary of Events and Information	Remarks and references to Appendices
LA GORGUE	5/6/4		and 4 points in bagon tents 10 hours 1500 feet in condition, long [illegible] and thirty have oft on phonol line 2 miles 100 feet in condition, 2 sphd horses on wagon lines very feet had condition. Units 2 shown to be had cond. the First had [illegible] First station 12 animals grazing these three have [illegible] placing sufficient room grown - but only 1 target 3 posts or 3 ft. high 3 small [illegible] of where Not established [illegible] 1 small high. 1 Target behind 3 - 3 Muzzy Garrets he commands he general name of men to be sent to a kint of instruction in shoeing interviewed Mayor Gerald A.E. B" Buriah are men who are inspection of "g" Batty. 121 A Bn. R.F.A.	
	6/6/4		Office Routine. Units eg : Weeks vety practical.	
	11/6/4		Lance 155th Kernish drivers limber attached to 82nd Division formed strength ditto 1 case puncture wound on foot 1 case continued lameness solution 19th Brinol B.N. Shoeings good, placing good. artillery good.	
	14/6/4		Office Routine. Units eg : Weeks Veterinary control	

Army Form C. 2118.

WAR DIARY
or
INTELLIGENCE SUMMARY.
(Erase heading not required.)

Instructions regarding War Diaries and Intelligence Summaries are contained in F.S. Regs., Part II. and the Staff Manual respectively. Title pages will be prepared in manuscript.

Place	Date	Hour	Summary of Events and Information	Remarks and references to Appendices
LA GORGUE	9/6/16		Officer posting features William Morris	
	10/6/16		Inter to be sent to Canada inviting 7 minerals 1 sent etc	
			Units 49 & Middx Regt relief Canada arrived back to evacuation	
	11/6/16		To reach B" Batty. 121" Bde. R.F.A. Parties infantry in invitation	
			Units 49 N.F.S. South A.O.13 61st Division	
	12/6/16		Divisional move to ST. VENANT as resting place for 3 days. Office	
			Parties.	
ST. VENANT	13/6/16		Received visit from B.R.I.S. East Army front to my detachment to	
			anchor Army	
			Units RUSNES composite M.M.P — 49" M.G.S.	
	14/6/16		Visited 49" Middx 25th Section starting at ST FLORIS Billeting Matron	
			Visits Section to 28" R.O.b. B" Battery 121 Bde - B" 122 Bde Twice	
			Batteries 119" Bde. 127" Bde 127" Bde 9 F.A. Evacuates 5 losses	
	15/6/16		Divisional move from ST VENANT to BOELLECOURT and ST MICHEL here	
			S.A.A.S. 2nd Army Hart of arrival	
			Visited 33rd and 23rd Hos. a/c and inspected arriving Trainings Interviewed	
ST. MICHEL	16/6/16		Asst Admt. J.C.E. 38" Divn. + A.A. "app.2" with reference to training opt issued	

Army Form C. 2118.

WAR DIARY
or
INTELLIGENCE SUMMARY.
(Erase heading not required.)

IV

Instructions regarding War Diaries and Intelligence Summaries are contained in F. S. Regs., Part II. and the Staff Manual respectively. Title pages will be prepared in manuscript.

Place	Date	Hour	Summary of Events and Information	Remarks and references to Appendices
ST MICHEL	16/6/16		Troughs and steam and cond. Phone at list of units not yet numbered required, and forwarded to A.A. + Q.M.G. Units 89th M.T. yet covered on their not told. ST MICHEL	
"	17/6/16		Visit Oxen Re Res + Agent for Veterinary Visit to more the stallions at Arsenal courtyard. Visit B.O.T.S. Tenth Army. Fixed instructions re Relieves etc.	
	18/6/16		Visit 6" Section. 19th Field Park attend 15 + 28th Division Supplies. Most of the animals are out. Francais Forage 3 Flies. 105 H.D. in Sub Line. Cavalry 2 uns – 2 Quartel. Leonard Louis in Sub Line. 1 Lambressis in Borcut. Visit Battalion 19th Field Park Francais B. Jutton. 3 Fries 105 H.R. Meetings good condition forward Cavalry 1 tone R+N Lens city summons. Two instructions to marinate. Visit 3rd Corp Artillery visit 129th Field Artillery. Battalion park. Issues potato haricot again which they ask to be fixed. Learned 1 horse Called horodogum which was circulated to the Vert. 1 horse Mourin on this avenue was circulated – was stretched mistreated for light dust. suffering from Colica on arrival.	

Army Form C. 2118.

WAR DIARY or INTELLIGENCE SUMMARY.

(Erase heading not required.)

Instructions regarding War Diaries and Intelligence Summaries are contained in F. S. Regs., Part II. and the Staff Manual respectively. Title pages will be prepared in manuscript.

Place	Date	Hour	Summary of Events and Information	Remarks and references to Appendices
ST. MICHEL	15/8/16		1 Officer &1 OR. Leave warrant forwarded Application for D.R.L.S. Bath & race of Mange had received at the Chateau ROELLECOURT. Motor Cars — interviewed D.O.L. 35th Divn & A.A. & Q.M.G. to arrange for animals to be put out to farm at once.	
	19/8/16		Visited CAMBLIGNEUX and inspected the camp where Horses had been affected. Proceeded to shoot to A.A. & Q.M.G. to inspection applied. Visited 38th D.B.S. Park of Ares. Ages 6, 7, 8 – 9's. 6 animals under feet not condemned. Visited D.B.L.S. 3rd army.	
	20/8/16		Visited C.B.	
	21/8/16		Visited 21/122 Bde & 6/122 Bde., accompanied with Lieut M. Harlop A.V.C. Vet Officer Inspected animals Stabilian good. Examined 3 Lame horses. Sent for treatment.	
	22/8/16		In accordance with instructions received from D.R.L.S. civilian Matern Camp. Visited civilian BOUZEUX — DRY. CORNAILLES. No horses were seen to be affected with Mange. Premises visited in BOUZEUX were not up to mark. Premises not up to a fair class 1 animal was	

T2134. Wt. W708—776. 500000. 4/15. Sir J. C. & S.

Army Form C. 2118.

WAR DIARY
or
INTELLIGENCE SUMMARY.
(Erase heading not required.)

Instructions regarding War Diaries and Intelligence Summaries are contained in F. S. Regs., Part II. and the Staff Manual respectively. Title pages will be prepared in manuscript.

Place	Date	Hour	Summary of Events and Information	Remarks and references to Appendices
ST. MICHEL	22/6/16		Found suffering from Mange. Arranged for the other animals to be at the same time following morning for S.A. inspection. Visited 49th D.T.S. gave the February Mange report. Madam bury	
"	23/6/16		BAILLEUL - AUX - CORNAILLES. inspected 2 animals stated to be Mange cases. Gave instructions for isolation & treatment	
"	24/6/16		Visited D.D.V.S. 4th Army. Visited 49th M.V.S. Neuvest Report S.B.V.S. re inspection of 2 animals affected with Mange at BAILLEUL - AUX - CORNAILLES.	
"	25/6/16		Office Routine. Visited 49th Mobile Vety. Section	
"	26/6/16		Divisional Move from ST MICHEL to LE MELLARD	
LE MELLARD	27/6/16		Visited Divisional Hd Qrs - Signal Co. Animals conditions good. Visited 49th M.V.S. at BOFFLES. Office Routine.	
"	28/6/16		Visited 49th Mobile Vety. Section at LANCHES. Visited Div. H.Qrs. & Signal Co. Office Routine. Visited signal Co. Evacuated 2 animals	
"	29/6/16		Office Routine. Visited signal co. animals	
"	30/6/16		Visited Div. H Qrs & signal Co. animals in fair condition	

Office Routine

A.D.V.S. 38th (WELSH) DIVISION.

CONFIDENTIAL

WAR DIARY

OF

A. D. V. S. 38th. (WELSH) DIVISION

FROM

1st. JULY 1916

TO

31st. JULY 1916

(VOLUME VIII.)

[signature]
Major. A.V.C.
A.D.V.S. 38th. (Welsh) Division.

Army Form C. 2118.

WAR DIARY
or
INTELLIGENCE SUMMARY.
(Erase heading not required.)

Instructions regarding War Diaries and Intelligence Summaries are contained in F. S. Regs., Part II. and the Staff Manual respectively. Title pages will be prepared in manuscript.

Place	Date	Hour	Summary of Events and Information	Remarks and references to Appendices
LE MEILLARD	1/7/16		Divisional move from LE MEILLARD to RUMEMPRE. Visited A/120 Bde R.F.A. Evacuated 1 horse (sick). Visited B/121 Bde. B.F.A. Evacuated 2 horses for debility. Visited B/120th Bde. R.F.A. Demolition of animals content. Visited 13/122 Bde. B.F.A. Evacuated 1 horse suffering from blue tack joint. Visited A/122 Bde B.F.A. Evacuated 3 for debility, 1 picked up nail. Visited D/120. Bde B.F.A. Evacuated 1 for debility + 1 badly pricked. Visited Ho Qrs 122. Bde B.F.A. Evacuated 1 horse suffering from lacerated wound, caused by accident by metal tang. Visited D/122 Bde B.F.A. Evacuated 3 animals 2 lame and 1 rifle gall.	
RUMEMPRE	2/7/16		Divisional move from RUMEMPRE to LEALVILLERS. Office Routine.	
LEALVILLERS	3/7/16		Divisional move from LEALVILLERS to TREUX. Office Routine.	
TREUX	4/7/16		Visited 49th Mobile Veterinary Section, just moved in billets at TREUX. Office Routine.	
"	5/7/16		Divisional move from TREUX to MORLANCOURT. Visited 49th Mobile Vety. Section at TREUX. Office Routine.	
MORLANCOURT	6/7/16		Visited Div. H.Q. + M.M.P. + Signal Co. Horses. Animals consistent fair.	

Army Form C. 2118.

WAR DIARY
or
INTELLIGENCE SUMMARY.
(Erase heading not required.)

Instructions regarding War Diaries and Intelligence Summaries are contained in F. S. Regs., Part II. and the Staff Manual respectively. Title pages will be prepared in manuscript.

Place	Date	Hour	Summary of Events and Information	Remarks and references to Appendices
MORLANCOURT	6/7/16 cond		Visited 129th Field Ambulance. Evacuated 3 camels. 1 suffering from lame shoulder, 1 Uneasiness saddle? & 1 suspected skin disease.	
	7/7/16		Weekly conference of Veterinary Officers. Accompanied with D.D.V.S. to Mobile Veterinary Section. visited M.V.S. and inspected at GROVETOWN. Visited Headquarters.	
"	8/7/16		Office Routine. Visited Divisional H.Q., Liguet Co., and H.Q.R.P. Animals condition good.	
"	9/7/16		Received visit from D.D.V.S. Fourth Army, and A.D.V.S. 7th Division. Visited 2nd Indian Cavalry Record Post and 3rd Cavalry Reserve Post. Visited H.Q. Divisional Train & Jo & Co. 12 Animals seen during my inspection.	
"	10/7/16		Visited 9th Reserve Park. Made arrangements for Captain J. SELLERS A.V.C. to be accommodated, who is taking over Veterinary charge. Number of cars in Sick lines. Visited 21. Field Ambulance. Passing for 2 sows horses. Visited 131. Field Ambulance Evacuated Black gelding offside shoulder suffering from Abscess on withers. 1 sore foot & 1 cracked heel.	

Army Form C. 2118.

WAR DIARY
or
INTELLIGENCE SUMMARY.
(Erase heading not required.)

Instructions regarding War Diaries and Intelligence Summaries are contained in F. S. Regs., Part II. and the Staff Manual respectively. Title pages will be prepared in manuscript.

Place	Date	Hour	Summary of Events and Information	Remarks and references to Appendices
MORLANCOURT	10/7/16		Visited 49th Mobile Vety Section at TREUX. Examined 3 animals from Sergeant RICHARDS Instructor 6/6 M.V.S. to feat. Found indication from Lieut. MACFARLANE A.V.C. that 1 horse belonging to 131 Field Ambulance was shot by this fire. This animal was one of a number at the A.D.S.	
"	11/7/16		Captain J. SELLERS A.V.C. reports for duty with 9th Reserve Park. Discussed move from MORLANCOURT to TREUX.	
TREUX	12/7/16		Discussed move from TREUX to PONT-REMY.	
PONT-REMY	13/7/16		Arrived and taken up billets at PONT-REMY. Officer Routine.	
"	14/7/16		Discussed policies received to P.D.V.S. Fourth Army. Officer Routine. Visited No Dis. & Signal Co. Visited 49th Mobile Veterinary Section.	
"	15/7/16		Discussed move from PONT-REMY to COUIN. Attended A.Ds.V.S. Conference at Q.B.V.S. Fourth Army Office. Officer Routine.	
COUIN	16/7/16		Visited Divn H.Q. & Signal Co. 49th Mobile Veterinary Section left COUIN for Army Mob. Vety. Staff Captain 113 Infantry Bde. that 1 horse had been shot whilst on the march. Proceed to FAMECHON. Secured verification from Staff Captain at CANDAS whilst on the march.	

O/c 49th M.V.S. to collect.

T2134. Wt. W708-776. 500000. 4/16. Sir J. C. & S.

Army Form C. 2118.

WAR DIARY
or
INTELLIGENCE SUMMARY.
(Erase heading not required.)

Instructions regarding War Diaries and Intelligence Summaries are contained in F.S. Regs., Part II. and the Staff Manual respectively. Title pages will be prepared in manuscript.

Place	Date	Hour	Summary of Events and Information	Remarks and references to Appendices
Eouin	17/7/16		Units and experts report Mobile Veterinary Section at FANECHON strength 57/6 bo. Auxiliary Horse Transport strength 34 I.D. 10 mules L.B. 7 1 Riad. Animals not fit to render. Units signed to received for sick cases. Unusual number of sales of forelimbers. Office routine. Inspected animals between headquarters.	
"	18/7/16		Units 46th Mobile Vety. Section at FANECHON. Units 130 Field Ambulance 101 THIEVRES. Animals in fact condition except two. Gave instructions for 1 to be evacuated and the other one quiet special treatment. Visits 19th Picquet Bn. Found the watering management unsatisfactory water freeing to be carried	
"	19/7/16		by marsfer sins to watch troops. Estimated transport effect to mobile fittel arrangements by obliging own men Mse. Spo etc. Casualite am how suffering from Dunist. Units 123 bo f.b. Animals condition fair with exception 3 ct 4. Give instructions for two to be evacuated Units No 2. Section, 46th Reserve Park who have just march into this area Made arrangements for Veterinary attendance.	

Army Form C. 2118.

WAR DIARY
or
INTELLIGENCE SUMMARY.
(Erase heading not required.)

Place	Date	Hour	Summary of Events and Information	Remarks and references to Appendices
COULIN	20/7/16		Veterinary Officers. Lieut. Armstrong + Lieut. Hartey + Lieut Finch who went sick with Field Mules. Reserve unit from Capt R.H. Smith A.V.C.	
	21/7/16		Mis + sick with Field Mules. V.O. to VIII Corps Headquarters. Nelly inspected of Veterinary Officers after Routine. B/ Battery which has just returned from the lines at MAMETZ furnished very poor turnout to form Burial + Punishing Parades.	
	22/7/16		Accompanied with B.R.V.S. General Dump inspected + Sections 38th D.A.C. Animals in excellent condition. Inspected 103/120 Bde. R.F.A. Montgomery. my report of these animals the day before. Animals feet in condition shown signs of being hard worked. Feulle 119 3rd M.V.S. and inspected the sections.	
	23/7/16		Office Routine.	
	24/7/16		Units and subjected to patrols 120. Bde. R.F.A. A Battery. Horses in fair condition, showed signs of hard work, coats - in general fairly good. B. Battery. Very poor condition "pulled up". Hide bound lean + "staring out". Hollow flanks and evidence of extreme debility.	

WAR DIARY or INTELLIGENCE SUMMARY.

Army Form C. 2118.

(Erase heading not required.)

Instructions regarding War Diaries and Intelligence Summaries are contained in F. S. Regs., Part II. and the Staff Manual respectively. Title pages will be prepared in manuscript.

Place	Date	Hour	Summary of Events and Information	Remarks and references to Appendices
Cousin	24/7/16	ant	C. Battery in fairly good working condition, with exception of two Riscumsters got one to to casualties.	
			D. Battery saw Med's an in good health & condition, and gunners all shed rapple evidence of care, attention and acclimatizing generally.	
			Reserve afrent to C.F.A. and quoted herds of animals condition in the 4 Batteries. Recommended for animals to receive special attention.	
	25/7/16		Units 122 Bde R.F.A. B/Batty. Evacuation one Reighne an Debilg. All animals are receiving green forage. B/122. Ben sensitive fast. Animals receiving green forage. Evacuated two for Debily. C/122. Bee sensitive fast. No green forage. A/122. Condition fair. Evacuation in Debily. Few & animals are recently Maine from the D.a.b. when newly from.	
			Units FAMECHON and interned J.A.O. afterce to green forage, supply for Mules. Units 49's D.S. at FAMECHON.	
	26/7/16		Units 35th Divn. A.D. + M.M.P. Evacuate 1 Piet. Douvill 100. Evac. M.M.P. 1 (Piet) Punitive arrival Cave. Queens Group (attached to M.M.P.) the 1 Piet. Finden. Units D.D.V.S. Fourth Army. Branchin hen will afterce to relieve for until. R.F.A. Petal 100 and afterture behind from our afterture to 2nd Army.	

T2134. Wt. W768-776. 500000. 4/15. Sir J. C. & Sons

WAR DIARY or INTELLIGENCE SUMMARY.

Army Form C. 2118.

(Erase heading not required.)

Instructions regarding War Diaries and Intelligence Summaries are contained in F. S. Regs., Part II. and the Staff Manual respectively. Title pages will be prepared in manuscript.

Place	Date	Hour	Summary of Events and Information	Remarks and references to Appendices
COUIN	27/7/16		Inspected 10's 38th Division. Received visit from A.D.V.S. and D.D.V. Reserve Army. Accompanied by Lieut J. Finch A.V.C. V.O.y/c. inspected animal case Sungholt Skin disease. Got instructions for animal to be evacuated.	
"	28/7/16		Visited D.H.Q. + Signal Co. visits TAMECHON and interviewed O/C. N/g.S. Mobile Vety Section and visited operation cases regarding mar to SAXTON	
"	29/7/16		Received wire from COUIN to BUS. Arrived a new at D.H.Q. Received wire from P.V.N. Upricarded for same. Visited O/C. N/g.S. Mobile Vety Section, met O/C. N/g.S. MARTIN SAUVAL. Visited + issued instructions for section to move to JEARUAL.	
			instructed O/C. N/g.L. H/g.S. M/N.L. to evacuate 24 Reinsents's sents instructions received from D.R.P. Reserve Army.	
BUS	30/7/16		Office Routine.	
"	31/7/16		Divisional move from BUS to ESQUELBECQ, (NORTH OF FRANCE).	

[signature] MAJOR.
A.D.V.S. 38th (WELSH) DIVISION.

Confidential.

General Staff,
    38th. Division.

———————————————

A.D.V.S.,
38th (WELSH)
DIVISION.

No. ....
Date ....

    Attached please find Original War Diary
Volume IX. compiled by A.D.V.S. 38th. Division,
for month of August 1916.
        Please acknowledge.

                            [signature]
                            Major. A.V.C.
        A.D.V.S. 38th. (Welsh) Division.

1st. September 1916.

CONFIDENTIAL.

WAR DIARY

OF

A. D. V. S. 38th. (WELSH) DIVISION.

FROM

1st. AUGUST 1916.

TO

31st. AUGUST 1916.

(VOLUME IX.)

[signature]
Major. A.V.C.
A.D.V.S. 38th. (Welsh) Division.

August 31st. 1916.

Army Form C. 2118.

WAR DIARY
or
INTELLIGENCE SUMMARY.
(Erase heading not required.)

Instructions regarding War Diaries and Intelligence Summaries are contained in F. S. Regs., Part II. and the Staff Manual respectively. Title pages will be prepared in manuscript.

Place	Date	Hour	Summary of Events and Information	Remarks and references to Appendices
ESQUELBECQ	1/8/16		Office Routine. Visited B.S.M. Second Army. Had tea when I called.	
"	2/8/16		Visited 49th M.V.S. Own H.Q. & Signal Co. Animals in good condition. Inspected for sick animals. Office Routine.	
"	3/8/16		Visited 29th M.A.S. Lieuts. ARMSTRONG, A.V.C. & Lieut. P. HOWARD, A.V.C. gazetted Captains. Visited I.O.A. Section 25th D.A.C. Total strength 245. Horses - 70 mules. 1 L.B. mustard wound, 1 L.B. bad blood. Stopped wound couch. Animals just completed a long journey into this area. Formation very good. Visited O.H.Q. Some lines prescribed for sick send. 2 P.M. & Sick Posts.	
"	4/8/16		Conference Veterinary Officers. Visited 89th M.V.L. Office Routine.	
"	5/8/16		Visited WATOU and inspected 129th Field Ambulance transport troop. 1 case Anchored wound (slight). 1 case bruised wound (slight), animals found unknown. 1 horse had wart, just recovered from Strangles, unsuitable for this work. Visited 130 Field Ambulance at WORMHOUDT. Condition good, 1 suspect. 1 stallion. The other horses being away. 1 case of strangulitis, due to drunkenness, the to amount in train.	

WAR DIARY or INTELLIGENCE SUMMARY.

Army Form C. 2118.

(Erase heading not required.)

Place	Date	Hour	Summary of Events and Information	Remarks and references to Appendices
ESQUELBECQ	6/5/17		Visited B.H.Q. Animals & Office Routine.	
"	7/5/17		Office Routine. Visited HQ. M.M.P. & Signed to.	
"	8/5/17		Visited 333 Co. M.L.C. Condition of animals good. 1 puncture wound. Thigh. 1 lacerated wound accident. Animals fitting coat. Visited HQ. M.M.P. & B.H.Q.	
"	9/5/17		Visited 17th Bn S.W.F. Animals in stables in good standings good. 1 Officers' charger lame. 2 cases Rope gall. Visited 11th Bn. S.W.B. Animals in good condition. 1 sand sore. Staff Sickling rifles tied to lines. Instructed transport Officer, if any damage is done to the lines, same will have to be paid for. Visited 140 Section, 38th D.A.C. Animals in good condition. Received visit from D.O.V.S. Second Army. Visited HQ. M.M.P. Instructed O/C. HQ M.M.P. to move into new and better accommodated huts at WORMHOUDT.	
"	10/5/17		Conference Veterinary Officers. Office Routine. Visited B.H.Q. HQ. M.M.P.	
"	11/5/17		Attended conference of A.D.V.S. Second Army. Office BRILLEUL. Visited HQ. M.M.P.	

Army Form C. 2118.

WAR DIARY
or
INTELLIGENCE SUMMARY.
(Erase heading not required.)

Instructions regarding War Diaries and Intelligence Summaries are contained in F. S. Regs., Part II. and the Staff Manual respectively. Title pages will be prepared in manuscript.

Place	Date	Hour	Summary of Events and Information	Remarks and references to Appendices
ESQUELBECQ	13/5/17		Visited R.H.Q. 7 M.G.A. Medl. Regt. Section. Office Routine.	
"	14/5/17		Visited 153 Bde. Vet. Regt. Shoeing good. Sanitation good. No cases on sick list. Visited 339 Coy. M.T.C. Evacuated 1 case mange. Condition of road animals with Army Station. Visited 10 % S.W.B. Sanitation of animals good. 1 case scratches arm. Everything satisfactory. At request of L.F.E. examined a mule, animal from Remounts for 124 Coy. R.E. very lame off fore. Burnt on frog. Would not have been shod. Evacuated to 49 M.V.L. for treatment. Visited 49 M.V.L. Examined fresh remount cases sent up by Remount Dep. Found number of old injuries also during ten cases + a number of fresh cases suffering from treatment. Gave instructions for treatment.	
"	15/5/17		Visited 114 Bde. Field Regt. Stables very good. Shoeing good. Visited 154 Bde. Med. Regt 1 Remount extremely poor in condition. Visited 114 Bee M. Gun Co. Evacuated 1 for Rabies. 7 + 1 for Lameness. Others in good condition. Found animals in a few old Units. Noor Stables. Gave instructions to remove animals in a few cases being unhealthy and made the Ascompet report the matter to	

Army Form C. 2118.

WAR DIARY or INTELLIGENCE SUMMARY.

(Erase heading not required.)

Place	Date	Hour	Summary of Events and Information	Remarks and references to Appendices
ESQUELBECQ	15/5/17	cont.	D.O. + A.D.M.S. to recommend animals to be available in a field most fit. Visits 331 Fd. Amb. Sanitation good. 1 case Pyrexia, fresh Remounts + 1 Horse. Visits 15th Bn. R.W.F. 2 mules very poor, other in good condition. Visits 13th Bn. R.W.F. Saw sanitation & 1 horse to be evacuated, grey old. Them half fed a long time. Visits to 16th Bn. R.W.F. Sanitation & animals good. No cases on sick lines. Saw Montreal, nearly seven cwt. no good long. Visits 14th Bn. R.W.F. All in excellent condition except one red Percheron, which is working on press cart, and has a slight knee gall. This mule as constantly sweating when fresh horses in miss cart, and miswearing them reported matter to A.D. + D.A.D.V.S. Visits 113 Bde. M. Gun Co. Animals in very good condition. 1 case poll, chose 1 Regt. Blemish had given frost in the mouth. Pinna - mouth membrane &c. Horse unable to feed. Spoilt recommends that an Infantry mule should be substituted with a late gunner. All above units are conditions to be Now Raised. Visits No 2 Mobile Vet. Section. Official Routine.	
	16/5/17		Visits 120. Fld. Ambulance. 3 cases sick - 1 case Tetanus, 1 Pyrexia and 1 Recy. Animals in artillery good.	

War Diary or Intelligence Summary

Army Form C. 2118.

Place	Date	Hour	Summary of Events and Information	Remarks and references to Appendices
EQUELBECQ	18/8/4		Conference Veterinary Officers. Office routine. Visits 104 Fm. Ambce Posk. extract the Shatters steps to be traced in foot rent. 1 mule casualty taken in. Condition of animals good. Visits 129th Field Ambulance. 1 case sick + refs gall. Visits 130 Field Ambulance. Examined a tetanus case. Visits HQ. W.M.1 & D.H.Q.	
	19/8/4		Visits HQ W.M.1. & H.D. Office routine. Received Divisional Circular No. 55. 2 move mules not ready and area.	
	20/8/4		Visits B/119 Bde R.F.A. Condition of animals only fair. Moving good. 3 cases saddle galls. Examined for Mange. no cases. B/119 Bde R.F.A. Condition good. except sick tethered. 1 bad case hundred remark. To Mange cases. C/119 Bde R.F.A. Condition good except 2 or 3 having Mange. Examined for Mange, no cases. B/119 Bde R.F.A. Condition good. 12 feed animals been sprayed for special attention. HQ 119 Bde R.F.A. Condition good. Moving indifferent. C/177 Bde R.F.A. Condition fairly good. Examined for Mange, no cases. HQ 177/Bde F.F.A. Condition good. B/177 Bde F.F.A. Condition good. Examined for Mange, no cases.	

WAR DIARY or INTELLIGENCE SUMMARY

Army Form C. 2118.

Place	Date	Hour	Summary of Events and Information	Remarks and references to Appendices
ESQUELBECQ	20/8/17 (contd)		8/121 Bde. R.F.A. 1 animal scalded though, condition of animals good. Horses suffering. 1 or 2 six feet condition. A/121 Bde. R.F.A. condition much improved. Horses good. No mange seen. Received mare from ESQUELBECQ to ST SIXTE (Belgium). Office routine.	
"	21/8/17		49th M.V.S. cat place allotted. Found the other of M.V.L. 41st Division. The missing Lieutenant O.C. + D.M.S. to enquire into this missing mq. M.V.L. Found the M.V.L. of 4 Division. Met Mr. Receiving mare from C.O. 4 Division, saying D.R.V.S. Army agreed that both sections should share duties.	
ST. SIXTE	22/8/17		Wrote 129. Quite satisfactory. Examined fat mange. All feet satisfactory. 3 strangles. Art. corrected, futile with things. Halt thought fever heat and sweat shivers. Visited 124 Co. R.E. 1 case ringworm from removed in 11/8/17. Mange R.S.C. Co. also suffering from partial leaf fatigue near Poperinge. Instructions given to isolate this animal. Examined for mange. All free. Condition of animals fairly good. Watering arrangements not satisfactory.	
"	23/8/17		Visited 151 Co. R.E. Animals in good condition. No mange. Same	

Army Form C. 2118.

WAR DIARY
or
INTELLIGENCE SUMMARY.
(Erase heading not required.)

Instructions regarding War Diaries and Intelligence Summaries are contained in F. S. Regs., Part II. and the Staff Manual respectively. Title pages will be prepared in manuscript.

Place	Date	Hour	Summary of Events and Information	Remarks and references to Appendices
ST. SIXTE	23/8/16	Cont.	...all Arrangements. As 124. C. F. E. Visited 131. Field Ambulance. This is situate on not far newly occupied by 104 Field Ambulance. Met the O.C. the six whom Gunson spoke and Arranged with O.C. to put his findings in a different field, and use different hiding place on the same farm.	
"	24/8/16		Received visit from Lieut Harley R.V.C. who intimated copies of letters being sent to O/C 121 Bdu R.F.A. these I kept to O.O. & R.M.O who promised to interview A.O.O. R.O. in connection with this. Visited HQ. M.V.S. and informed that Lt. Goodwin, A.V.C. was wanted at once for duty with Sergt. Hart & Sergt. Rivers. On my return interviewed D.O.O. & R.M.O. and asked for instructions regarding this want. Wrote O/c HQ. M.V.S. to detail a successor for F.G.C.M. Receive wire from O.O. & C.M.S. who asked me if I could accept Lieut. HARLEY A.V.C. to which I replied. Lieut. HARLEY would report i.e. Conference Veterinary Officers. Office Routine.	
"	25/8/16 26/8/16		Visited D.H.Q. & M.M.P. animals. Visited HQ 2 M.V.S. Office Routine.	

Army Form C. 2118.

WAR DIARY
or
INTELLIGENCE SUMMARY.
(Erase heading not required.)

Instructions regarding War Diaries and Intelligence Summaries are contained in F. S. Regs., Part II. and the Staff Manual respectively. Title pages will be prepared in manuscript.

Place	Date	Hour	Summary of Events and Information	Remarks and references to Appendices
ST. SIXTE	27/8/17		Accompanied A.D.V.S. & A.D.T.D.V.S. met train from CALAIS. Remounts 68 animals L.B. JB Pétés & Loose English remounts. Mare to be a fair lot. One or two rather poor in condition. Visited D.H.Q. & Lancs Horse Comp. Evacuated 1 to M.V.S. for treatment suffering from sore back.	
"	28/8/17		Office routine. Visited D.H.Q. & 99th M.V.S.	
"	29/8/17		Visited 38th D.A.C. found Tarbecloney sick mule with a oedema of the larynx. Visited D.H.Q. animals. Office routine.	
"	30/8/17		Office routine. Visited Divisional Artillery H.Q. & D.H.Q. animals.	
"	31/8/17		Visited Sta. Ops. 35th D.A.C. & No.2 Section. Animals in good condition. No skin diseases. Visited No.3 Section. Condition of animals very good. No skin disease. Visited No.4 Section. Animals in excellent condition. No skin disease. No.1 Section. Animals in animals very good. No skin disease. Office routine.	

F. W. Gann
MAJOR,
A.D.V.S. 38th (WELSH) DIVISION.

CONFIDENTIAL

WAR DIARY

OF

A. D. V. S. 38th. (WELSH) DIVISION

FROM

1st. SEPTEMBER 1916.

TO

30th. SEPTEMBER 1916.

(VOLUME X.)

-:-:-:-:-:-

[signature]
Major. A.V.C.
A.D.V.S. 38th. (Welsh) Division.

September 30th. 1916.

WAR DIARY or INTELLIGENCE SUMMARY

Army Form C. 2118.

Place	Date	Hour	Summary of Events and Information	Remarks and references to Appendices
ST. SIXTE	1/9/16		Office routine. Visited D.H.Q. horse lines. Le Jolie Jeegis. A.V.C. on re-organization of Divisional Artillery Brigades.	
"	2/9/16		Visited A/119. B/119. accompanied with O/C. 119. Bde. R.F.A. Inspected animals. Evacuated 3 to M.V.S. Surplus animals inspected prior to distribution to other units in Division. Present.	
"	3/9/16		Visited 382 Div. Amm. Column. - Inspected surplus animals not in fair condition. Artillery Brigades Evacuated 3 to M.V.S. for details. Visited 49th M.V.S. animals to other units for requirements.	
"	4/9/16		Visited 38 C.o.R. and inspected the remounts of animals supplied to establishment, in re-organization of Divisional Artillery. Decreased 3 horses from B/121 for details. 2 horses B/121. 2 horses from B/121. 2 mules from B/122. 3 from B/122. 2 mules from 133 Co. ASC. 1 R. 1 R to 129 Co. ASC. 1 LB to 10th Bn. 1 Horse. battery unknown issued 1 L.D. to 333 Co A.S.C. 1 L.B. to 10th Bn. to 114 Bde. R.F.A. Howi. Sec. L.B. to 10th Div A/S.B. Midd. Regt. 1 R to 129 Field Ambulance. 3 L.B. to D.A.C. 1 R. to D.H.Q. Regt. Fined. Proceeded to-day on Official leave.	

WAR DIARY or INTELLIGENCE SUMMARY

Army Form C. 2118.

Place	Date	Hour	Summary of Events and Information	Remarks and references to Appendices
ST. SIXTE	5/9/16		Visited 1st Bn. R.N.F.; Inspected 1 cow suspected of being diseased. No lesions of Ringworm. No skin disease. Office routine.	
"	6/9/16		Visited 10th Entrenching Bn. Inspected animals. Condition fair. 1 case Mastitis on cut out. Gave instructions for this animal to be sent for treatment to M.V.S. and advised as to skin disease.	
"	7/9/16		Visited No. 5, 2nd Pontoon Park. Animals in good condition. Visited 124th & 160th F.E. Animals in good condition. No skin disease. No skin disease.	
"	8/9/16		Visited 49th Mot. Vet. Sec. Received mail from A.D.V.S. 5th Belgian Divisional Office routine. Office routine.	
"	9/9/16		Conferred Veterinary Officers. Visited 6/122, through 183. No skin disease. 9/122 considerably sick though condition fair. Communicated with effect on the complaint, that horses have been taken away in place of "begs" (?claim), also states that men taking away in place of Mrs Mary dating, one 2 N.B. animals attended shortage of men.	

Army Form C. 2118.

WAR DIARY
or
INTELLIGENCE SUMMARY.
(Erase heading not required.)

Instructions regarding War Diaries and Intelligence Summaries are contained in F. S. Regs., Part II. and the Staff Manual respectively. Title pages will be prepared in manuscript.

Place	Date	Hour	Summary of Events and Information	Remarks and references to Appendices
ST SIXTE	9/9/14	cont.	not amount of hay out cut grazing C.R. rations. Units B/122. Condition fair. Animal Strength 184 horses. ant strength. No shoeing necessary. Units 9/122. Animal strength 182. ant strength. Farrier 6 ft Pulteley. 1 Abscess. The rest of the animals in fair condition. Effect to Units. Units he gets no green forage and supply of hay is insufficient. To Main Kisswe	
"	10/9/14		Units E.H.Q. Asron Aies + 492. Effect Vet fur Officer Practice. Units D.H.Q. + M.G.P. Rest Lines.	
"	11/9/14		Officer Practice.	
"	12/9/14		Reconnaisance with C/c 363 Park train. Inspected 333 C. ASC. Ammunition cry good except 2. rather foot. Shoeing and grooming good. No cases in sick lines. No skin disease. 331 C. ASC. Condition of animals excellent, with exception of 2. Shoeing and grooming good. 9 cases in sick lines. 4 P.U.O. 1 Tread. 1 Harness gall. 1 Section fairly good. 2 sec. good. = 3 sec. very good. Shoeing sufficient. but left too long. 1 case Suspected Mange. examined 1 Ryle gall. 2 suspected cases of Mange	

Army Form C. 2118.

WAR DIARY
or
INTELLIGENCE SUMMARY.
(Erase heading not required.)

Instructions regarding War Diaries and Intelligence Summaries are contained in F. S. Regs., Part II. and the Staff Manual respectively. Title pages will be prepared in manuscript.

Place	Date	Hour	Summary of Events and Information	Remarks and references to Appendices
ST SIXTE	12/9/17		Inspected & left server Hospitalier. 332 Co. A.S.C. Class of horses in this Co. not to good, at the chef does, although condition of animals is good. 2 or 3 old horses on loan being good. 2 cases of scabies at Lans Hussar Yeomy. (attached.) Inspected for Mange. no cases.	
"	13/9/17		Visits Lans Hussars Yeomy attached to E.H.Q. 1 case colic. Visits E.H.Q. & M.M.P. Office & stores.	
"	14/9/17		Visits Sico pols. Inspected for evacuation of Horse Baths. 1 mal POPERINGHE and 1 near WESTOUTRE. Reported sick to A.D.V.S. (No. 2.) and quoted the best site.	
"	15/9/17		Conference Veterinary Officers. Office Duties. Army Letters.	
"	16/9/17		Visited No. 9. Vet. Vet. Sec. Inspected 19 horses. Office duties. Army Letters which were returned from Remounts. — Sent on court by D.V.A. (certain horses from Re-organisation Artillery) these animals were not inspected prior to dispatch, consequently they are not returned in but cast for transfer for Details. 5 claimed for re-issue.	

T2134. Wt. W708—776. 500000. 4/15. Sir J. C. & S.

Army Form C. 2118.

WAR DIARY
or
INTELLIGENCE SUMMARY.
(Erase heading not required.)

Instructions regarding War Diaries and Intelligence Summaries are contained in F. S. Regs., Part II. and the Staff Manual respectively. Title pages will be prepared in manuscript.

Place	Date	Hour	Summary of Events and Information	Remarks and references to Appendices
ST. SIXTE	17/9/16		Visited 49th Mob. Vet. Sec. Visited 19th Armed Bre. Animals in good condition. 2 cm off lift line. 1 H.D. & 1 Mule No skin disease.	
"	18/9/16		Office Routine. Visited 49th Mob. Veterinary Section. Sick animals first to Ambulance to 1st Vety Hospital.	
"	19/9/16		Visited 49th Mob. Vet Sec. Office Routine.	
"	20/9/16		Visited D.A.D Horse lines. Office Routine.	
"	21/9/16		Visited 38th D.A.C. Animals in good condition. Inspected 23 newly arrived remounts. Visited 123 Field Coy R.E. Inspected 41 animals. resept 3 – issued instructions for one animal to be classified.	
"	22/9/16		Inspected Veterinary Officers. Visited D.T.D. 7 M.M.P. horse lines. Office Routine.	
"	23/9/16		Visited 49th Mob. Veterinary Section. Office Routine.	
"	24/9/16		Held post-mortem examination on mule died at D.H.Q. previous day. Been due for Battles of Shamash.	

Army Form C. 2118.

WAR DIARY
or
INTELLIGENCE SUMMARY.
(Erase heading not required.)

Instructions regarding War Diaries and Intelligence Summaries are contained in F. S. Regs., Part II. and the Staff Manual respectively. Title pages will be prepared in manuscript.

Place	Date	Hour	Summary of Events and Information	Remarks and references to Appendices
ST. SIXTE	25/9/16		Office Routine. Visits 49th Mobile Veterinary Section.	
"	26/9/16		Visits D.H.Q. & M.M.P. Office routine.	
"	27/9/16		Visits 38th Divisional Signal Co. Animals in good condition.	
"	28/9/16		No sick horse dressed. Office Routine.	
"	29/9/16 to 30/9/16		On leave.	

J. W. Blair
A.D.V.S. 38th (WELSH) DIVISION.

C O N F I D E N T I A L

WAR   DIARY

OF

A. D. V. S.   38th.   (WELSH)   DIVISION

FROM

1st.   O C T O B E R   1 9 1 6.

TO

31st.   O C T O B E R   1 9 1 6.

: : : : : : : : : : : :

(V O L U M E   XI.)

: : : : : : : : : : : :

(Original)

[signature]
Major. A.V.C.
A.D.V.S., 38th. (Welsh) Division

31st. October 1916

WAR DIARY or INTELLIGENCE SUMMARY

Army Form C. 2118.

Place	Date	Hour	Summary of Events and Information	Remarks and references to Appendices
ST. SIXTE	1/10/16		On leave from Octbr 1st to October 8th 1916.	
"	9/10/16		Visited D.H.Q. & M.M.P. Horse lines. Office Routine.	
"	10/10/16		Visited up Met Vet Sec. Examined Jennings mule microscopic slides from horse belonging to 332nd Coy A.S.C. Found no specific parasite (nematode). Wire WO Officer i/c of this Unit, to interview me regarding this case. Visited D.H.Q. & M.M.P. Horse lines.	
"	11/10/16		Visited 10th Bn Black Regt. Animals in good condition. Standings good. 1 A.D. Coy sent to M.G. for training. Visited 332nd Coy A.S.C. Horses command in splendid condition. Saw instructions to NCOs & Co. Commandant, to use care, to inspect all brushes, grooming utensils, ropes, hair collars and harness, to issue Horse Standings to and position to lift all horses. Gave instructions for 1 horse to be examined for Debility.	
"	12/10/16		Visited 142nd Bn. B.W.F. - Standings good. Condition very good. No sick.	

Army Form C. 2118.

WAR DIARY
or
INTELLIGENCE SUMMARY.
(Erase heading not required.)

Instructions regarding War Diaries and Intelligence Summaries are contained in F.S. Regs., Part II. and the Staff Manual respectively. Title pages will be prepared in manuscript.

Place	Date	Hour	Summary of Events and Information	Remarks and references to Appendices
ST. SIXTE.	12/10/16	cont.	Visited 16th Bn. R.W.F. Standings good. Animals condition good, with exception of 3 of 4. 3 cases Ringworm. 1 case Dermatitis. Have instructions for the three Ringworm cases, to be sent to M.V.S. for treatment. Visited 15th Bn. R.W.F. Condition of animals good. 1 horse suffering from open joint — sent instructions for animal to be evacuated. 1 horse too small to be suit to M.V.S. for testing by D.D.V. Army.	
"	13/10/16		Visited 49th Fld. Vet. Sec. by appointment with D.D.V. Army, and assisted in inspection of animals casting of animals from micro units in the Divison. Visited Brig. Bde. R.F.A. Made post-mortem examination with Capt. J. Macfarlane, A.V.C. V.O. i/c, on horse found dead in the lines. This memory post-mortem revealed [acute?] nephritis in the left kidney.	
"	14/10/16		Accompanied by Capt. W. Harley, A.V.C. V.O. i/c, visited 115th Bn. Machine Gun Co. Animals in excellent condition. Standings good. Grooming good. Visited 7 unspected animals of 115th Bde. H.Q.	

T2134. Wt. W708—776. 500000. 4/15. Sir J.C. & S.

Army Form C. 2118.

WAR DIARY
or
INTELLIGENCE SUMMARY.
(Erase heading not required.)

Instructions regarding War Diaries and Intelligence Summaries are contained in F. S. Regs., Part II. and the Staff Manual respectively. Title pages will be prepared in manuscript.

Place	Date	Hour	Summary of Events and Information	Remarks and references to Appendices
ST. SIXTE	14/10/16		Condition excellent. Standings good – grooming good – shoeing good. 10th Bn. S.W.B. Animals in good condition with exception of one or two. I.D. Mules shoes standings good. 16th Bn. Welsh Regt. Standings good – grooming good. Condition of animals excellent. 17th Bn. R.W.F. Condition very good. Standings good – grooming good. 11th Bn. S.W.B. Condition of one exception of two. 1 very old – gave satisfaction at same to be cast. NB. Some of their animals have begun to slip, another have they stopping machines to shoe that that. Advised Transport Officers to purchase or shoe a machine. Field 131. Fuln Ambulance. Condition good. – grooming good. – shoeing good. General management excellent. None of their units show signs of ......
"	15/10/16		Officer Routine. Visited M.T.B. and Lancs Yeomy.
"	16/10/16		Visited 19th Trench Bn. Standings not yet completed. Conditions good.
"	17/10/16		By appointment, accompanied D.D.V.S. Army, I inspected F.F.B. units

WAR DIARY or INTELLIGENCE SUMMARY

Army Form C. 2118.

(Erase heading not required.)

Instructions regarding War Diaries and Intelligence Summaries are contained in F. S. Regs., Part II. and the Staff Manual respectively. Title pages will be prepared in manuscript.

Place	Date	Hour	Summary of Events and Information	Remarks and references to Appendices
ST. SIXTE	17/5/16		2/119 Bde. Number of animals sent in foot condition selected animals properly evacuating. 6/119 Bde. condition good. Evacuated 3 A/171. No condition good. B/119. Bde. condition fair. To recruit to quota for evacuation. A/119. Bde. condition good. B/121. Bde. condition very good. Number of horses legs clipped. Contrary to G.R.O. — No call for clipping given by an Luit. THOMAS. 5/121. Bde. condition good. One to be evacuated. Legs clipped by Batty Commandant, instruction contrary to G.R.O. D/122. Bde. condition very good. A/122 Bde. condition good. with excellent 1 section to recruit out other 2 recruit for evacuation. B/122. Bde. condition fair. 1 to be evacuated, clipping of legs contrary to G.R.O. C/122 Bde. condition good. Tent lengths of nettel. Now being in use for remedying salt to insects. Reported R.E. Medical Officer salvaged sun lifting for this purpose. Men living under canvas to weather caused do damage. D/122 Bde. condition good. Legs clipped contrary to G.R.O.	

WAR DIARY or INTELLIGENCE SUMMARY

Army Form C. 2118.

Place	Date	Hour	Summary of Events and Information	Remarks and references to Appendices
ST. SIXTE	17/10/16		38th D.O.G. & Sec. 2 & Hd. Qrs. Animals in excellent condition. Section 1. Animals in excellent condition. Lesions 3 and 4. Animals in excellent condition. No faults to find in any of these sections.	
"	18/10/16		Visited D.H.Q. Horse lines. Office Routine	
"	19/10/16		Office Routine. Visited M.M.P. & D.H.Q. Horse lines	
"	20/10/16		Accompanied D.D. & D.M.S. to HOPOUTRE STATION and examined 84 Remounts arrived for this Division. Mules & L.Ds. average good. H.Rs. well good. Inspected Veterinary Officers.	
"	21/10/16		Visited B/119 Bde. R.F.A. Selected 24 Debilis cases for evacuation. B/119 Bde. Picked out 26 for evacuation. Visited #5 M.V.S.	
"	22/10/16		Visited A/122 Bde. F.A. Picked out 30 Debilis cases for evacuation. Placed then horses on separate lines for special attention, all Debilis cases.	
"	23/10/16		Visited 4/2 Lateral Bn. Animals in excellent condition. Matting not good. 1 Horse sent to MVS for treatment. Skin case.	

WAR DIARY
INTELLIGENCE SUMMARY.
(Erase heading not required.)

Army Form C. 2118.

Place	Date	Hour	Summary of Events and Information	Remarks and references to Appendices
ST. SIXTE	24/10/ic		Office Routine.	
"	25/10/14		Visited Cases Isolation Camp — two cases Itch.	
"	26/10/14		Office Routine. Visited O.H.D. Horse lines. Office Routine.	
"	27/10/14		Visited 12H. to R.E. - examined horse reported suspected glanders, by local J. Culmare. A.V.C. view of opinion the suspected horse is of a unusual nature. Extra instructions to be sent to M.V.J. for isolation & to be told by matron (suspected method). Visited H9. M.V.J. and again examined horse from 12H. to R.E. 11th & showed the horse is friendly. Epistaxis has now supervened.	
"	29/10/14		Meanwhile animal to be isolated 9.0 a.m. this morning. Fresh instructions for first horse to be Visited 331 to A.S.C. elected at once. - 1 Horse with Mange to be examined with Manket. Sanitary to my instructions, horses clipped and Blankets were in use, washed and immersed in oil. 78% Disenfect Iamp requesting this practice to cease.	

Army Form C. 2118.

WAR DIARY
or
INTELLIGENCE SUMMARY.
(Erase heading not required.)

Place	Date	Hour	Summary of Events and Information	Remarks and references to Appendices
St. SIXTE	29/10/16		Visited no. 1st Vet. Sec. Examined horse kicked with Mallein 26 hours after. Not the slightest reaction. Visited D.H.Q. Horse Lines. Office Routine.	
"	30/10/16			
"	31/10/16		Visited no. 1st Vet. Sec. Visited 333 Co. A.V.C. Most of the animals out. Horses not made a satisfactory completion.	

signature
A.D.V.S. 38th (WELSH) DIVISION.

CONFIDENTIAL

WAR DIARY

OF

A.D.V.S. 38th. (WELSH) DIVISION

FROM

1st. NOVEMBER 1916.

TO

30th. NOVEMBER 1916

::::::::

(VOLUME XII.)

::::::::

(Original)

[signature]
Major. A.V.C.
A.D.V.S., 38th. (Welsh) Division.

30th. November 1916.

Army Form C. 2118.

WAR DIARY
or
INTELLIGENCE SUMMARY.
(Erase heading not required.)

Instructions regarding War Diaries and Intelligence Summaries are contained in F.S. Regs., Part II. and the Staff Manual respectively. Title pages will be prepared in manuscript.

Place	Date	Hour	Summary of Events and Information	Remarks and references to Appendices
St SIXTE	1/10/14		Visited 12th Co. R.E. Standings disgracefully bad, situated in a wood. Partially under water. Not ones long completed in higher position. Condition of animals good. Stopping has not yet commenced. End meal ones in log lines. Visited 129 Field Ambulance. Horses in good condition, with exception of two stopping not yet carried out. Visited Lancs. Hussars Yeomy. Exceeds for two days animals. Visited D.H.Q. horse lines.	
"	2/10/14		Inspected Veterinary Officers. Attend conference at OC. Divisional Train, with S.S.O. (Dickson) to reduce scale of forage. Conference came to conclusion that the best arrangement for equivalents to replace that 5lbs of hay which is not long to time from rate of feeding, 13 1/2 lb Linseed cake and 7 lbs stand for 24 hours for 20 horses 1/2 lb class Linseed cake and 6 lbs Hay, so that the ration for 24 hour class would be 12 lbs oats, 6 lbs Hay, 1/2 lb. Linseed Cake + 7 lbs Straw. For L.E. horses 17 lbs Oats, 6 lbs Hay 1/2 lb. Linseed Cake + 6 lbs Straw	
"	3/10/14			
"	4/10/14		Visited 130 Field Ambulance. Standings good, Sanitation + animals	

WAR DIARY or INTELLIGENCE SUMMARY

Army Form C. 2118.

Place	Date	Hour	Summary of Events and Information	Remarks and references to Appendices
ST. SIXTE.	4/11/17		Grooming and Shoeing good. Visited 332 Co. A.S.C. Animals excellent. Still in old lines - up to their hocks in mud; unfortunately evacuation and most for billets. A proper inspection at the present time - impossible. Visited H.Q. Not. Sec. and examined leavings of a horse lost on by the aforesaid Sec., as suspected mange. Found many were without difficulty. On passing along the road, I was called in by a Corporal of the 2/1st Co. R.E., 55 Division to look at a Bay mare which had died during the night. My opinion - Infants' colic.	
"	5/11/17		Ambulance with D.A.D.M.S. to them and examined 91 newly arrived Remounts, to be distributed to various Units in this Division - Animals on the whole - fair.	
"	6/11/17		Visited H.Q. 49th Mil Vet. Sec. Listened to Transport & Wagon Line Officers and N.C.Os. on Horse and Stable Management. Visited D.H.Q. Horse lines. Office Routine.	
"	7/11/17		Visited D.H.Q. and M.M.P. Horse lines. Office Routine.	
"	8/11/17			

WAR DIARY or INTELLIGENCE SUMMARY

Army Form C. 2118.

Place	Date	Hour	Summary of Events and Information	Remarks and references to Appendices
St. Sixte	9/11/16		Visited Lange. Horses seemy. Conference Veterinary Officers. Office routine.	
"	10/11/16		Visited 114 Bde. Machine Gun Co. Animals in fair condition. Shoeing indifferent. Visited 15th Bn. Welsh Regt. Condition of animals good with exception of — H.Q. horses which are very poor. Good ventilation for one H.Q. to be circulated. Standing good. Shoeing good. Visited 13 Bn. Welsh Regt. Standing good. Shoeing good. Animals in good condition. Visited 114th Bde. Vet.Sect. Animals in very good condition. Visited 114 Bde. H.Q. Condition of animals and shoeing good. Standings excellent. Visited Q.H.Q. Visited 12H Co. R.E.	
"	11/11/16		Visited 149 M.W.S. Lecture to transport and Wagon Lines Officers & N.C.O's on Horse and Stable Management. Second lecture.	
"	15/11/16		Visited B/122 Bde. R.F.A. Examined horses reported by V.O. Yos. 16 to 20 affected by influenza. Attended to typical cases of a virulent type. The affected animals isolated, - receiving special attention	

WAR DIARY
or
INTELLIGENCE SUMMARY

Army Form C. 2118.

Place	Date	Hour	Summary of Events and Information	Remarks and references to Appendices
ST. SIXTE	12/11/16		My Special attendants Six more under suspicion. Men were segregated in separate lines. Gave instructions to be taken in this falling every day and on no account of any Temperatures being observed. The animal to be isolated and reported to this office. Had several returned with L.F.U. and informed him of the outbreak. Also notified D.M.S. Army & A.D. + D.M.G. Divn. Acquainted the former of steps which have been taken to restrict the outbreak. Visited 9/Iny. Bde. with Col. PATTERSON 96. Bde. - Inspected animals. I found very poor and just recovered from attack of colic. Gave instructions for sick animal to be placed on sick lines. Visited B/Iny. Bde. Animals in good condition, with exception of 3 or 4, which I viewed instructions, - to receive special attention.	
	13/11/16		Visited B/Iny. Bde. Animals in good condition. No fresh cases. Visited B/122. Bde. Animals food of influenza in B/122. Bde. Visited B/122. Bde. Animals food	

2353 Wt. W2514/1454 700,000 5/15 D. D. & L.   A.D.S.S. Forms/C. 2118.

WAR DIARY or INTELLIGENCE SUMMARY

Army Form C. 2118.

Place	Date	Hour	Summary of Events and Information	Remarks and references to Appendices
St. Sixte	13/11/16		in condition. Visited 114. Bde. H.Q. And judged for "turn-outs". Visited B/122. Bde. Inspected the animals are taken from the lines this morning	
"	14/11/16		2 additional cases were taken from the lines this morning. Isolated and receiving special attention. High temperatures. Among the 7 suspected cases, no further developments.	
"	15/11/16		Visited B/122 Bde. Examined the animals affected with influenza. Several showing signs of improvement. One fresh case admitted. Those remaining suspicious – no further developments. Visited D.H.Q. horse lines. Office Routine.	
"	16/11/16		Conference Veterinary Officers. Office Routine	
"	17/11/16		Visited 123rd Battery R.F.A. with Capt. Prebster, etc V.O. 4/c.	
"	18/11/16		Condition of animals excellent, with exception of two – which I ordered to be sent to M.V.S. for evacuation. Animals were receiving 3 feeds – put on during the night by orders of O/c. Battery. Contrary to S.R.O.I. Sorted this matter out to-	

WAR DIARY or INTELLIGENCE SUMMARY

Army Form C. 2118.

Place	Date	Hour	Summary of Events and Information	Remarks and references to Appendices
ST. SIXTE.	18/11/16		2R.V.S. Army. One horse segregated - Mange - face irritations for animal to be sent up to Mob. Vet Sec. for evaluation	
"	19/11/16		Visits No. 2 Section 38th D.A.C. - Examined two ponies by Capt. FINCH. A.V.C. V.O.'s. 1 new influenza and confirmed diagnosis. Every and every precaution taken to prevent spreading of the disease. Visits 1 B/122 Bde. and examined two animals isolated suffering from influenza. Signs of improvement. Visits Lancs Hussars Yeomy. One case of Mange remains. Visits D.H.Q. Horse lines. Officer Conding.	
"	20/11/16		Accompanied onto Q.M. Q.M.S., visits POPERINGHE Station and inspected 46 Remounts arrived for Mrs. Deacon. Fairly average lot. 1 horse very foot. Flees. Slightly dull Mare lame left hind. Vaulte	
"	21/11/16		B/119 Bde. with A.D.R. & inspected animals in view to casting for view. Visits A.D.R. 122 Bde. S.F.R. Inspected - one suspected to the R.S. examined and case of Influenza origin traceable to B/122 Bde. where the disease is animals being shed at B/122.	

WAR DIARY
INTELLIGENCE SUMMARY

Army Form C. 2118.

Place	Date	Hour	Summary of Events and Information	Remarks and references to Appendices
ST SIXTE	21/11/18		Arrol is the outbreak on Miss falling. Gave instructions for Mrs animal to be removed from the stable and to placed under treatment in B/122 Bde. B.F.A. Other horses in contact to be placed on infectious lines at B/122. Bde. J.V.O. Visited B/122. Bde. B.F.A. and inspected animals with influenza under treatment there. General all were improving — no complications. Visited 119th Mob. Vet. Sec. and inspected unit.	
"	22/11/18		Visited Section 4. 38th D.A.C. Inspected remounts — detected flaring out of these horses in mud kaths in mud. Examined one — found Influenza. Visited Section 2. 38th D.A.C. and examined the affected animal with Influenza, much improvement.	
"	23/11/18		Conference Veterinary Officers. Visited B/122. Bde. Inspected animals with Influenza, and inspected cases. Has 2 infectious cases remove to affected lines. All animals showing marked improvement. Visited 129th Field Ambulance. Examined one at request of Capt. CULHANE. Horse signs of Pneumonia. Prognosis fatal.	

Army Form C. 2118.

WAR DIARY
or
INTELLIGENCE SUMMARY.
(Erase heading not required.)

Instructions regarding War Diaries and Intelligence Summaries are contained in F.S. Regs., Part II. and the Staff Manual respectively. Title pages will be prepared in manuscript.

Place	Date	Hour	Summary of Events and Information	Remarks and references to Appendices
St Sixte	24/11/16		Office Routine.	
"	25/11/16		do.	
"	26/11/16		Visited 122 Brigade R.F.A. A. & B. Batteries. Inspected Animals affected with Influenza. 34 cases in sick lines at present, all doing well. That suspected animals from Standby Div Open L Standing under cover. Visited No 2 Section D.A.C. and inspected the sick horses affected with Influenza, both doing well. Visited 129 Fld Amb. and examined sick horse with shy galler, progressing satisfactory.	
"	27/11/16		Attended C. Sgt. Ormond M.O. Service. Office Routine. One horse picked up nail, 1 prevent A.D. Horse there ... leave officer, she foot strained ?, sore rubdown, stripper sale, and after antiseptic.	
"	28/11/16		Office Routine. Visited Lancashire Hussars ..., and stated horse which has met with an accident, he could wants on elbows and stifl, detailed C operate, also spavin horse which failed to go out and came back lame. Suspicious spavin should inside.	
"	29/11/16			
"	30/11/16		Visited and inspected horse in 332 C.A.S.C. poor horse for oversea, 1 deliver almost in ... for by, awai Jundice use in stifle, awai for additional axial for ... Suspence of N.O.	

Signed W.H. Lewis
MAJOR,
A.D.V.S. 38th (WELSH) DIVISION

Original.

CONFIDENTIAL

WAR DIARY

OF

A. D. V. S. 38th. (WELSH) DIVISION

FROM

1st. DECEMBER 1916.

TO

31st. DECEMBER 1916.

: : : : : : : : : :

(VOLUME XIII.)

: : : : : : : : : :

[signature]
Major. A.V.C.

31st. December 1916   A.D.V.S., 38th. (Welsh) Division

WAR DIARY or INTELLIGENCE SUMMARY

Army Form C. 2118.

(Erase heading not required.)

Place	Date	Hour	Summary of Events and Information	Remarks and references to Appendices
ST SIXTE	1/12/16		Office routine. Inspected Veterinary Officers.	
"	2/12/16		Office routine. Army Relieves. Visits D.H.Q. Acc. Lines.	
"	3/12/16		Visits 123 Bde. B. Battery. Inspected the animals with Stephenson. Not - improvement.	
"	4/12/16		Visits 124 Fd. F.C. Met A.D. the animals had been moved into new Standings - much better. Full standings. Condition of animals fair. Shoeing good.	
"	5/12/16		Visits 38th Div. Amm. Column. Inspected Stephenson. Examined two cases - Strangles - not much improvement.	
"	6/12/16		Visits "D" Battery 122nd Bde. R.F.A. Found indications for Stephenson. Visits "A" and "B" Batteries and inspected remounts for Remedies. Satisfactory improvement.	
"	7/12/16		Accompanied A.D. + D.M.S. to POPERINGHE and met the Remounts arriving for Divisions - party veterinary for Conference Veterinary Officers - influenza cases - not attended to. Much influenza cases - Cold - wet feet.	
"	8/12/16		Visits 2nd Fd. Amb. and attended to Much influenza cases - Cold - wet feet.	

Army Form C. 2118.

WAR DIARY
or
INTELLIGENCE SUMMARY.
(Erase heading not required.)

Place	Date	Hour	Summary of Events and Information	Remarks and references to Appendices
ST SIXTE	8/1/16		Parkes: etc - and I and Inoculated Around 1.	
"	9/1/16		Office Routine. Visited D.H.A. Horse Lines.	
"	10/1/16		Visited "B" Battery 122 Bde R.F.A. Examined Influenza cases, Inferring satisfactorily — No fresh cases. Any 9 Men in charge 34 horses — insufficient — Paid attention of Sergt. Major — being no Officer present — visited Lanes. However, ponies duly two bags of Oats as ration form of the horses in good condition.	
"	11/1/16		Visited EGANELBECQ, and arranged for Waiting for the A.V. Horses. Called on M.R.V.S. 39th Division. Infected site at present occupied by 50th Mob. Vet. Sec. Decided to place 39th Mob. Vet. Sec. at the site site LEDRINGHEM. Arranged for posting to change over on 14th inst. An my return to office I found instructions awaiting me from R.A.M.S. Army to detail O/C. 49 M.B. to take charge of Sick Horse train on 13th inst. Issued instructions to O/C. 49 M.V.S. and about date of move from 14th to 15th. Advised O/C. 49 Mob. Vet. Sec. and arranged with A.D.V.S. 39th Division and O/C. 49 Mob. Vet. Sec.	

WAR DIARY or INTELLIGENCE SUMMARY

Army Form C. 2118.

Instructions regarding War Diaries and Intelligence Summaries are contained in F. S. Regs., Part II. and the Staff Manual respectively. Title pages will be prepared in manuscript.

(Erase heading not required.)

Place	Date	Hour	Summary of Events and Information	Remarks and references to Appendices
ST. SIXTE	12/7/16		Visited R.H.Q. Mob. Vet. Sec. Officer Routine.	
"	13/7/16		Inspected Veterinary Officers. Visited R.H.A. Horse lines. Officer Routine.	
"	14/7/16		Divisional moved from ST SIXTE to ESQUELBECQ. Officer Routine.	
ESQUELBECQ	15/7/16		Visited 49th Mob. Vet. Sec. at LEDGINGHEM. Visited R.A.C. remount Hollies in various stables. Officer Routine.	
"	16/7/16		Visited 131 Field Ambulance. Corrected new horse - Lamenels. Visited Div. Signal Co. & R.H.Q. Horse Stables.	
"	17/7/16		Visited 49th Mob. Vet. Sec. Div. Mob. Vet. Horses. Divl Signal Co. Horses. Purchasing Board Horses. Sent to M.V.S. for Inspection. Animals in a dirty condition. Ordered that a clipping machine should be obtained.	
"	18/7/16		Visited R.H.Q. Stables. M.M.P. 49th Mob. Vet. Sec. & Signal Co. 1 case of Colic at Divl Signal Co.	
"	19/7/16		Inspected 149 Rev. F.A. & 147 130th marching off for Training Amimets in good condition. Detailed Capt. J. MACFARLANE. AVC. in Veterinary charge. Inspected Ho. Os. & No. M. Section 38th Divl. Amm. Column.	

WAR DIARY or INTELLIGENCE SUMMARY

Army Form C. 2118.

Place	Date	Hour	Summary of Events and Information	Remarks and references to Appendices
ESQUELBECQ	19/7/16		Animals in excellent condition. Visited B/122 Bde. R.F.A. and inspected animals. Reported on account of Influenza and found them in excellent fettle. Recommended half ARMSTRONG. A.V.C. to continue the care of Jenie's with them. Meanwhile to report service to Capt. Rice shows a Jap. Visited 130. Field Ambulance and inspected animals in the lines. Report of the animals not at work. Condition good. I have taken Lieut. Lyffe, during the night. Visited Divl. Signal Co. Examined the animal suffering from Colic — improving.	
	20/7/16		Visited HQrs. Mot. Vet. Sec. Visited VIII Corps Purchasing Board. 3 mange cases. Forwarded to 25th Division D.T. re authority to supply Stewart Stripping Machine for this unit. Visited HQrs. Mil. Vet. Sec. Visited 131. Field Ambulance. Ret.	
	21/7/16		Signal Co. ~ VIII Corps Purchasing Board.	
	22/7/16		Visited HQrs. Mil. Vet. Sec., accompanied by D.A.A.–Q.M.G. and inspected Cases required attention. Trenches to be put in. Visited Divl. Signal Co.	

2353 Wt. W2544/1454 700,000 5/15 D. D. & L. A.D.S.S. Forms/C. 2118.

WAR DIARY or INTELLIGENCE SUMMARY

Army Form C. 2118.

Place	Date	Hour	Summary of Events and Information	Remarks and references to Appendices
ESQUELBECQ	23/10/16		Visited R/1/M. Res. P.F.A. Condition good. Many horses unclipped - legs clipped. Evacuated 3 horses for Debility and 1 surgical case. R/1/M. Condition good. Evacuated 5 surgical cases. 6/1/M. Condition not so good as the other two batteries. Evacuated 2 horses for Debility. 8/1/- Condition good. Evacuated 2 Debility cases, and 2 surgical cases. One 12.2. Res. Bde. Examined cases Influenza. All doing very well. One additional suspected case. A/1/M. Res. One additional suspected case. B/1/M. One additional case of Influenza and 2 additional suspected cases. Condition slight. Visited No. 50 Vet. Vet. Sec. and suspected batt. Linhings. Returned to A.D.V.S. 63rd Division. Major Ball Armstrong. Noted to NELLAVIZE to report to duty. Nothing - D.V.S. Lept. A.V.C. to duty. No. 2 Veterinary Hospital now kept. Brigade No. 2 Section. 38th D.A.C.	
	24/10/16			

Army Form C. 2118.

WAR DIARY or INTELLIGENCE SUMMARY.

(Erase heading not required.)

Instructions regarding War Diaries and Intelligence Summaries are contained in F. S. Regs., Part II. and the Staff Manual respectively. Title pages will be prepared in manuscript.

Place	Date	Hour	Summary of Events and Information	Remarks and references to Appendices
ESQUELBECQ	24/12/14		Visited Divl. H.Q. Divl. Signal Co. - M.M.P. Office routine.	
"	25/12/14		Office routine.	
"	26/12/14		Visited Divl. H.Q. Office routine.	
"	27/12/14		Proceeded with G.O.C. R.A. & Brig. Major F.W. to WISSANT and inspected 119. Bde. F.T.W. Met in training. Animals fairly well. 20 T 3 cases Lame adjourned. Recommended keeping new togs on to prevent animals picking up sand from the ground.	
"	28/12/14		Returned from WISSANT to ESQUELBECQ. Office routine.	
"	29/12/14		Visited Divl. H.Q. Divl. Signal Co. 1 case P.U.N. + 1 case casting nil. Visited 49th M.V.S. Corps purchasing Board. 1 case wound contusion - hip. Visited 49th M.T.S. Divl. Signal Co. Div. Vet. Officer ← M.M.P. Lieut. F.R.	
"	30/12/14		PAGE. A.V.C. reported for duty next this Div. Asst. Vet PAGE. to 122. Rev. F.T.W. for duty. arranged for his accommodation. Weekly State acc.t ending 25/12/14. East return to - Animals since 102 - Cured 51 - Evacuated 33 - Died 2 - Destroyed 1 - Remaining under treatment 9t.	
"	31/12/14		Visited 49th M.T.S. D.H.Q. Office routine.	

[Signature]
A.D.V.S. 38th (WELSH) DIVISION. MAJOR.

Original.

CONFIDENTIAL

WAR DIARY

OF

A. D. V. S. 38th. (WELSH) DIVISION

FROM

1st. JANUARY 1917.

TO

31st. JANUARY 1917.

: : : : : : : : :

(VOLUME XIV.)

: : : : : : : : :

Major. A.V.C.
A.D.V.S., 38th. (Welsh) Division.

31st. January 1917.

Army Form C. 2118.

WAR DIARY
or
INTELLIGENCE SUMMARY.
(Erase heading not required.)

Instructions regarding War Diaries and Intelligence Summaries are contained in F.S. Regs., Part II. and the Staff Manual respectively. Title pages will be prepared in manuscript.

Place	Date	Hour	Summary of Events and Information	Remarks and references to Appendices
ESQUELBECQ.	1/1/17.		Visited HQ. Mob. Vet. Sec. Div. Hd. Qrs. & M.M.P.	
"	2/1/17.		Office routine. Visited HQ. Vet. Sec. I saw Ringworm Capt. F. Smith' Charger. Out the Qrs. for treatment. A.P.M. charged Driver sending horse to M.V.S. for treatment. 19th Bde. R.F.A. report Horn. Among ESQUELBECQ on way to HERZEELE. 10 cases taken on march 9 cases left behind.	
	3/1/17		Visited D.H.Q. Sent report to F.A. 38th Division (copy to A.D.V.S. 2nd Army, 38th D. & V.O. & 19th Bde.) informing method of treating sick animals of 19 Bde. R.F.A. at WISSANT. Recommendations for stabling temporary measures to prevent further outbreak in 121 Bde. R.F.A. and one at WISSANT. Also questioned the supply of using this place for training purposes sent further accommodation for freezing & watering of animals to be made. Visited 19. M.V.S. I arranged for collection of horses left behind by B/D1. Bde. suffering from opthalmia. Made application for cab. informed one not available.	

Army Form C. 2118.

WAR DIARY
or
INTELLIGENCE SUMMARY.
(Erase heading not required.)

Instructions regarding War Diaries and Intelligence Summaries are contained in F. S. Regs., Part II. and the Staff Manual respectively. Title pages will be prepared in manuscript.

Place	Date	Hour	Summary of Events and Information	Remarks and references to Appendices
ESQUELBECQ	4/1/17		Visited H.Q. N.F.S. & arranged for collection of sick horses left by 119. The R.F.A. on return to this area at EPERLECQ. Visited BOLLEZEELE & inspected 10th Bn. S.W.B. Animals in good condition. Past sick insufficient - Filled all out this place, very unsatisfactory. Also - no Mant line coming into this area. Inspected 16. B. WELSH REGT. Billeted in dispersal manner as 10th Bn S.W.B. Condition of animals good. No Mant Lines coming to this area. No new arrivals to this Unit. Inspected animals 115th M.Gun Co. condition good. Starting out in full no clothing To Mant Lines and coming to this area. Received way - 01 dental. - no new ticket Ments. - Inspected 10. yo. & report the matter. visited 17. Bn. R.W.F. Animals in excellent condition no standings - in field - no clothing - no Mant lines lines coming to this area. the Qr 115. BDE. Animals in excellent condition. - Animals water cool. Visited Also 7 animals of 131. FIELD AMB. - No Mant Mann Ry this Unit. Peculiar	

2353 Wt. W2544/1454 700,000 5/15 D. D. & L. A.D.S.S. Forms/C 2118.

WAR DIARY or INTELLIGENCE SUMMARY

Army Form C. 2118.

Place	Date	Hour	Summary of Events and Information	Remarks and references to Appendices
ESQUELBECQ	4/1/17		to WATTEN and inspected 123. Co. R.E. condition of animals good, with exception of one. No Head Groom by this Unit.	
"	5/1/17		Conference Veterinary Officers. Visited Lt. Col. the O.i/c. & M.M.P. Horses. Sent application for boots, informed one not available. Joined H.Q. C.A.F. & R.O. 115. Recd. jnl. Capt. J. Culhane. T. Capt. T. FINCH to change and on 7th inst.	
"	6/1/17		Visited Lieut.H. 384 R.O.G. & inspected Remounts segregated there. Gave permission for the dispersal to various Brigades, with exception of four affected with ringworm. Intended Capt. T. FINCH. to send them to M.V.S. for treatment. Visited Lieut. F. PAGE. Vc. 122 BDE. — to unit to make inspection. Handed over Capt. W. ARMSTRONG. called refc. Advance from Lieut. PAGE. 2 Field Ambces. to tie foot M.D.	
"	7/1/17		of P.W.N. Visited Hq. M.V.S. + and Met A.D.V.S. 55 Division who came to run the Hosp. for two Months. Visited PROVEN, accompanied by R.O. + A.M.A. & inspected 5th Reserves.	

WAR DIARY or INTELLIGENCE SUMMARY

Army Form C. 2118.

(Erase heading not required.)

Place	Date	Hour	Summary of Events and Information	Remarks and references to Appendices
ESQUELBECQ	1/1/17		Average foot. Low in general condition. Chris showing some defect of Ringworm palates, possibly used.	
"	8/1/17		Visited Col. Ed. Cav. Hd. Grs. & M.M.P. Smokers Regt. to D.A.B. re large protection to mules & mares to horses. B.O.C. ed stolen horn hair.	
"	9/1/17		Visited Hq Mob. Vet. Sec.	
"	10/1/17		Office routine. Visited D.S.O. & M.M.P. horses	
"	11/1/17		On absence of leave from 11/1/17 to 21/1/17.	
ST. SIXTE	22/1/17		Visited R.O. 42. shot 1 horse & 1 M.V.S. 1 case suspected Mange. Visited 3rd Bat. Leicest. Examined horses had feet. Informed officer concerned & informed him of neglect. Visited Lanc. Hussars Comp. 1 saw cracker heels, through clothing lays. 1 case suspected Ku disease. General examinal animals from R.V.S. army viz :- That to certify to freedom of Mange. This to communicate No. of animals examined. B.V.S. 11/2nd6/17. A.D.O. Memo re suggestions	B.V.S. C.M. 195

Army Form C. 2118.

WAR DIARY
or
INTELLIGENCE SUMMARY.

(Erase heading not required.)

Instructions regarding War Diaries and Intelligence Summaries are contained in F.S. Regs., Part II. and the Staff Manual respectively. Title pages will be prepared in manuscript.

Place	Date	Hour	Summary of Events and Information	Remarks and references to Appendices
ST. SIXTE	22/1/17		Phone msg. by Majors A.V.C.	
"	23/1/17		Received communication from Capt. MACFARLANE offered to horse slaughter reported immediates — anyone to proceed to the unit & condemn infected Animals. The animal to-morrow. Rained cat — informed me not available. Visited H.Q. V.S. & inspected animals sent to condemn. Instructed Mr. N.S. to return mule from No's Sec. 39th D.A.K. & to be tested in unit seen left limb. Was informed by off M.L.S. that the V.O. of this unit had ordered an ambulance to be sent to remove this animal, — which was carried out — the mule was standing fairly sound taking this matter in hand at next conference. Received memo from Capt. B. MUNDLAS, requesting me to visit & inspect Hays Heavy Artillery under his charge. This I postponed doing on visiting HERZEELE	
"	24/1/17		Visited 6/121 Bde P.A. & inspected the animals. V.O. 96 was not present — out visiting other units. Some animals suffering from Enzheuma — 5 horses in an emaciated condition, most of them are	

WAR DIARY or INTELLIGENCE SUMMARY

Army Form C. 2118.

Place	Date	Hour	Summary of Events and Information	Remarks and references to Appendices
ST. SIXTE	24/1/17		Ante-Mortis and scab inspects. Animals Ante Morten to be slaughtered. Animals in the right section were in much better condition. Orderly Cpl. — informed and not available.	
"	25/1/17		Accompanied with the D.D.V.S. Divn. A.D.V.S. + Off. I/c. attached works. Inspection of the Corps Commandant's Reference subject of Mange. Horses in animals in this Division. Visited C.H.Q. Lines.	
"	26/1/17		Conference Veterinary Officers. Office routine. Visited 81st Bde R.F.A. No. of cases Dermatitis.	
"	27/1/17		Visited 81st Bde. R.F.A. return 5 for examination. Details. Animals in good condition. Examined horses suffering Dermatitis by Vety. Officer etc — conclusion not Dermatitis. B/121 Bde. R.F.A. Animals in Jnr. Section, animals in excellent condition, others moderate. Animals in food Station, in Mange — 2 pairs to be remounted. Lost report to Offr. I/c. Accomm. Horses from B.R.S. No. to R.B.V.S. — D.D.V.S. + D.D.V.S. Re these Horses — 16 animals. A.D.V.S. 17/222/17. Re these Horses — 16 animals.	

Army Form C. 2118.

WAR DIARY
or
INTELLIGENCE SUMMARY.

(Erase heading not required.)

Instructions regarding War Diaries and Intelligence Summaries are contained in F. S. Regs., Part II. and the Staff Manual respectively. Title pages will be prepared in manuscript.

Place	Date	Hour	Summary of Events and Information	Remarks and references to Appendices
ST. SIXTE	28/1/17		Visited B/122 Bde R.F.A. Animals in good condition. Mangings not good, but what cool. B/122 Bde. 1 horse in poor condition. Are animals have recently been transferred on re-organizing of Artillery. 1 case Quitor mandated. Lost carry to destinations recovered from R.F.L. — no casualties to late. Have until further orders. horse surface animal not sent for the present. Used dogs on : for Mange. Visited B/122 Bde. Passed sub continued animal until negs on : for Mange, which are not was found. the any these funed into microscopical examination. failed and 10 suspected cases — for treatment — my train. Gave orbit estimations to treat animals and report to F.O.yo.	
"	29/1/17		Visited Vet. Cert's How the × examined same durations not yet recommend which eg. Ast. Vet. See. and examined leashings of horse from 11 Bn. S.W.B., horse's firm Sarahie Mange. this case was chronic by F.O.yo. 115 Bde. further instructions to to F.O. H.Q. re Mange in B/122. Ade. when sent to	

WAR DIARY or INTELLIGENCE SUMMARY

Army Form C. 2118.

Place	Date	Hour	Summary of Events and Information	Remarks and references to Appendices
ST SIXTE	29/1/17		C.O.11. - D - + N.O.ib. Sent report to D.D. 115 Div. to Major in 11. Bn. S.W.B. - copies to C.O.11. - D. - + N.O.ib. Received intimation from Capt. MACFARLANE of a further outbreak of Mange in A/124 Bn. R.F.A. 2 slight cases. Inspected all N.C.s to take precautions.	
"	30/1/17		Visited A/124 Bde. Inspected 2 cases Effengis + 1 suspected case of a Mange form – probable. All removed for the moment in this Camp. – 3 in hoot condition – (not debilitated). I am a satisfied condition. The remainder were in good condition. Had instructions let the Bitty men to to be removed when circumstances will admit. Inspected 16th Bn. Welsh Regt. All animals in very good condition. Inspected 115 Bde. S.C. + various cases received ment in connection of Mange; having efficient in this unit. 2 horses showing signs of symptoms – treatment – Mustings. All animals in good condition. 17 Bn. N.W.F. Animals in good condition. Mustings fairly good. Visited 11. Bn. S.C.B. Case of Mange having been communicated in this	

WAR DIARY or INTELLIGENCE SUMMARY

Army Form C. 2118.

Place	Date	Hour	Summary of Events and Information	Remarks and references to Appendices
ST. SIXTE	2/1/17		Unit. No animals unfitted. Gave instructions to hand over feed to at once. Room for great improvement in this unit. Quality of hay issued about the same. Animals feeding up hay ration by mls. considerable wastage here.	
"	3/1/17		Visited VIII Corps horse Ah. attached 39th Division. Horse lines through. Out at in Hospital getting cold — H. this morning going to frost. Vet Sergt. F. PAGE A.V.C. N.O. ½ 122 Bde. R.F.A. and accompanied him to Bde. HQ. Examined horses reported as suffered mange — nothing seen — cannot bring that to an absolute and had horses thin although taking ammunition night and day to the front. Examined Regiment — Mange — not seen in contact with any animals. Gave instructions for animal to be isolated & most careful examination. Examined 18 cases. Rejected — Suspected Montagne — confirmed diagnosis — all 18 from taken for examination. Field 332 Co. A.S.C. Isolated the animals. N.B. — Majority out at soft Frontline good. No Mange. Isolated 331 Co. A.S.C. 2 cows Suspected Mange. —	

Army Form C. 2118.

WAR DIARY
or
INTELLIGENCE SUMMARY.
(Erase heading not required.)

Instructions regarding War Diaries and Intelligence Summaries are contained in F. S. Regs., Part II. and the Staff Manual respectively. Title pages will be prepared in manuscript.

Place	Date	Hour	Summary of Events and Information	Remarks and references to Appendices
ST SIXTE	31/1/17		Inspection of animals gen. Visits 333 Co RSC. Animals in good condition - 3 cases slight Mange. Visits 330 Co RSC. At least 1/3 regt. very suspicious cases of Mange. Condition good. 6 cookers of the 21 Divisional A.S.C. Working in next field - just arrived. All infected cases were pulled out, isolation & instructions given for treatment. Many of the animals in these companies are still unclipped.	

(signature)
MAJOR
A.D.V.S. 38th WELSH DIVISION

CONFIDENTIAL

WAR DIARY

OF

A. D. V. S. 38th. (WELSH) DIVISION

FROM

1st. FEBRUARY 1917.

TO

28th. FEBRUARY 1917.

: : : : : : : : : :

(VOLUME XV.)

: : : : : : : : : :

(Original)

[signature]
Major.

28th. February 1917.   A.D.V.S., 38th. (Welsh) Division.

Army Form C. 2118.

WAR DIARY
or
INTELLIGENCE SUMMARY
(Erase heading not required.)

Instructions regarding War Diaries and Intelligence Summaries are contained in F. S. Regs., Part II. and the Staff Manual respectively. Title pages will be prepared in manuscript.

Place	Date	Hour	Summary of Events and Information	Remarks and references to Appendices
St Sixte	1/3/17		Visited D.H.Q. Horse lines. Alfred Routine	
"	2/3/17		Office Routine. Visited R.H.Q. + M.G.C. Horse lines	
"	3/3/17		Visited 119th Bde. Vet. Sec. Office Routine	
"	4/3/17		Visited D.H.Q. Horse lines. 1 case casted mule. Visited H.Q. F.A. 1 case colic 1 case lame. N.Y.D.	
"	5/3/17		Visited 10th Bn. Welsh Regt. condition of animals good. Shoeing good. Loose animals. All inspected. Clipping machine sent for. To be kept out of Regimental Lines. Visited C.O. 11th Bn. The Hastings and condition of animals good. 1 case Influenza. T.O.b. charged. Condition of animals and Horse Standings good. Visited 11/5 Bn The Welsh Regt. Condition only. Fair – this Unit does not conform in any respect to ... – this Unit. Visited 13th Bn Welsh Regt. condition only. This Unit. Cases of dumping the feet of animals. Attention later – that Mules. S.S. and frontal cut faults to him. Not fit. horses. Br. a recent. Remarked 6 mule horses. mules in N. Mc. Gut with this Br. a recent. Remarked 6 mule horses. mules in fair condition	
"			Also – Mules in good condition, riding horses in poor condition	

WAR DIARY or INTELLIGENCE SUMMARY

Army Form C. 2118.

Place	Date	Hour	Summary of Events and Information	Remarks and references to Appendices
ST. SIXTE	5/2/17		Gave instructions for 2" horses to be evacuated.	
"	6/3/17		At request V.O. of "R" Bde Heavy Artillery visited & inspected 123 Heavy Bde R.G.A. & cast mange cases of Kiatment. Rest of the animals in this Bty in excellent condition. 141 St Heavy Battery R.G.A. 10 cases mange, cases under treatment. Rest of animals in excellent condition. Re animals in 141st H.A. Col. are not in so good Issue Kings to animals in good condition. Spoke to men later re Battery animals in mange nettrearst, disinfection, isolation etc. to by V.O. of "D" to mange suffering animals and their manger, nose lines & R.A. M.D. lines. Visited 352 Divisional Shell.	
"	7/3/17		1 case inspected then issues.	
"	8/17		Office Routine. Visited 6/121 Rein & inspected animals on the lines. Condition poor. Number of cases of Recurable improving. 18/123 Bde R.F.A. not inspected on the animals, condition good. Lieut F. PAGE. M.O. of examined for Mange. 2 cases Ulcerative Stomatitis, 1 improving.	

WAR DIARY or INTELLIGENCE SUMMARY

Place	Date	Hour	Summary of Events and Information	Remarks and references to Appendices
St Sixte	8/2/17		The chief saw Veterinary Officer Bliss Bon. R.F.A. Animals in good condition with exception of left section whose newly joined. This Brigade on an emergency of (A) with artillery Brigade. At animals in this section fair. 2 or 3 cases mange slight symptoms. Liaison and meetings officer, can boil in extremely crowded condition, arrangements for animals to be evacuated. Had Sgt. Major in this Battery, who offered to be an excellent man, and and impart state of affairs in this unit.	
"	9/2/17		Veterinary Officers Conference. Visited 51/21 Div. R.F.A. inspects animals affected with Remedies. Bliss Bon. R.F.A. Inspected all animals - all indications for mange present to be put up. animal animals segregated for Mange. also examined 2 cases animal animals segregated for Mange. also examined 2 cases Artillery. 51/22 Bde R.F.A. Inspection the animals. Bliss Bon. R.F.A. animals in a very dirty condition, showing evidence of want of Stable management. Wagon Line Officer sent to see charge.	

WAR DIARY or INTELLIGENCE SUMMARY

Army Form C. 2118.

Place	Date	Hour	Summary of Events and Information	Remarks and references to Appendices
ST SIXTE	9/2/17		2/122 Bde R.F.A. Inspected all animals. Gave instructions for [illeg] horses to be sent to the Mob. Vet. Sec. for scabies. Inspected Mange. Visited 4 gds Mob Vet Sec. By appointment met D.D.V.S. French Army at 122 Bde R.F.A. Reported on scabies cases & D.D.V.S. had to return to A.H.Q.	
"	10/2/17		Secret then expected. Unable to mobilise expected. Visited 15th Bn R.G.A. Examined animals. 2 cases slight Mange. 16th Bn R.G.A. Last vaccinations for all animals to be clipped. Verifying not yet completed. No — cases. 14th Bn R.G.A. Vaccination & feeding gate. 13 Bn R.G.A. Vaccination still some trouble in these Units. Met oft with difficulty. Received information from R.R.M.I. — classifications by road is now open again.	
"	12/2/17		Visited 16/121. Bde R.G.A. Issue animals eating off the ground. Recd. A/Major attention to it. this issue was met. he was having upon the hay nets not unusually [illeg] I pointed out much of the hay was picked out and wasted. the cuts remedies are	

WAR DIARY or INTELLIGENCE SUMMARY

Army Form C. 2118.

Place	Date	Hour	Summary of Events and Information	Remarks and references to Appendices
ST SIXTE	12/2/17		Inspecting favourably. Visited Horse Hosp and ascertained A.D.V.S. 39 Division who agreed that any officers cases of Mange in our Divison may be sent to his R.H. Four continues to all H.Qs. concerned together with Horse Hosp instructions. Visited 3/122 inspected the animals remaining under treatment for Mange. Several of them had been unseen for the past time and none being escorted to any them. Pointed out that it was useless dressing animals not clipped. Arranged out to officer in charge Mange Lines, left for clipping machine would not cut, + he states he has maintained already for blades. Gave me a certified copy of he amount dated 2/2/17 and 13 for 3 hours for shower clipper t H hand clippers. Inspected Sleing R.A.D.S. to ask them to hasten delivery. Saw another horse symptoms suspicious pulmonis - animal segregated. Advised evacuation two animals for kidney animal and Mange. Visited H.Q. Net. Vet. Sec. inspected animals prior to evacuation.	
"	13/2/17		29 Animals to be evacuated. Gave instructions for R.V. horse to be	

Army Form C. 2118.

WAR DIARY
or
INTELLIGENCE SUMMARY.
(Erase heading not required.)

Instructions regarding War Diaries and Intelligence Summaries are contained in F. S. Regs., Part II. and the Staff Manual respectively. Title pages will be prepared in manuscript.

Place	Date	Hour	Summary of Events and Information	Remarks and references to Appendices
ST SIXTE	13/3/17		Nothing quiet no to report.	
"	14/3/17		Visited R.V.O. Horse lines. Accompanied by O.C. A.V.S. proceeded to POPERINGHE and met Num. 100 General. for this Divisions. Average number of animals good – two actual feet.	
"	15/3/17		Proceeded to ST OMER, and attended reconnaissance on Mange at No. 23 Veterinary Hospital.	
"	16/3/17		Conference Veterinary Officers. Visited Affies Reoline. visited R.V.Q. Horse Lines.	
"	17/3/17		Received from Q.M.G. No. Mob Vet. Sec. receipt for No. S.E. 1018 bought JONES C. A.V.C. for Mulcet Veterinary. Visited R.V.O. + M.M.P. Horse Lines. Received from R.V.O. 2nd Army Veterinary Officer Standing Orders for Evacuation of Sick Horses by rear. Traversed roly to O.C. H.Q. Mob. Vet. Sec. Visited M.M.P. stables at DRUMORE CORNER examine Horse reported by A.P.M. as unfit. seems nothing the matter with the animal, except he is too heavy for police work. Visited 19th Lancer Bn. Implest Lines. Animals in good condition. No sick	

Army Form C. 2118.

WAR DIARY
or
INTELLIGENCE SUMMARY
(Erase heading not required.)

Instructions regarding War Diaries and Intelligence Summaries are contained in F. S. Regs., Part II. and the Staff Manual respectively. Title pages will be prepared in manuscript.

Place	Date	Hour	Summary of Events and Information	Remarks and references to Appendices
ST SIXTE	17/7/17		No appearance of Mange. Search note from Offr. 49 M.V.S. announcing Mange Parade has been fixed for one horse belonging to No. 1 Sec. 382 R.A.C.	
"	18/7/17		Visited No. 1 Sec. 38th R.A.C. & examined each individual animal in the Section – found one such animal affected with minor Notined to be evacuated as a sore case & continues case – slight – for treatment. No. 2 Sec. 382 R.A.C. – inspected each individual animal and failed to discover any traces of Mange. No. 3 Sec. 382 R.A.C. and examined each individual animal. 1st that this section is affected with Mange although more Isolated cases symptoms. Settled out 6 slight cases for treatment. Bad conditions as animals in this section. Hats to be taken to N.C. R.E. by to be shot receiving Hats to be taken to N.C. R.E. by 382nd Div – & D.D.V. announcing the arrival of 2 men from Capt. Macfarlane A.V.C. announcing the arrival of 2 men from Capt. Ambrose in A/119. (D) F.A. Bde.	

WAR DIARY or INTELLIGENCE SUMMARY

Army Form C. 2118.

Place	Date	Hour	Summary of Events and Information	Remarks and references to Appendices
ST SIXTE	19/2/17		Reported to P.M. R.E. The exchange of Nominates Interpreted in R/up (A) F A Rev. Sent cop. to R.A.D. - 354 Q" - + R.O.4. FA Rev. visited 331 Co. A.S.C. and inspected sick lines over an the states. 1 case of Mange had just been sent through the Horse Ell hospital of animals foil. visited 332 Co. A.S.C. - inspected sick animals were an the lines. Found 4 or 5 cases of undoubted Mange standing in the lines with other animals. Gave instructions to Capt HARLEY R.O.Y.c. to isolate + deal in isolation the affected animals. Many horses in this Co. still unclipped. secret time two animals have evidently acct been clipped. Has an O/c Rev. tain cov of merchant such this matter.	
"	20/2/17		Visited 13 Rm. Rides. Regt. in schemes to remmechant received from O/c. SG. M.L. that Lensenfies tyme had been disewered in two animals. Gave a nominal of animals Gave instructions for excellent anch treatment. Lent rept to 20.7. 114. Sep. Rev. - copy to R.A.D. - 385 Q" - + 1.0.4c. Visited 19	

T2134. Wt. W708—776. 500000. 4/15. Sir J. C. & S.

Army Form C. 2118.

WAR DIARY
or
INTELLIGENCE SUMMARY.
(Erase heading not required.)

Instructions regarding War Diaries and Intelligence Summaries are contained in F. S. Regs., Part II. and the Staff Manual respectively. Title pages will be prepared in manuscript.

Place	Date	Hour	Summary of Events and Information	Remarks and references to Appendices
ST. SIXTE	23/3/17		Met Lt. Lee and inspected the animals for slaughter. I drew notice to the fact F. PAGE. A.V.C. at being time - animal sent out this time in one eye and enucleators for this animal to be by returned cruelty at mistake has been made.	
"	24/3/17		Took R.S.C. Arty Cart. Ambulance by D.A.D.V.S. Proceeded to HOPOUTRE lying and inspected 27 Remounts arrived for this Division. Very good lot.	
"	25/3/17		Took A/Vet Sec. F-76. Mazar Lines for purpose of inspecting at request of P.R. H.Q. of the disinfectant. Went to animals lines. Stopped to all lines. Same disinfection had been carried out in a satisfactory manner. I left and I met the A.D. Vet Servs. pointed out faults and commissions to the D.V.S. who stated he was trying for more disinfectant. Informed Staff Captain P.R. H.Q. and informed him of his M.C. Os. Holmwood & Ireland to give certificate required until the disinfection has been carried out. Took 12th Co. R.E. and inspected animals. Profin out one animal which has already been dressed with	

T2134. Wt. W708-776. 500000. 4/15. Sir J. C. & S.

WAR DIARY or INTELLIGENCE SUMMARY

Army Form C. 2118.

Place	Date	Hour	Summary of Events and Information	Remarks and references to Appendices
ST SIXTE	22/2/17		Held sick parade. Good nominations for isolation and forage dressing offices. Visited A/iug the R.J.B. examine two cows Monett's bathycan. I selected one from the shed my doubtful. Also examined 2 cows rejected for dermatic follicules. In my opinion I will diagnosis is correct. No other cows doubtful. Two animals are isolated. I recommend proper attention. Accompanied by R.O.B.M.S. met D.B.S. by Chrchenwood who inspected lines for view. Second arm from V.O. No. Horses, inspected horses by to give the Division all day on Sunday 25th inst. for use of Horse Sept. This arrange at conference with C.Os.	
"	23/2/17		Accompanied D.D. Arranged for Lieut Col. MACFARLANE to utilize horse R.H. on 25/2/17 Units - 332 Co. A.S.C. 115 Res B.E. & 11th Sqn J.R.B. Units R.H.S. Horse lines.	
"	24/2/17		Visited R.H.B. Horse lines. translate R.A.O.B. chapel suffering from debility. Visited Lancs Hussars lines 1 case Mange - this animal has been sent by the troop on 15th inst to this field Isolation.	

T2134. Wt. W708–776. 500000. 4/16. Sir J. C. & S.

WAR DIARY or INTELLIGENCE SUMMARY

Army Form C. 2118.

(Erase heading not required.)

Place	Date	Hour	Summary of Events and Information	Remarks and references to Appendices
ST SIXTE	24/2/17		A.P.M. and requested animal to be returned to Irish and notify the V.O. i/c. Visited Divisional School and Anthony Co. their accommodation is disgraceful. Visited Scots Pets Rifle subcommander animals of 11 Div. A/S.B. - 115 Bde A.D. and 332 Ho. A.S.C. + D.A.C. - Nothing.	
"	25/2/17		Visited 123 Co. R.E. labelled animals - found one case isolated by Capt. CULMORE V.O. i/c as suspicious Mange. Picked out 7 other cases - located and dressed 4 Mange dressing applied. Horses State retaken to stalls disinfected. Visited 114 M. Gun. Co. Animals are getting in bad condition - without supervision is insufficient. Many animals feet - 1 case laminitis - 1 case biting. On the whole the animals in this Co. are in fairly good condition 1 charger reported sickled by Lieut. DAVIES is very foot and serious suspicion symptoms Mange. Visited 151 Co. R.E. Condition of animals good. Vet. Sergt. missing Mange symptoms. Visited 115 Bde L.F.C.	

Army Form C. 2118.

WAR DIARY
or
INTELLIGENCE SUMMARY.
(Erase heading not required.)

Place	Date	Hour	Summary of Events and Information	Remarks and references to Appendices
St Sixte	26/2/17		Inspects animals after having been through Horse Lift yesterday. All men and kit inspected after the Lift. Found 11 Bat. I.M.G.B. and inspected animals which were also at Horse Lift. 3 mules still unclipped. Several others not yet had their second clipping. Saw transport officer - who as usual are not in the lines, and told him of these animals not yet clipped when not working well when the mules to I.O.C. Bde. Mules were not properly disinfected. A statement made by Lytabat in 11x26 line. - Its heard were - scabs not yet being formed. No trace of broken in the lines.	
"	27/2/17		Visited 49th Mot M.T. Coy and inspected all animals tot vaccinated. Ordered to sub coys at R.H.B. horse lines.	
"	28/2/17		Visits 2/119 Army Brig Artillery Bde. Inspected the animals. Ordered 5 horses to be schemated for scabies. About 8 animals to be clipped. A few were infected with Itch, had very heavy coats - to be intrabbed to me for motorbicn when clipping is completed. Nos. are - 1145. 1146. 1143. 1144	

T2134. Wt. W708—776. 500000. 4/15. Sir J. C. & S.

Army Form C. 2118.

WAR DIARY
or
INTELLIGENCE SUMMARY.
(Erase heading not required.)

Place	Date	Hour	Summary of Events and Information	Remarks and references to Appendices
Sr SIXTE	28/2/17		158.160.37 I also ordered the following to be shorn *viz.*: Nos. 129. No. 73 as they were affected with Mange No.75. had already been clipped not infected with lice. Good interesting very difficult site to apply dressing. He remained of the animals in this battery are in good condition. Majority un-clipped. 119th Bde A.F.A. the J-front, the following animals to be in a very concerned condition affected with Mange 1. and two of them affected with climatic pneumonia. I advised situation as they were much too fat gone to meat. Nos 119. 163. 122 the animals in this battery are fat, the most part in a poor oil mutilated condition. Only a few have had their clothes stripped. In all remaining animals to be clipped and further orders given. This is the battery that was mobilized by 39½ Division to complete 119th Army firm artillery Brigade.	

F.W.B. Davies
MAJOR.
A.D.V.S. 36th (WELSH) DIVISION.

(Original)

CONFIDENTIAL

WAR DIARY

OF

A.D.V.S. 38th. (WELSH) DIVISION.

FROM

1st. MARCH 1917.

TO

31st. MARCH 1917.

(VOLUME XVI.)

[signature]
Major.

31st. March 1917.   A.D.V.S., 38th. (Welsh) DIVISION.

Army Form C. 2118.

WAR DIARY
or
INTELLIGENCE SUMMARY.
(Erase heading not required.)

Instructions regarding War Diaries and Intelligence Summaries are contained in F. S. Regs., Part II. and the Staff Manual respectively. Title pages will be prepared in manuscript.

Place	Date	Hour	Summary of Events and Information	Remarks and references to Appendices
ST SIXTE	1/3/17		Visited and inspected B. Inf. (Army) Sick Convoy Stn. Animals treated on the whole in very good condition. 1 case Mange. Advice given as to treatment and use (5% sp?) lot LetSec. 1 reduced case of Mange to be isolated. 1 pulvinous ear ulcerative dermatitis separate. Issued animals to be vaccinated for Rabies. Gave instructions for a number of horses to be staked at rest and to be inspected A.Inf. (Army) V.A. Stn. Stopping preceding recent Visited and inspected A.Inf. (Army) V.A. Stn. Stopping preceding recent animals in feet condition. Not as numerous count in this stnt. Re Rabies case cant be ensured. Several cases suspected Mange. Gave instructions for them to be clipped and dressed. Visited R.H.Q. horse lines.	
"	2/3/17		Veterinary Meeting Officers. Office routine.	
"	3/3/17		Visited 123 Ba. Bc. Recovered marked case of Mange — gave instructions for horse to be sent to No 9 Mob Vet Sec.	
"	4/3/17		Visited R.H.G. & M.M.P. horse lines. Office Routine.	
"	5/3/17		Visited and inspected lines of 102 Interesting Bn. - Incidence of Mange	

WAR DIARY or INTELLIGENCE SUMMARY

Army Form C. 2118.

Place	Date	Hour	Summary of Events and Information	Remarks and references to Appendices
51 SIXTE	5/3/17		very good. Mules and surroundings in clean condition. 1 horse isolated until treatment for Mange.	
"	6/3/17		Visited and inspected the animals of 113 Machine Gun Co. Condition of horses good. Shoeing proceeding. Shoeing bad. In the manner of trimming transport affected. Had Co/C shoeing smith and told shoe present and hind out feet. Recommended to transport officer to select animals who had been shod ready to take disciplinary measures. Visited 114 Machine Gun Co. Some animals in roughish hot condition - shoeing had several cases lumping this fat too long. Another bad accident as 113 M.Gun Co. Clipping proceeding. Visits and inspected 115 Machine Gun Co. Condition of animals g'd. Shoeing indifferent. Similar procedure taken to 113 M Gun Co. Visited animals of 151 to RF. Clipping proceeding and also manufacture of Mules by real lamb. Ascois g'd - several cases slight mange, being treated of Mules by real lamb. Visited up Moth Vet Sec. Inspected all animals report to evacuation.	

T134. Wt. W708—776. 500000. 4/16. Sir J. C. & S.

Army Form C. 2118.

WAR DIARY or INTELLIGENCE SUMMARY.

(Erase heading not required.)

Place	Date	Hour	Summary of Events and Information	Remarks and references to Appendices
St. Sixte	1/5/17		Office Routine. Visited D.H.Q. and A.M.L. Acre lines	
"	2/5/17		Visited 331. Co. A.S.C. Found Artic No 531. who had been dressed few days before, not yet cured. Mixing in lines No. 349. First sling himself and refusing to medicine. Also in the lines Mule No. 404. Put the two animals to the sickyard. Dressed and worked with the other horses until treatment for Mange whisker animals in question, not yet cured. Mules Nos. 381 & 369 also working in lines afflicted with Mange - retired the animals to be put in isolation. Mules for treatment. Received a case of Dermatitis. Re animal and transferred from the Sergent Bns. - The mule is isolated - instructions given to keep all precautions etc. Visited No. 332 Co. A.S.C. Mule No. 405 with Mange. Mixing in lines - ordered to be retired and isolated. J 17-18 animals in this Co. were transferred from 330 Co. A.S.C. in very poor condition. Visited 333 Co. A.S.C. Mule No. 584. Parasitis - II - to be observed. Visited 330 Co. A.S.C. Animals are losing condition, evidently others	

WAR DIARY
or
INTELLIGENCE SUMMARY

Army Form C. 2118.

Place	Date	Hour	Summary of Events and Information	Remarks and references to Appendices
St Sixte	9/3/17		Signs of want of improvement had instructions for the following animals to be evacuated. Nos. 115 & 221 for Debility & No 41 for dermatitis.	
"	9/5/17		Conference Veterinary officers. Office routine. Visits R.S.O. M.D.V. horse lines.	
"	10/3/17		Visited A/122 Bde R.F.A. Condition of animals very good – more improvement. 2 horses in poor condition evacuated for Debility. One horse showing symptoms of Mange. Still no notified Government stables. Dipping and treatment for Mange. Dressings clean, teeth well attended and line mostly. Visited B/122 Bde R.F.A. Sign of improvement in the condition of lines. Clipping not yet completed. Many it is alleged difficulty in obtaining hairs for clipping machine. No cases Mange nasal treatment – a cult too. Visited C/122 Bde R.F.A. Condition of animals very good with exception of one reduced to be evacuated for Debility. One horse sent to field this morning direct to my inspection for microscopical examination. Informed the Farriers Sergt had been found.	

Army Form C. 2118.

WAR DIARY
or
INTELLIGENCE SUMMARY.
(Erase heading not required.)

Instructions regarding War Diaries and Intelligence Summaries are contained in F.S. Regs., Part II. and the Staff Manual respectively. Title pages will be prepared in manuscript.

Place	Date	Hour	Summary of Events and Information	Remarks and references to Appendices
St. Sixte	10/5/17		Saw three retain - unretailed case of Mange. Good installations for animals to be clipped - instructed to not let led. Recommended all animals to be clipped at once. Visited 8/22 Bde R.F.A. Animals in fairly good condition. I have to be clipped with ointment. Shook and another lose for Debility. Sent report of sanitation and accommodations to H.Q. R.A. - replied to R.O.'s army - E 35th Division & R.O. ye.	
"	11/5/17		Visited 124 Co. R.E. Examined two cases under treatment for Mange. Progress satisfactory. Also examined case reported by Capt. Cuthoys A.V.S. as suspicious case Stomatitis - no salivation at the mouth - seen off food for 4 or 5 days. Colt fairly bright and required feeding. Temperature 101. Good instructions & continue isolation for further developments. Visited 14th Bde R.E. and made enquiries of the horse examined by Capt. T. Finch A.V.C. for Mange. This horse came from H.Q. Signal Co. Some weeks ago. To other cases in lines all animals clipped - recommended isolate all contact until the	

WAR DIARY / INTELLIGENCE SUMMARY

Army Form C. 2118.

Place	Date	Hour	Summary of Events and Information	Remarks and references to Appendices
ST. SIXTE	11/3/17		Sent thoroughly disinfected. Visited No. 2 Rgnt Co. with Capt P. Howard A.V.C. - sent for Vet. to make examination of animals on Horse Lines &c - suspicious case Mange - animal returning to isolation. Saw horse with Ophthalmia - on examination of hay found large quantity of very musty hay being stuffed - drew attention and ordered the forage barn and stables out - danger of feeding animals on such stuff. My fingers - Ophthalmia due to bad hay.	
"	12/3/17		Visited A/121 Bde. R.F.A. Examined each individual horse. 45 horses at Battery. Good feather. 173 horses in Lines. - sickness 5 to be isolated and sent for Mange - 1 horse sent to M.V.S for strangles to be destroyed. 66? Army visited St. Sixte by appointment and inspected officers charges withdrawn from 113 Mx. & 115. Machine Gun Co. and arranged for Mx. Inspect.	
"	13/3/17		Visited 119 M.V.S. and examined sick animals fit to evacuation. Arranged for 332. Co. A.S.C. & No. 2 Section 28 B.A.C. animals to go through	

Army Form C. 2118.

WAR DIARY
or
INTELLIGENCE SUMMARY.
(Erase heading not required.)

Place	Date	Hour	Summary of Events and Information	Remarks and references to Appendices
ST SIXTE	13/3/17		Motor Horse Rest on Wednesday. Also arranged for 157 Co. R.E. 330 Co. A.S.C. 114 Bde M.G., 114 Machine Gun Co. & 13 Bn. Welsh Regt. to put their animals through Rest on Thursday.	
"	14/3/17		Turks Morbo Horse Dip and Inoculated animals of this Command for Mange. The Dip Med 350 animals Passed Mange. Officer Inspecting.	
"	15/3/17		Attended Conference of A.Ds.V.S. at R.H.Q. Army Mean BAILLEUL.	
"	20/3/17		Further Rest animals from 114th & 115th Bde were passed at R.H.R. for castration by R.O.P. By arrangement R.A.M.C. unable to attend owing to the absence intervening entrainment of 113 Bde. to BOLLEZEELE.	
"	21/3/17		At 12.m.p.m. Veterinary Sergeant anived from R.H.Q. to say unable to come. Asked me to castrate the animals and send on with self. Proceeded to Field Remount Station. 115 Bde sent 6 animals. No Officer accompanied same. 1 of their animals had escaped from which was totally blind to abscess. Returned animal to Unit as being a Veterinary Case. 114 Bde sent 7 Mules and 1 Horse. Two officers

Place	Date	Hour	Summary of Events and Information	Remarks and references to Appendices
ST. SIXTE	21/3/17		Accompanied Lieut. [...] descriptions of all the animals 13 in number and forwarded same to RAQMG with Veterinary certificate from I. Os. Ye. Bns. Received animals to units sending recruiters from "D" as to date of despatch to full period of issue. In accordance with Circular memo from B.O.S. had 2 horses paid on Lieut. PRATT-BARLOW charge. No difference in fitting them. Examined charger belonging to Lieut. CHANDLER HQ. R.A. – Hasley – was shot by R.A.C. on Wednesday. Complaint was [...], and teams kept lame. No loss shoes removed – treats nothing the old horse had lost, on the way of recurring. Nails had been driven too close. Doing little work for the next he set. Not put in panniers. Returns from D.S.O. [...] animals to be seen to private farriers – Re Poly Appliances – Re samples – Re "B" cases (elucidation) Received [...] return to "A". Sent memo to "D". Re clipping, happening	

WAR DIARY / INTELLIGENCE SUMMARY

Army Form C. 2118.

Place	Date	Hour	Summary of Events and Information	Remarks and references to Appendices
ST. SIXTE	21/3/17		Daily sick No. 1 Section 38th R.A.C.	
"	22/3/17		Three ponies sent to "D" to hide & skin from carcass - efforts may be made to save hides and distributed to Base for Tanneries. Horse	
"	23/3/17		Inspected V.Os. Subjects:- Relieving warmbloods by rest and mail cleans "A" "B". Skin carcass - to remove hairs for horse hair. Arranged for Dipping at Horse Pan. Visited B.O.C. H.Q. A.F.A. Bde. Inspected the animals - only about 50 clipped. Mange started in this Unit in January (instructions for Relief). Men found for clipping. Returned 1 horse to 2 wounded. Visited Sect. 1 38th R.A.C. and about 1/3rd animals rubbed. Returned to be clipped on day when Mange was discovered for continuous for 1 horse to be evacuated for Details. Rest of animals in good condition. Visited Sect. 2 38th R.A.C. all animals have been clipped and seem fairly through the Regt. 1 animal in poor condition, the rest moderate.	

Army Form C. 2118.

WAR DIARY
or
INTELLIGENCE SUMMARY.
(Erase heading not required.)

Instructions regarding War Diaries and Intelligence Summaries are contained in F.S. Regs., Part II. and the Staff Manual respectively. Title pages will be prepared in manuscript.

Place	Date	Hour	Summary of Events and Information	Remarks and references to Appendices
ST SIXTE	23/3/17		Visited 123. C. P. C. Red Hearing not yet completed. for 8 Men's had been sent. Work preceding my stay. men on the job. Matting had been inserted in accordance with B.R.O. N. 1467. Note O/C N Mir Co. on this matter. Evacuated 2 men for Debility.	
"	24/3/17		Visited H.Q. R.W. 1 New Lown - Bady Meth. - Congestion of Lamines and fencing - not enough water. Visited But. Signal Co. 1 Horse out with accident - maurning.	
"	25/3/17		Alfred Rowling. Visited C.A.D. Hotel Vines. Examined & drove for Remounts - 2 Margue withdrawn from But. Chaplains. Gave necessary certificate. Alfred Rowling.	
"	26/3/17			
"	27/3/17		Visited Hq3 Mit. Til. He. Examined hurses for evacuation. Enlarged 3 cases from class "A" to "B". Inspected men's quarters - cookhouse Latrines. found everything very satisfactory.	

Army Form C. 2118.

WAR DIARY or INTELLIGENCE SUMMARY.

(Erase heading not required.)

Place	Date	Hour	Summary of Events and Information	Remarks and references to Appendices
ST. SIXTE	28/3/17		Visited A/Vet. Mo. R.F.A. at request of C.R.A. with a view to remedial measures carried in my report to VIII. Corps, as to the condition of the animals in this Battery. Had no reason to alter any views on Nothing is preventing said animals are slipping out full of lice. Visited D/171. Mde R.F.A. On the whole stallion is fair. Numbers of animals are poor — but the down lines are well managed. Showing signs of care and comfort to the animals. Visited 131. Mo. R.F.A. I.G. Animals in good condition with exception of two rather poor. Visited 176.? Machine Gun Co. Mls. mint armed. His missing from home 54 mules in good condition with two exceptions. Made arrangements to inspect Mont to the Pibehal Mallens A/31 on Saturday morning. Details kept J. Cuthane to late Veterinary charge of this unit. Has been shoeing feet — A cold shock and a Mud Bath.	
"	29/3/17		Office Routine. First report to D.A.D. Army. As final notes of feet States for Arrowlant of P.U.N.	

WAR DIARY or INTELLIGENCE SUMMARY

Army Form C. 2118.

Place	Date	Hour	Summary of Events and Information	Remarks and references to Appendices
ST. SIXTE	30/3/17		Inspected V.Os. Arranged for shifting 70 animals for horse fair on Sunday. Subject - entrance - Re horse Henry Irvine - Province - Re collection of time. Received certificates from V.Os. certifying mules fit in inspection. A.V.C. Sergeants are in good order with one exception. Lieut Page whose 1 All. sept up the new test. I had dressing sessions. Men 3/- for allowance form - with animal to Paris. Send extract from O.O.Q. Vet. Service by aged that men arrived with Bucket? Culture of Mallein, with instructions not to issue same with the view to give to any horse that anticipates - any stranger forward in lairs to be treated with suspicion. Enquired of any units lan wallies clipping - in order to utilized clipping machines as per O.R.O. visits 12H. Co. R.E. some 6 animals in poor condition. Informers R.O. to pay special attention to these animals	
	31/3/17		Visited 176 Machine Gun Co. Issued 54 animals with Mallein by Subcutal method. Visits HOPITAL farm with a	

WAR DIARY or INTELLIGENCE SUMMARY

Place	Date	Hour	Summary of Events and Information	Remarks and references to Appendices
St. SIXTE	31/3/17		Went to inspect 192 Tunnel Rv. transport animals — found the place recently barricaded with shell craters. Made enquiries in neighbourhood from the Mait. and obtained all transport lines of 151 Co. R.E. yesterday. The transport lines are very unsatisfactory having very many pairs unsuitable for supplying horses and had manger. Interviewed A.D.V.S. and explained the danger of introducing clean animals into affected stables. Recommended immediate ceasing taking up & stabling fed down, which he agreed. Wired to dept. from information from D.R.L.S. dept these lines allotment of 6 sheds for 32 4/17	A.D.V.S 36 DS.

X.W. Mann
Major

(Original)

CONFIDENTIAL

WAR DIARY

OF

A.D.V.S. 38th. (WELSH) DIVISION.

FROM

1st. APRIL 1917.

TO

30th. APRIL 1917.

(VOLUME XVII.)

[signature] Major.
A.D.V.S., 38th. (Welsh) Division

Army Form C. 2118.

WAR DIARY
or
INTELLIGENCE SUMMARY.
(Erase heading not required.)

Instructions regarding War Diaries and Intelligence Summaries are contained in F. S. Regs., Part II. and the Staff Manual respectively. Title pages will be prepared in manuscript.

Place	Date	Hour	Summary of Events and Information	Remarks and references to Appendices
ST. SIXTE	1/4/17		Visited Chap. A.F.A. Res. stables animals with C.R.M. & Off. i/c A.F.A. Res. Asked one horse to be isolated. "Buddy" lost. Gave instructions for evacuation & blood serum to be sent for found dead(?) 1 fat bastard horse "Billy" and 3H of "Billy" to animals in Mod. Italian with heat reactions not in rest section. Visited 176 Railway Gun Co. Exhibit animals, diet, are inoculated and Mallein tested. No reaction.	
"	2/4/17		Visited M.V.S. Exhibit animals for Elevation plance list. Gave paint. Selects 45 class "B" cases & 117 class "A" No animal from 19H.B. Med. P.S.D. Sent down by last O'Brien M.V.L. to went to be shown it to L.f.C. Ordered Off. i/c 40 M.V.S. to return horse to Host until sent to M.O. i/c to this effect.	
"	3/4/17		Office Routine. Visited D.A.D. horse Camio.	
"	4/4/17		Visited tm cases Horse Epil. Tried 173 Co. R.E. Making & leash Mannings.	
"	5/4/17		Inspecting Horsey. Very unsatisfactory. Sent report to A.C. & Q.M.G. re 173 Co. R.E. horse dressing, etc.	

Army Form C. 2118.

WAR DIARY
or
INTELLIGENCE SUMMARY.
(Erase heading not required.)

Instructions regarding War Diaries and Intelligence Summaries are contained in F. S. Regs., Part II. and the Staff Manual respectively. Title pages will be prepared in manuscript.

Place	Date	Hour	Summary of Events and Information	Remarks and references to Appendices
St Sixte	5/9/17		Veterinary conditions. Visited 332 Co A.S.C. Inspected shoe horses here in the stable. I am very pleased with animals. 331 Co A.S.C. Most of the horses out working. Found 3 horses in hot condition, retired one to the stud. 119 M.V.S. for treatment for mange. Visited 109 Field Ambulance. Found no animals in great standings. 10 horses in isolated stables - examined 11/24 - no trace of disease. Being cases of mitis. Visited at Dimeille.	
"	6/9/17		Conference Veterinary Officers affair Indian Cavalry.	
"	11/9/17		Visited No. 3 Sec 113 C.A.C. Inspected all the animals examined carefully. Most on this unit including horses and mules [?] 13 Remounts standing in their lines were sent forward taken one animal from 113 Res. for treatment — the latter was lacking in establishment owing to sickness. Most of these animals are unfit for Classification — probably. Classes maintained to the being to evacuate any be considered unfit. Vide No. 2.	

WAR DIARY or INTELLIGENCE SUMMARY

Army Form C. 2118.

Place	Date	Hour	Summary of Events and Information	Remarks and references to Appendices
ST SIXTE	7/4/17		Inspected 38th B.A.C. Animals showed some improvement from last visit. No 1 Sec. 38th B.A.C. plus lost mare and mule in infection. Mules recently affected with Mange. Some of the animals not yet under treatment had suffered not even badly + showing in this section — Average temp Nulla 175. Returned in late afternoon to field, shelved condition in gun "Horses" — Eastward to R.E. Moss on Rd. Mornings proceeding very slow. Horses still 2 others in late trenches and looking onto cut, but last but started down — found Mon. Italy horses. Occasional feeds to continue and figure haul lots given at night.	
"	8/4/17		Visited A/vet Sec B.A.C. 50 animals sick unlooked, condition of animals improving. Posse and 7 animals to be recommended to receive relief of forage rations. Numbers are — 93. 62. 155. 86. 18. 19. and 32. Nulla "Blue Sec B.A.C. Section of animals appearing from animals — clipped out badly. Section of animals "-for manning — 6 horses taken from patient. No are — 77. 130. 114. 131. 118. 128. 133. 161. and 27. Visited C/131 Bde Ambulance	

WAR DIARY or INTELLIGENCE SUMMARY

Army Form C. 2118.

Place	Date	Hour	Summary of Events and Information	Remarks and references to Appendices
ST. SIXTE	8/4/17		Insp'd g[eneral] details g animals for cold forage ration. Men av - 30 lb. 10. 19 ins. 139. 155. 13n g?. Visite 15.th. Welsh Regt. Animals hard, lost condition. Some g hoof infected. Him. Visite 16.th Div Welsh Regt. Condition g animals excellent. Visita 13. Div. Welsh Regt. Condition g animals good. Visita 14.th Div. Welsh. Regt. Animals condition good.	
"	9/4/17		Office Routine. Visita D.A.D. S. & T. Asked him to inspect animals prior to Evacuation.	
"	10/4/17		Charged 2 horse from Cas. "A" to "B".	
"	11/4/17		Received wire from Capt I. MACFARLANE A.V.C - outbreak g poisoning at E/121 Div. R.F.A. on night of 10/4/17. 3 horse died. MY [started?]	
"			20 shore affected. Proceeded to his Unit & made investigation as regards to feeding, watering, hay - good. oats hard in quality, but fresh and good. Men fed meteor ammunition of horse who had their tabs &?... I was in the depot since train Men ??... lustenus was much softened throughout although about ??

T2134. Wt. W708-776. 500000. 4/15. Sir J. C. & S.

Place	Date	Hour	Summary of Events and Information	Remarks and references to Appendices
ST SIXTE	12/4/17	cont.	Murray continued being easily moved by drawing fingers along it. Lymphatic threads of Tarsetto discerning. A large short caecum + three were very much inflamed. Not bottle in chest, abt — Spleen w/ body animal. Schemes of Rabit being present at several points in cals. A.P.M. notified and making inquiries. Horse van put on van much valued from another farm. Emphatic report of the outbreak from ABP Army - Eng - Cy to "D." 25th Division + H.Q. 38th Div. Royal R.A.V.C. Cmdt informing him of outbreak.	×
"	13/4/17		Evacuation to R.E.D. Camp - reply to "Q" - list of settling ewes recommended to also And cat ration for Billeted Animals no H.1 A.R.D. 1399. AVC Corps called at ST SIXTE with Capt. P.S. Menard AVC. together arrived to Flor Res. Branch Officer Animal(?) with [fevering?] not matter examined all Mark on one animal who died and that [?] [?] were samples are taken by R.A.V.D. for analysis and examination	×

WAR DIARY or INTELLIGENCE SUMMARY

Army Form C. 2118.

Place	Date	Hour	Summary of Events and Information	Remarks and references to Appendices
ST SIXTE	12/4/17		[illegible handwritten entry regarding success of the Sergt. & small tank and cylinder... rings... one horse was very ill during the... and exhibit symptoms which had not been noticed in the Indian cases - namely - profuse sweating, heavy breathing, acute... cerebral abnormal... Noted had developed symptoms... ... from my place from... ...from 7 O'ct that all the two horses were... showing symptoms of laminitis.]	
"	13/4/17		[Temperature of retained Micro Units 38° but febrile & ... Reinforcement camp. Received letter... message from R.S.O. Army 10 h.m. that he had received the rest of analysis. The specimens received No. 13 & 17 from Major Sims @ F.SH a 69 (Wed 27) 8/12/. Both R.F.A. had been examined for malitic serum disease & reaction with negative result. The ...cal test for vegetable... parasites was also negative.]	
"	14/4/17		[Sergt. 2/131 Pte. R.F.A. S and found the success which was so very...]	

T2134. Wt. W708—776. 500000. 4/15. Sir J. C. & S.

Army Form C. 2118.

WAR DIARY or INTELLIGENCE SUMMARY.
(Erase heading not required.)

Instructions regarding War Diaries and Intelligence Summaries are contained in F. S. Regs., Part II. and the Staff Manual respectively. Title pages will be prepared in manuscript.

Place	Date	Hour	Summary of Events and Information	Remarks and references to Appendices
ST SIXTE	14/4/17		At the time of writing all lumps [illegible] marching out. Roads much impracticable at the [illegible]. Hard but solid and loud [illegible] causing the troops to strike with each foot. Areas at [illegible]. Attend an unusual fire shot, horses looking took 7 high [illegible] quiet today — all cars are facing [illegible] [illegible] as little hay. With a view to testing the hard road hay — the hole which was left out returned to my horses which were sent up to HQ MLS and then to the horses which were ordered to destroy food then their forward.	
"	15/4/17		Visited HQ MGC, accompanied by O.C. 7 L.M.G. & 20 L.G. and inspected billets, horse lives and surroundings. [illegible] were very still. J. MACFARLANE. — reached here of River Aw [illegible]. Sod out this new one of the horses which was suffering from fever.	
"	16/4/17		Visited [illegible] [illegible] [illegible] horses [illegible] off there feed. Feed shed [illegible] and inspected [illegible] etc. These two horses are [illegible] little [illegible] much and [illegible] has shown signs of	

T2134. Wt. W708—776. 500000. 4/15. Sir J. C. & S.

WAR DIARY or INTELLIGENCE SUMMARY

Army Form C. 2118.

Place	Date	Hour	Summary of Events and Information	Remarks and references to Appendices
ST SIXTE	16/4/17		Inspection, but all yet free from serious outbreak. All the shed horses are cleaned, feeding out. Saw linseed mash and cooking mixed rations. Visited 1 B/119. A.F.A. Are... and inspect the horses. Picked out 3 horses affected with mange. Stables has not been established for two weeks and attention is needed to.	
"	17/4/17		Visited ... Major Innes, who has just taken over. Not very... Visited A/122 Bde. 4 horses with sarcoptic mange mixed among horses. Light general improvement in stables to animals. Visited H.Q. M.V.S. Examined horses for vacancies. Purchased 2 yrs of Russia Vet. and Veil Riquette from POPERINGHE for treatment to several cases. Lost 8.80 horses.	
"	18/4/17		Office routine. Visited R.H.A. Army Lines.	
"	19/4/17		Office routine. Gave lecture to students at 3rd Divisional School on lines 1 Mule Management.	
"	20/4/17		Inspection of V.O.S. Visited 8/122 Bde R.F.A. All ... of Mr.	

Army Form C. 2118.

WAR DIARY or INTELLIGENCE SUMMARY.

(Erase heading not required.)

Place	Date	Hour	Summary of Events and Information	Remarks and references to Appendices
St. Sixte	20/4/17		Arrival camp and horsing lines of the animals show a little dull but units own to R.E. and improved animals. Much improvement noticeable. Quite that I have the classed stable for rest subs. stainless.	
"	21/4/17		Units up to per Farriers and subsists animals. Inspection good. Animals accommodated in horse standings. I seen M.O. & had seen attended to. Farrier artificier from 21 Mtd Bde R.F.A. paid for all animals not by stamp red 22/4/17. 5 mules poor mil articles. Notified all V.S. for such information.	
"	22/4/17		Proc. H.Q. M.S. from there proceeded to BAMBECQUE accompanied by O/C. ng. M.S. and situate a site suitable for R Horse Trans. accommodation for 300 horses. 20 of which can be under cover. Nothing accommodation for the dead and large farm for Noss & forage. Shall notify attention round fuel YSER. This place is situated between BAMBECQUE and WYDER on the Rivt YSER. The only difficulty is situate its forage as a

WAR DIARY or INTELLIGENCE SUMMARY

Army Form C. 2118.

Place	Date	Hour	Summary of Events and Information	Remarks and references to Appendices
ST SIXTE	22/11/17		Light and fed horses. Sent to to Artillery Forage Depot. The usual Railhead RUMBEKE. At arrangements made for mules brought from Supply Column. General — 1 Sergeant A.V.C. and 1 man. Equipment material A.V.C. and rope. Mule wagon 4 camp carts. Built 129 Field Ambulance at Remy Siding. Got 3 horses are on feet condition good, little sentiment.	
"	23/11/17		Visited D.H.Q. Horse Lines. Also Reuliu.	
"	24/11/17		Visited 49 M.D.S. Examined animals. Sent to evacuation. Tremloink 2 cases from mange 13' to 'B'. 2 Visited 333 Co. A.S.C. — inspected animals. 2 cases mange not yet reported, recommended wheel drivers to get 3 cases not reported, tendency, lendings good. 332 Co. A.S.C. — very bad cases of i, - 1 bad influence. 334 Co. A.S.C. conditions of animals improving. Extra Div. Bde R.F.A. all remains of the animals which had been suffering from — all now to be seeing soon — but have lost slightly in condition, and inspection of this Battery very good.	

T2134. Wt. W708-776. 500000. 4/15. Sir J. C. & S.

Army Form C. 2118.

WAR DIARY
or
INTELLIGENCE SUMMARY.
(Erase heading not required.)

Instructions regarding War Diaries and Intelligence Summaries are contained in F.S. Regs., Part II. and the Staff Manual respectively. Title pages will be prepared in manuscript.

Place	Date	Hour	Summary of Events and Information	Remarks and references to Appendices
St Sixte	24/4/17		Visited 1/1st Bde R.F.A - condition of animals improving. Wastage not great. Visited C/283 Bde R.F.A - great many flies in this Battery - are in poor condition.	
"	25/4/17		Visited 13 Bn R.H.T - condition of animals good. 14 Bn R.H.T. Animals condition of 101 x horse heat. 15 Bn R.H.T. Horses in hard condition, but suffering great many flies. Visited 11 Bn 1.M.B. Horses in 16 Bn R.H.T. condition of animals very good. Visited 113 Bde hospital good condition. This unit is at Vincent battle-upwards. Visited 17 Bn R.F.A. and A.C. 115 Bde. Condition of horses very good. 15 Bn Field Regt. Animals in very moderate condition - relieved from the Reserve Area and this wastage. Animals reported for the information of the Corps Commander in reference to this Matter, as requested.	C/v.84/121. ? 9/r.13/122
"	26/4/17		Visited Tlh Coys Royal Engrs. Also R.F.A. horses lines through the D.H.	
"	27/4/17		Conference V.O.S. Visited R.U.B. Road lines	
"	28/4/17		Visited H.Q. 38th D.A.C. Condition of animals very good. No. 1 Section D.A.C. condition on the whole good - Z animals to be evacuated, the	

T2134. Wt. W708—776. 500000. 4/15. Sir J. C. & S.

WAR DIARY or INTELLIGENCE SUMMARY

Army Form C. 2118.

Place	Date	Hour	Summary of Events and Information	Remarks and references to Appendices
ST SIXTE	28/10/17		[illegible handwritten entries regarding animal inspection, shoeing, harness and horse lines. References to 131 Field Ambulance — condition good. Shoeing wasteful — sent for Farrier Sergeant. Heels feet were too long. No remarks of this and seen to by the time I re-visit. No report on matter.]	
"	29/10/17		[Visited H.Q. 115 Bde. — condition of animals very good. 7 Bn R.W.F. condition very good. 10 Bn S.W.B. stables on the whole good, but small. Saw simulations for this animal bite casualties. 16 Bn. Welsh Regt. stables & transport of animals visited, shoeing not good had Farrier Corporal and Transport Officer to scrape and inform them the faults. 11 Bn. S.W.B. condition on the whole good. Many of the Cavalry on a delapidated condition — one of the legs out on Geldings — consequence being loss of one/gas feet for transport. Officer the duty fault of nothings — too late, had extended for them — had not yet been visited. Interviewed A.D.V.S.]	

T2134. Wt. W708—776. 500000. 4/15. Sir J. C. & S.

WAR DIARY
or
INTELLIGENCE SUMMARY.

(Erase heading not required.)

Army Form C. 2118.

Place	Date	Hour	Summary of Events and Information	Remarks and references to Appendices
St. Sixte	29/4/17		a.m. Noted all Mule had been supplied with nosebags.	
"	30/4/17		Visited 330 Co. A.S.C. 4 or 5 horses in poor condition. Movie execution of two horses for debility. Visited 49 Mtd. Fd. Ambce.	

Sd/ W.J. Gwin
MAJOR.
A.D.V.S. 38th (WELSH) DIVISION.

(Original)

CONFIDENTIAL

WAR DIARY

OF

A.D.V.S. 38th. (WELSH) DIVISION.

FROM

1st. MAY 1917.

TO

31st. MAY 1917.

(VOLUME XVIII.)

Major.

1st. June 1917.   A.D.V.S., 38th. (Welsh) Division.

Army Form C. 2118.

WAR DIARY
or
INTELLIGENCE SUMMARY.
(Erase heading not required.)

Place	Date	Hour	Summary of Events and Information	Remarks and references to Appendices
St. Sixte	1/5/17		Visited Hqrs Mot. Vet. Sec. Inspected sick animals sent to Casualty Offrs Pouline	
"	2/5/17		Visited 38th R.A. Horse lines. Offrs Pouline	
"	3/5/17		Visited 119 A.F.A. Bde. with R.A.F. Liason Army, who inspects this Bde. for Remount Horses.	
"	4/5/17		Conferences Veterinary Officers. Visited O.I.C. M.M.P. Horse lines.	
"	5/5/17		Held conf. Lt.Col. Hutchinson S.S. "G" 119 A.F.A. Bde. as Vet. Staff Captain A.B. R.A. Made arrangements raised by me as to completing shelters with Brit. Gas Officer to fit on 2 horses - Horse Respirators. Two animals coughed a little, while my men on that part of the Horse Respirator to elastic band. Arranged with C.T.R. Dept for documentation.	
	7/5/17		Transport Officers Offrs i/c Horse Respirators on Mondays Visited G. Bdr. R.O.T. One cow Island Affrs i/c Waggon lines + Vety Offrs to collect to be distinguished Vet Instructions for animals	
"	6/5/17		Visited 38 D.I.R. Horse lines. Offrs Pouline	
"	7/5/17		Proceeded on leave. Notified NOVS Army departure	

Army Form C. 2118.

WAR DIARY or INTELLIGENCE SUMMARY.

(Erase heading not required.)

Instructions regarding War Diaries and Intelligence Summaries are contained in F. S. Regs., Part II. and the Staff Manual respectively. Title pages will be prepared in manuscript.

Place	Date	Hour	Summary of Events and Information	Remarks and references to Appendices
ST. SIXTE	18/5/17		Conference Veterinary Officers. Visited 8.F.A. & M.M.P. Rest lines.	
"	19/5/17		Visited Drainage Farm. Examined Rear M.M.P. reported sick & swollen leg and lame. Visited and inspected 130 Field Ambulance. Condition of animals excellent.	
			M.M.P. 1 case ulcerated corn lanced for hoofwound. Visited 129 Field Ambulance. Most of the horses in fair condition — still a number in fair condition. Visited O.H.B. Rear lines.	
"	20/5/17		Visited A/121 Bde. Animals improving in condition. Visited C/119. A.F.A. Bde. — some of the horses in fair condition.	
"	21/5/17		Visited 149th M.T. Vet Sec. Inspected sick animals for evacuation 1 cow changed to "B" line (sick).	
"	22/5/17		Visited B/121 Bde R.F.A. and inspected the animals — improving in condition. Animals picketed out in the open. B/121 Bde F.F.A. Animals have improved immensely in condition and are picketed out. Class 120 R.F.A. Shews great improvement. The Mule horses are picketed out. Mower lines very clean.	

WAR DIARY or INTELLIGENCE SUMMARY

Army Form C. 2118.

Place	Date	Hour	Summary of Events and Information	Remarks and references to Appendices
ST. SIXTE	24/5/17		Visited 134th Siege Co. R.G.A. Animals in very fair condition. Firrier Sergt. told in Sheffield. Horses are excellent. Visited 10. Bn. S.G.B. and 16th Bn. Welsh Regt. Animals in excellent condition.	
ST SIXTE	25/5/17		Visited M.M.P. attachment. Yorks Yeomy. Corps Tps. Sect. Sect. no Shoeing smith. Conferred Veterinary Officers A.V.C.	
"	26/5/17		Visited 11. Bn. S.W.B. Animals condition fair & N. Div. also visited 17. Bn. R.W.F. condition middling good. 115 Bde. H.Q. Condition of animals excellent.	
"	27/5/17		Mules pulling hard. R.M.B. horse lines.	
"	28/5/17		Visited B/122 Bde R.F.A. Inspected number of remounts arrived from CALAIS. The mules were good, this condition fair. Many were suffering from girth galls - result from marching from CALAIS. The rest of the animals in this battery were in good condition. Inspected and in the field one bn. being very new. C/122. Bde R.F.A. Inspected animals - majority in very good condition. All are picketed out in the open.	

WAR DIARY or INTELLIGENCE SUMMARY

Army Form C. 2118.

Place	Date	Hour	Summary of Events and Information	Remarks and references to Appendices
ST. SIXTE	28/5/17		Visited B/122 Bde. R.F.A. – animals scabies moderate, good – considerable improvement since my last inspection. Visited A/122 Bde. R.F.A. condition good. 2 O.R. hors two which are related by themselves for special attention. All new batteries are up to strength.	
"	29/5/17		Visited up Mot. Vet. Sec. and inspected sick animals kind of transactions. Visited 129 Field Ambulance. Infected animals – must improvement in condition. 14 animals selected to proceed to QUELMES with U.S. Vet. Bde. All in horses are in good condition.	
"	30/5/17		Visited 217 Army Tropo Coy R.E. Inspected 27 horses. All in very good condition. horses suffering from punctured wound on fore-arm, result from kick. 1 horse recent lame. Visited 19 Bn. Faniers. Mules looking very well. Visited R.H.Q. + M.M.P.	
"	31/5/17		Visited 332 Co. A.S.C. Signs of very great improvement in condition cattle at 331 Co. A.S.C. horse times : 3 horses sick, doing very well.	

[signature] MAJOR.
A.D.V.S. 38th (WELSH) DIVISION.

(Original)

CONFIDENTIAL

WAR DIARY.

OF

A. D. V. S. 38th. (Welsh) DIVISION.

FROM

1st. JUNE 1917.

TO

30th. JUNE 1917.

(Volume XIX.)

[signature]
Major.
1st. July 1917.   A.D.V.S., 38th. (Welsh) DIVISION.

Army Form C. 2118.

WAR DIARY
or
INTELLIGENCE SUMMARY.
(Erase heading not required.)

Place	Date	Hour	Summary of Events and Information	Remarks and references to Appendices
ST SIXTE	1/6/17		Inspected 1 OS. Visited 18 Labour Companies just arrived and attached to this Division. Arranged for Veterinary charge.	
"	2/6/17		Visited 333 Co. A.S.C. — Horses in good condition. Visited D.A.D. Horse lines. Visited Horse Lines attached to M.M.P. Hard arranged for Horses Sick Lines. Went for C.M.O. Col. 1st RE, for 143 Labour Co. R.E. attached to this Division.	
"	3/6/17		Office Routine. Visited R.A.D. Horse Lines. Received wire from ADV.S. MACFARLANE that a number of Horses are suffering from gas shells.	
"	4/6/17		Visited 143rd Co Labour R.E. - inspected Horses. Made arrangements for the Horses to be treated. Went at D.H.Q. Visited 122 Bev. R.F.A. B/Bary. Argent Line. Inspected Horses affected not Acute. Numerous - nothing front Shell gas. One case serious - prognosis Hopeful. Visited C/121. Bev. R.F.A. 5 Horses affected similarly in not acute. Visited K/121. Bev. R.F.A. Found 8 Horses affected from Gas Shells 5 of which are serious. Gave directions for Horses care and treatment. Went U.V.S. Second Army in above Affects went Sheep Dog and proposed to ascertain what when few particulars are

WAR DIARY or INTELLIGENCE SUMMARY

Army Form C. 2118.

Place	Date	Hour	Summary of Events and Information	Remarks and references to Appendices
St SIXTE	4/6/17		Ascertained Visits B" and F.O. the Bdes and ascertained the causes of horses affected by Mal de Sute.	
"	5/6/17		Visits 119* Mth Bde - Inspected sick animals. Had to evacuate	
"	6/6/17		Visits D/117 Bde. RFA and examined animals which were gassed. Great improvement. D/121 Bde RFA Co Bull cases still very bad, a few acres showing signs of improvement. 330 Co ASC and surplus horses all new in lines, condition good, 1 horse down from colic, 1 case of ascites; schemed by Army Purchasing Board, suffering from parasitic Mange - gave instructions for those to be sent to 49 Mtl Vety Sec. Intended horses to be dressed. Visit D/121 Bde RFA. 1 gun cow still very bad, other improving. Attended to horse reported by APM - slight case & recommended for evacuation. Injected Anti-Tetanic serum into charged which had been attended by Mustard gas.	
"	7/6/17		Visits 8th DAC - Examined several cases of horses suffering from [—]	

SECRET.   53rd. Infantry Brigade No. B. 934.

War Diary

Amendment to 53rd. Inf. Brigade Order No. 130.

8th. Norfolk R. will not enter NOYON before 3.0 p.m.

Billets will be taken over from 13th. Middlesex R. in RUE de ORROIRS.

8th. Norfolk R. will leave behind in SABOEUF, 1 Officer and 75 other ranks for work on 13th and 15th insts.

Work - unloading petrol at SABOEUF under orders of R.S.O. NOYON.

This party will rejoin its battalion on the evening of the 13th inst. or morning of the 14th inst as most convenient.

Instructions in Brigade Order No. 130 not cancelled by the above, hold good.

ACKNOWLEDGE.

10th. Feb. 1918.   Captain,
                            Brigade Major, 53rd. Infantry Brigade.

Issued at 10.45 a.m.

Copies to :-
    8th. Norfolk R.
    Staff Captain.
    Brigade Transport Officer.
    161st. Coy. A. S. C.
    Camp Commandant IX Corps.
    R. S. O. NOYON.
    18th. Division "G".
    War Diary.
    File.

WAR DIARY or INTELLIGENCE SUMMARY

Army Form C. 2118.

Place	Date	Hour	Summary of Events and Information	Remarks and references to Appendices
Mobile Camp	14/6/17		Bde. Horses in excellent condition. Mules require a little attention. Visits 15 Can. Fd.F. Find improvements in condition; stay due to in foot condition and are aged. Visits B/122 Bde. and examined the animals which have not yet recovered from the effects of gas shell. Find to evacuate these two mares when they are fit to be moved. Visits C/122 Bde. RFA. Examined 5 horses which have been gassed and have recovered with the exception of one which will be released for treatment.	
"	15/6/17		Conferred with Executive Veterinary Officer. Visits HQ 9th Mtd. Ser. Office routine.	
"	16/6/17		Visits HQ Mtd. Vet. Ser. Received mail from DADVS 5th Army re. I.R.C. 5th Army. Visits 330 Co. ASC. Horses improving in condition. 1 horse very lame to be evacuated. Another horse to be detached for debility. Visits Train detachment and employed the horses are lame. 1 animal to be evacuated. Visits 333 Co. ASC. All horses in good going condition.	

Army Form C. 2118.

WAR DIARY
or
INTELLIGENCE SUMMARY.
(Erase heading not required.)

Instructions regarding War Diaries and Intelligence Summaries are contained in F.S. Regs., Part II. and the Staff Manual respectively. Title pages will be prepared in manuscript.

Place	Date	Hour	Summary of Events and Information	Remarks and references to Appendices
Nox Vrie Farm	17/6/17		Visited A.D.R. Horse lines. Visited 49th Mob Vet Sec. Explained to O.R.C.S 5th Army a scheme and suggestions as regards the Evacuation of sick animals by road and rail. Also forwarded pro forma reference to sick rates.	
"	18/6/17		Visited 49th Mob Vet Sec. and inspected sick animals prior to evacuation.	
"	19/6/17		Visited M.V.S. Visited No.2 Sec. 78th D.A.C. Animals in excellent condition. Visited No.3 Section Condition of horses & mules excellent.	
"	20/6/17		Attended Conference by A.D.S. of MASS and ADVS re sick afterments of MRUS — Visited at No 13 Veterinary Hospital ST OMER. For 17th Setting - at midnight field 2 horses & other sickness required lad to be destroyed. 6 horses were shot by Skpard. Animals belongs to 38th F.A. the Div.	
"	21/6/17		Visit 2nd H.Q. A.M.P. & And. Signal Co. horse lines.	
"	22/6/17		Conference of Veterinary Officers. Made arrangements for Vety attendance for H.S. Med. to be taken over by Capt Blair & Capt Cochrane during all ranks attended on leave.	

WAR DIARY or INTELLIGENCE SUMMARY

Army Form C. 2118.

Place	Date	Hour	Summary of Events and Information	Remarks and references to Appendices
Van Vries Farm	23/6/17		Visited 113 Adv. M. Vet. Sec. Inspected the shoeing. Notwithstanding on my previous visit attentions drawn to the bad shoeing - the shoeing still unsatisfactory. Saw the Sergt. and informed him of the displayed shoeing. Saw instructions for and shoes to be removed - feet not to long - level not cut out down to normal level. Insisted upon the nailed lines to have the feet to walk out the animals and to observe to mark where this has been done before re-inspecting. Insisted me when this has been done. Much neglect.	
"	24/6/17		Visited R.V.S. 5th Army on inspection with [?] hose Hans Visited 49? Mob Vet Sec. D.A.D. M.V.S. + Capt C. Vict. Lucis.	
"	25/6/17		Visited Morrent Fontes. all infected and already 60 at Mobile Veterinary Sections about sheeing to Stavrone act.	
"	26/6/17		Visited 38th R.A.C. arranged for sheeing [?] visits by the pin and had mem sent to Mt. Vet. Sec. Ordered a number of animals to be sent to M.V.S. for treatment - suffering from chronic wounds. Called on D.M.S. 5th Army office who was out - arranged to meet	

WAR DIARY
or
INTELLIGENCE SUMMARY.
(Erase heading not required.)

Army Form C. 2118.

Place	Date	Hour	Summary of Events and Information	Remarks and references to Appendices
Vox Vrie Farm	16/6/17		Telephone call. Agreed to the arrangements. See made of men to the training area. Arrangements made were :- Capt Cobban remain with 38th D.A.C. + 330 Co. A.S.C. 173 + 151. Cos R.E. Capt McFarlane remain with 121 + 127. Bdes R.F.A. + 19 Pioneers. Capt Blair to accompany 115. Bde Group on the march to training area. Capt Hewart to accompany 116 Bde on the march to training area. Bought 115 Bde Group.	
"	17/6/17		Received sent from A.D.V.S. 49th Div. + A.D.V.S. 2nd Corps and made arrangements for 18th Mob.Vet.Sec. to dress up with 49th M.V.S. for instructions to O/c 49th M.V.S. to hand over and obtain necessary receipts.	
"	18/6/17		Rec'd 131. Bde. R.F.A. Ol Rout. Many of the horses not looking well and suffering. An a/c being credited. Serious until treatment for strained tendons, the animals and this battery must proceed sicker and are now fit to work. Chief Vet. Horses ov. this battery stating very bad. 1 case. Lastelle Alonate. Madol treatment very bad. 1 case Walnut wound. 19/191. Rev. The majority of the animals are away at HERZEELE. 18 remaining on lines at MANHES. Apron Bov. Very limited in condition	

WAR DIARY or INTELLIGENCE SUMMARY

Army Form C. 2118.

Place	Date	Hour	Summary of Events and Information	Remarks and references to Appendices
Vex Vrie Farm	28/6/17		To 28/6/17. New R.O. Hd Qrs. are occupying Mrs Hardinge having been turned out from Hardinge at Noyon Camp. Several animals suffering from Mange. Army Vet. Statn of animals good. I have seen Farriers. Army Vet. animals not so good in condition have moltinctions of it animals to receive special treatment, others. Any sick animals have to be evacuated. D/132 New Army Vet condition of animals good, no deeding condition.	
" "	29/6/17		Censored mod. from Noyon Camp to Margent Fontes.	
Fontes.	30/6/17		Visit 49th Mxd Vet Sec. Saw nine Mules at Fontes. After Routine.	

F.W.W. Lyons
MAJOR.
A.D.V.S. 38th (WELSH) DIVISION.

CONFIDENTIAL

WAR DIARY

OF

D.A.D.V.S. 38th. (Welsh) DIVISION.

FROM

1st. JULY 1917.

TO

31st. JULY 1917.

(Volume XX.)

[signature]
Major.

1st. August 1917.   D.A.D.V.S., 38th. (Welsh) DIVISION.

Place	Date	Hour	Summary of Events and Information	Remarks and references to Appendices
FONTES	1/7/17		Visited 330. Co. A.S.C. Inspected the horses standing in Wagon Lines – Animals in good condition. Arranged for Wagon Lines for 38th B.H.Q. Interviewed R.A.M.C First Army in reference to evacuation of sick animals.	
"	2/7/17		Visited 15th Bn. Welsh Regt. Animals standing in good field – in good condition – were looked after. C.O's charged suffering from flies, suitable dressing was not being applied, granulating to sweat nearly. I could extract gas – man suggestion to 10 each horse to putting oil hitting line, which would mate matters worse; 1 hr. line for dry animals 1 ft. wet mane. Visited 10th Bn. Welsh Regt. Animals only in moderate condition, standing in field. 1 horse with serious attack trench feet. 98. Mtd. Bde. – most of the animals were out. Few remaining cut lines in very good condition. 1 B.D. furnished animal due to this, 1 had plain field, 1 Bn. Welsh Regt. private cat fault of passing, 1 solder of animals good. 7th Co. Mtd. Machine Gun Co. condition very good with one exception, shoeing indifferent, farrier officer has been in my opinion shoeing has not been done	

Place	Date	Hour	Summary of Events and Information	Remarks and references to Appendices
FONTES	2/1/17		For 6 weeks - Journed and to transport Officer [?] march route 15th Bde R.F.A. Animal's condition indifferent supporting 2 R. & L.B. that of Establishment & Hastings arch. 113 Bty H.Q. Draught animals in good condition. Hastings — Field — the rest of the horse with the H.Q. are located in Valliers huts of the village in 2 or 3 lines in which they are [?] are moderate and miserably — [?] of [?] Stables [?] and [?] not moderately [?] for these animals to be taken to the field and [?] with the draught animals. Mostly lacking both cultivation & discipline. Hunter 13th B.H.E. 1 mule entertained Tarbally animal 1 slight [?] of Skin 6" across hanging across [?] inoculations for animals to be sent to 49 V.H. for evacuation. Will take at least 3 months to deal. This day is without a Farrier Sergeant at present. — Have 6 L.B. that of Establishment, I know three Horses have quarter, [?] instructions for the horse to be sent to HQ V.L.P. — Maple to be inoculated and say to return to unit.	

WAR DIARY or INTELLIGENCE SUMMARY

Army Form C. 2118.

Place	Date	Hour	Summary of Events and Information	Remarks and references to Appendices
FONTES	3/4/17		Visits to H.Q. Mob. Vet. Sec. Miss Fontes. D.A.Q. + M.M.P. Horse lines.	
"	4/7/17		Visits 38th Bde Signal Co. Animals in very good condition. Visits H.Q. Mob. Vet. Sec. Visits 38th D.A.C. + M.M.P.	
"	5/7/17		See Inspection Veterinary Officer. Visits C.I.D. + M.M.P. Horse lines. Visits 331 C.A.S.C. Most of the horses aged out - bad mouthing and condition any girth. Seen lame, good condition for valuation. Camp condition very good. I horse lame good conditions in the animals in this Visits H.Q. Field Ambulance - great improvement in the mounts.	
"	6/7/17		Visits 11th Bn. 4th I.B.B. Majority of the horses were lent on manoeuvres. Condition good of those remaining in transport lines. Visits 333 C. A.S.C. Animals in excellent condition. Hastings good. Visits 130 Field Ambulance, condition of horses excellent. Shoeing magnificently bad - had the cattle shoeing Smith himself before me - gave instructions to see that more supervision is exercised. He has had feet and found to him. The fault. Visits 162 Amb. R.A.M.C. looking good.	
"	7/7/17		Inspection of horses had mules good. Miss Fontes. Visits 38th V.M.P. + M.M.P. Horse lines	

WAR DIARY / INTELLIGENCE SUMMARY

Army Form C. 2118.

Place	Date	Hour	Summary of Events and Information	Remarks and references to Appendices
FONTES	8/7/17		Visited 129th M.V. Vet. Sec. 38th C.V.S. & M.M.P. Horse Lines	
"	9/7/17		Visited 130. Field Ambulance. Also shown all of the horses which I complimented on their early sharp action and inspecting the animals of this unit. Led new Ath. Safari Stores and three nursing field hospitals 38th Brit General Co. Horses in splendid condition – doing well.	
"	10/7/17		Visited 49th Mob. Vet. Sec. Inspected sick animals. Arrived at "Office Frontière"	
"	11/7/17		Visited C.H.Q. & M.M.P. Horse Lines. Capt. T. Finch arrived from Leeres. Made arrangements for him to proceed to 115th Bn. and safe and veterinary duties of 114. & 115. Bns. M.M. Vet. Sec. inspected sick animals about to evacuate from malarial units not fit for march on arr.t	
"	13/7/17		Visited R.A.M.S. East Army. Visit 73rd R.H.Q. M.M.P. & Sgnal C. Horse Lines. Capt. S. Wall, A.V.C. detailed from Mrs. Brown for duty to A.S. Veterinary Hospital on 10/7/17	
"	15/7/17		Visited 49th M.V.S. B.H.Q. & M.M.P. Horse Lines. Mrs. Fontine.	

Army Form C. 2118.

WAR DIARY
or
INTELLIGENCE SUMMARY.
(Erase heading not required.)

Instructions regarding War Diaries and Intelligence Summaries are contained in F. S. Regs., Part II. and the Staff Manual respectively. Title pages will be prepared in manuscript.

Place	Date	Hour	Summary of Events and Information	Remarks and references to Appendices
FONTES	14/7/17		Units of B.? Sqnd G. Horses in good condition. Men in ugh M.P. Enterts. No fitting animals sent to Escortion.	
"	15/7/17		Units and Detachment Ralk 1st Army LILLERS. in connection with 2nd Army. Held two - M.P.	
"	16/7/17		Units B.H.Q - M.P. held two. Made arrangements for R.M. From to proceed with Iomb 1-x and when to the forward area.	
"	17/7/17		Units ugh M.P. Went to motor to ammbhm of forward area. Arranged for Capt HOWARD to accompany to Para Military charge of Sends 2, 4 & 5, who are not relating to the Belgium Forward area.	
"	18/7/17		Units Office Routine. Visits 18th R.R. & M.P. to Sqnd G. Divisional more from NUGENT - FONTES to PROVEN.	
"	19/7/17		Conference at O.S. Units ugh M.P. - kits Sqnd G.	
"	20/7/17		Advanced mess from PROVEN to DRAGON CAMP.	
PROVEN	21/7/17		Units and interviewed A.D.V.S. XIV Corps. between him with reference to Evacuation of Sick and from Ui informed me in future all	
DRAGON CAMP	22/7/17		Sick cases were to be sent as arranged to Mobile Vet. Detachment	

T2134. Wt. W708—776. 500000. 4/15. Sir J. C. & S.

Instructions regarding War Diaries and Intelligence Summaries are contained in F. S. Regs., Part II. and the Staff Manual respectively. Title pages will be prepared in manuscript.

VI WAR DIARY
or
INTELLIGENCE SUMMARY.
(Erase heading not required.)

Army Form C. 2118.

Place	Date	Hour	Summary of Events and Information	Remarks and references to Appendices
DRAGON CAMP.	22/7/17		and that no road cases were to be moved without instructions received from D.D.V.S. Army. In future daily states in reference to Evacuations to be sent direct to D.D.V.S. Army. In consequence of suspected Mange been seen on one horse from C/122 Bde R.F.A., I visited this Battery and inspected all the animals. Found no trace of Mange in any of the horses. Animals are looking well and in good fettle.	
" "	23/7/17		Visited 38th D.A.C. Sec. 1. Standings in deplorable condition, exposed to hostile shell fire. Animals up to their hocks in mud. It is regretted, no other site for standings is available. Anticipate the condition of the animals will suffer if they are to remain here much longer. Large number of horses are under treatment for Gunshot Wounds. Section 2. Standings much better, on sloping ground. Condition of animals good. 3 foot cases - gave instructions for one P.U.F. case to be evacuated; & one with kick on stifle, ordered to be evacuated. Section 3. Animals in excellent condition. Standings good.	

WAR DIARY / INTELLIGENCE SUMMARY

Army Form C. 2118.

Place	Date	Hour	Summary of Events and Information	Remarks and references to Appendices
DIXMUDE CAMP	24/7/17		Accompanied by O/C Hd Mds visited site for Advanced Veterinary Post at CASDOEN FARM. Made arrangements for accommodation for men and to obtain water. Met A.A.Q.M.G. proceeded to PROVEN and Hd Med Hd Remounts. Arranged for this Advanced Remounts in a very good condition.	
"	25/7/17		The A.D.V.S. XIV Corps depot visited & inspected Hq 4 Mob. Vet. Section.	
"	26/7/17		Visited 14th Bn. R.W.F. Stables & animals good. I have very low sickness – recommend for Corps the Evacuator, 113 Bun HD. Animals in excellent condition with the exception of one. I know type and should – need to be obtained where condition & Visit No 2 Bn R.W.F. Stables & Animals have improved & O/C informed. Visit 113 Machine Gun Co. Animals in very good condition.	
"	27/7/17		Visit M.M.S. 5th Army Delivered him with reference to Div. Vet. Work, I was informed that Saturday at 1 during week at Advance Hq Mob. Vet. Sec. Totally sent and the arrangement Conference held.	

WAR DIARY or INTELLIGENCE SUMMARY

Army Form C. 2118.

Place	Date	Hour	Summary of Events and Information	Remarks and references to Appendices
DRAGON CAMP	28/7/17		Conference at A.D.V.S. Received instructions from A.D.V.S. to evacuate walking cases by rail to ST. OMER. Sick but at I.E. d.i.H. — Second half at NOORDPEENE after which have been walking and there cases and be sent to C.C.S. December finding evacuated from to them but to adopt the Aliceships said March in his instructions for Active Aliceships and evacuation from to C.C.S. in duplicate to submit will be sent as liaison and Receipts Vouchers	
"	29/7/17		Visits 1st 2nd 4th 5th & 6th Fd. Ambs. & A.M.P. base line. Conferred OC. D.H.P. & M.M.P. Sergeant for the succeed to be adopted on Jan day as Brds Casualties Animals. Also arrange for an C.O.S. to report to OC Fd Amb. a Absent sich plate made up to every 24 hours each day	
"	30/7/17		Visited Hqrs. Met. Col. Lee. Arrived Fd. 1 A.C.O. + men H. to proceed to Advanced Veterinary setting for CARDOEN FARM. Party arrived from Hq. M.V.D. – and took Kennel from G.H.Q.	

WAR DIARY or INTELLIGENCE SUMMARY

Army Form C. 2118.

Place	Date	Hour	Summary of Events and Information	Remarks and references to Appendices
Dragon Camp	30/7/17		The staff of the Motor Ambulance being short, was sent to assist Ferdapp for their mealtimes, and a half hour manned in WATOU. Received daily slips from 10th & 11th Fields which shows 38 admitted from Infantry and today, 3 are gunshot wounds. 7 were evacuated to Hqrs Mot. let. Sec. and 31 remaining until treatment on amb. 10th C.A.C. slip shows 23 admitted, 1 Belgian gunshot wounds, 1 evacuated to 149 M.D. and 31 remaining. 10 yds slip kept late. Mens 1 admitted gunshot wound — 1 evacuated. Evacuation Daily slip to A.D.M.S. 14th Corps showing total number of attendance 83. Evacuations to 142 C.C.S. Gunshot wound 1 included. Returned & 8 Evacuations and obtained permission for two Ambulances to see men 24. Died, and advanced dressing station waiting cases, during assist Belgian Ambulance. from A.D.M.S. was acceded. "3 hrs A.D.M." (5.30) Active Belgian Chilvern Regt Army Until 49th M.D.V. See. Card Advanced Dressing Station Belgian. Admitting total up to 3 p.m. (9½ hours) Rwounded 8 Sh. battle wounded, 5 remaining until treatment, not treatment on amb.	

Army Form C. 2118.

WAR DIARY
or
INTELLIGENCE SUMMARY.
(Erase heading not required.)

Instructions regarding War Diaries and Intelligence Summaries are contained in F. S. Regs., Part II. and the Staff Manual respectively. Title pages will be prepared in manuscript.

Place	Date	Hour	Summary of Events and Information	Remarks and references to Appendices
DRAGON CAMP.	31/7/17		Units: — 13 Staths. — 25 Wounded Animals, 1 Reserve Gas imbricated, 1 total bath evacuated. Ordinary duco carried out by 49th M.V.S. 3 Visited CANAL BANK, for the first day day 24.	

[signature]
MAJOR.
D.A.D.V.S. 38th (WELSH) DIVISION.

(Original)

CONFIDENTIAL

WAR DIARY

OF

D.A.D.V.S. 38th. (Welsh) DIVISION

FROM

1st. AUGUST 1917.

TO

31st. AUGUST 1917.

(Volume XXI.)

1st. September 1917.   D.A.D.V.S., 38th. (Welsh) DIVISION.

WAR DIARY or INTELLIGENCE SUMMARY

Army Form C. 2118.

Place	Date	Hour	Summary of Events and Information	Remarks and references to Appendices
DRAGON CAMP	1/8/17		Visits 49th Mobile Veterinary Section, Base Laundry plus for filling of Mobile Casualties. Wounded 16 deaths. 30 remaining under treatment. I.C.H. admitted 4-14. Gunshot wounds 43. 1 ordinary case wounded.	
"	2/8/17		Base Casualty Sub. for filing. Evacuated 6 sub. casualties. 12 deaths. 11 remaining under treatment. Total 33 Gunshot wounds. 1 ordinary case evacuated. Visits 49th Mobile Veterinary Section. 28th C.F.A. M.R.P. & H.Q. R.O. New Lines. Visits Advance Veterinary Section.	
"	3/8/17		Base Laundry plus evacuated 9 deaths 2. remaining under treatment 6. Includes Ordinary cases wounded 6. ordinary cases wounded. Include in Visits casualty stat. aic 13 Gunshot wounds + 5 Ardua Evacuated (sent). Visits 49th Mobile Veterinary Section. Visits Advance Veterinary Post. Conference 105.	
"	4/8/17		Base Laundry plus. Evacuated sv. deaths 5. remaining under treatment 1. Veterinary cases wounded. Evacuated H. Included in total casualty stat. Sent 1 Ordinary (Mule class). Visits Veterinary Section. Visits Advance Veterinary Section at A.D.S. Office	

WAR DIARY or INTELLIGENCE SUMMARY

Army Form C. 2118.

Place	Date	Hour	Summary of Events and Information	Remarks and references to Appendices
DRAGON CAMP	5/8/17		Route Casualty Stats. Evacuated 5 sick & remaining and treatment. Horses serious 8. Visits 19th Mtd Vet Sec. Signal Co.	
"	6/8/17		Bivouaced camp from DRAGON CAMP to PROVEN. Visits 19th Mtd Amb and arrived for site for 35th C.C.S. Visits and arranged for site for 35th C.C.S. horse lines.	
PROVEN	7/8/17		Visits C.M.B. + N.E. I.B. Evacuated sick hors[es] for Merens. Visits 19th Mtd Vet Sec. Visits and inspected 113 Bde M.B. Animals in good condition.	
"	8/8/17		Visits Dept Subn Casualty Station. Exhole List Stores sent to evacuation to Base Depot. Visits 19th Mtd Vet Sec for Fld. Amb ALTS cups. Field Ambulance. Animals in good condition.	
"	9/8/17		Visits 35th R.B. M.M.P. + 19th C.C. horse lines. Office Routine.	
"	10/8/17		Visits 15th Aus Mobile Vet Sect transport. Horses sick in good condition. Horse and mules — animals in rather good. Sgt & mins sick. Visit 19th B.R. Mobile Vet transport. Visit 19th Mtd than 15th Mobile — Visits Vets A.C.S Veg. Condition of animals received excellent. Conference W.O.S.	

Army Form C. 2118.

WAR DIARY
or
INTELLIGENCE SUMMARY.
(Erase heading not required.)

Instructions regarding War Diaries and Intelligence Summaries are contained in F.S. Regs., Part II. and the Staff Manual respectively. Title pages will be prepared in manuscript.

Place	Date	Hour	Summary of Events and Information	Remarks and references to Appendices
PROVEN	10/8/17		Inspected sick animals. About to evacuation.	
"	11/8/17		Visited A.D.V.S. later - Inspection. Visited 29th Mob. Vet. Sec. Visited 33rd C.C.S. M.M.P. horse lines.	
"	12/8/17		Visited certain Veg. Details Heavy Artillery. Inspected sick animals. Fired to dispatch to Base Hospital. Visited No 4 Vet Sec. D.H.Q. & fines to horse lines.	
"	13/8/17		Office routine.	
"	14/8/17		Visited Sub. Vety. H.Q. Station. Inspected sick animals. Fit to dispatch to Base Veterinary Hospital. Visited 179 Field Ambulance. Animals in good condition.	
"	15/8/17		Visited HQ Mob. Vet. Sec. Inspected animals. None to evacuation. Visited 16th. Div. A.D.V.S. - most of N animals sick. Most remaining not in good condition - except 2, - in fair condition - ordered placed sick by of heavy to be given. 15th Div. A.D.V.S. - most I.W.D. & hand sent strength. That attention for same to be sent to HQ 2. Mob Vety Sec. 113 Bre. R.A. - only 3 animals our lines.	

T2134. Wt. W708—776. 500000. 4/15. Sir J. C. & S.

Army Form C. 2118.

WAR DIARY
or
INTELLIGENCE SUMMARY.
(Erase heading not required.)

Instructions regarding War Diaries and Intelligence Summaries are contained in F.S. Regs., Part II. and the Staff Manual respectively. Title pages will be prepared in manuscript.

Place	Date	Hour	Summary of Events and Information	Remarks and references to Appendices
PROVEN	15/8/17		All checks out. 1 Artic. which had reed. Kreolin was ordered to be sent to A.M. Vet. Sec. for treatment. T.M. message recd. with A/Bdy. Marci to send the 1 Rebel Anne to MR Vet Sec at once. Mules 113. Machine Guns 6. 1 or 2 mules afflicted with Mange –	
"	16/8/17		Mules 113. Mange. Mules up. M.V. Vet. Sec. R.A.B. 1 cow Rent.	P.E. I.O.
"	17/8/17		Supplemental Veterinary Officer's Office Pockets. Alloted Supplement at A.M.L. Office 11. Vet. Sec. A.B.	
"	18/8/17		Division as Men from PROVEN to DRAGON CAMP. Mule Murrelly	
"	19/8/17		Left to to day – Evacuated 5. Deaths 6. Remaining under treatment 16 – Gunshot Wounds 29. R.A.G. Horse Lines.	
			Mules 109. M.V. Vet. Sec.	
DRAGON CAMP	20/8/17		Mules 109. M.V. Vet. Sec. Rebels Sick animals. Marci to Evacuating to Corps Veg. O.C.S. Mule Murrelly The Evacuated 3. Deaths 1. Remaining under treatment 5. Missing since received 13. Gunshot wounds 9. Mules Attacked Reg. Musling lost. Mules 113. 114. v. 115. A/ Div.	

Army Form C. 2118.

WAR DIARY
or
INTELLIGENCE SUMMARY.
(Erase heading not required.)

Instructions regarding War Diaries and Intelligence Summaries are contained in F. S. Regs., Part II. and the Staff Manual respectively. Title pages will be prepared in manuscript.

Place	Date	Hour	Summary of Events and Information	Remarks and references to Appendices
DRAGH CAMP	20/8/17		Inspected lines. Inspected all animals. Rec'd. Rose lines all filled close to Bridge further. Condition of horses & mules good. A number of rains. small strads are P.M. Gave instructions for serial issue to be sent to Mob. Vety Sectn for evacuation.	
"	21/8/17		Visit 121 & 133 Bdes. R.F.A. Gave instructions for 14 horses to be evacuated for debility. All the other animals are in fairly good condition. Saw shoeings at present are dry whilst Advance Vety. Supply collecting Post. Visit 49th Mob. Vet. Sec. Made arrangements for A.D.V.S. 14 Corps to inspect Artillery Regimental horses. Batte Animals Fair. Fired nit- Wounded 12.	
"	22/8/17		Accompanied A.D.V.S. 14 Corps on inspection of 121 & 133 Bdes. R.F.A. Recommended serial horses to be evacuated. Visit 49. Mob. Vet. Sec. & D.H.Q. horse lines. Battle casualty rate Killed 5 - Wounded 8.	
"	23/8/17		Visit HQts Mob. Vet. Sec. D.H.Q. horse lines. Battle casualty rate Killed 7.	

WAR DIARY
or
INTELLIGENCE SUMMARY

(Erase heading not required.)

Army Form C. 2118.

Place	Date	Hour	Summary of Events and Information	Remarks and references to Appendices
DRAGON CAMP	24/8/17		Inspected Veterinary Affairs. Office tendve. Visited 49th Mob.Vet.Sec. Ratto Casualty Slats. this mit no wounded.	
"	25/8/17		Attended conference at A.D.V.S. office in Cubo. Visits D.H.Q. horse lines. Visited 49th Mob.Vet.Sec. Mobile Casualty Slate. Killed mit - wounded 7.	
"	26/8/17		Visited advanced detraining station, Bridge Junction. Visited 49th Mob.Vet.Sec. R.H.Q. horse lines.	
"	27/8/17		Visited 49th Mob.Vet.Sec. Numbered with taff Howard V.O./c mules and mephets Nos 3 Sec. 3rd G.A.C. All animals in excellent condition nothing hill can be found, cannot have this feeling too high, location of lashings fail, very cost has been taken to change the lines about, and to reduce the risk of being cut up to much. With No. 8 field Annuals are but the most that is my last condition. This unit has suffered very much since my last inspection, caused in early camp T.S. Multiple cases of great dies of falling this way, in condition is attributable to bad lashings. they are altogether unsuitable.	

Army Form C. 2118.

WAR DIARY
or
INTELLIGENCE SUMMARY.
(Erase heading not required.)

Place	Date	Hour	Summary of Events and Information	Remarks and references to Appendices
DJAGUN CAMP	28/8/17		Sitting of the general court and animals canal sir down in context and attention to their welfare to Off. (Lt. Hayward) and also Staff Captain, R.A. - also permission to see the steps what can be done. No. 1 Sec. R.A.b. 3 Sub. Sections in fair condition, 1 sub. section better in condition. Sandwagon not very good, although better than M.S. Sec. Evacuated 12. The majority of the cases being febrile.	
"	29/8/17		Visits E. Mahomed Br B.S. - A.P. & M.L. Visits 49 MK. Vet. Sec. Visits 303 R.A. H.J. Animals in good condition Visited D.H.Q. Horse lines, & 49th Mt. Vet. Sec.	
"	30/8/17		Visits 38th F.A.b. to inspect mules horses which had to be removed, sent back to unit, about 10. As they were not fit for immediate work, hopeless horses cases - condition fairly good. Visits 19 Pioneer Bn. Animals in excellent condition, 1 saw M.Y. flexion tendons, 1 saw poll evil & 1 case fistulas Visits 49 MK. Vet. Sec. and D.H.Q. Horse lines.	

Army Form C. 2118.

WAR DIARY
or
INTELLIGENCE SUMMARY.
(Erase heading not required.)

Place	Date	Hour	Summary of Events and Information	Remarks and references to Appendices
DEPOT CAMP.	3/8/17		Inspected N.S. Visited Nos. 1 & 7. Sections, 38th D.A.C. & No. 1 Sec. 7 D.A.C. return to be devoured for Ridely. 1 pot and horse. Had feeling removed to farmed picket - much better standings - from Veterinary point of view - standings not in one area. Rmain horse sale turned out. Also several mild colitis Animals being fed. Not satisfactory with system. Chaff not much fed very small mix with oats. Recommended Mil while quantity of oats & chaff to be mixed and attention to be given to forage barn. For ventilation to be sure to fit on not meshbag. Any sick hay also on in No. Sec. No. 1 Sec. Attend 1 animal to be shot. Witnessed feeding, same faults as in No. 5 Sec. Active Report similar as in No. 1. Sec. D.A.C. Examined 1 horse & 1 mare mary, recommend casting by D.A.Y. 1 horse that gelding viscous and very difficult to handle, not above age to be handled. No. 5. Examined for Ridely. Pony - No. 347 unable to lane.	

D.D. & L., London, E.C. Sch. 52a. Forms/C/2118/4

Army Form C. 2118.

WAR DIARY
or
INTELLIGENCE SUMMARY.
(Erase heading not required.)

Instructions regarding War Diaries and Intelligence Summaries are contained in F. S. Regs., Part II. and the Staff Manual respectively. Title pages will be prepared in manuscript.

Place	Date	Hour	Summary of Events and Information	Remarks and references to Appendices
DRAGON CAMP.	31/8/17		Men supplied by me anonymously marked on 131 Field Ambulance from 4AM to 6AM night and meanwhile for fatigue work.	

signature
MAJOR,
D.A.D.V.S. 38th (WELSH) DIVISION.

CONFIDENTIAL

WAR DIARY

OF

D.A.D.V.S., 38th. (Welsh) DIVISION.

FROM

1st. SEPTEMBER 1917.

TO

30th. SEPTEMBER 1917.

(Volume XXII.)

[signature]
Major.

1st. October 1917.　　D.A.D.V.S., 38th. (Welsh) DIVISION.

Army Form C. 2118.

WAR DIARY
or
INTELLIGENCE SUMMARY.
(Erase heading not required.)

Instructions regarding War Diaries and Intelligence Summaries are contained in F. S. Regs., Part II. and the Staff Manual respectively. Title pages will be prepared in manuscript.

Place	Date	Hour	Summary of Events and Information	Remarks and references to Appendices
DRAGON CAMP	1/9/17		Conference at A.D.V.S. Office 11th Corps. Visits A.R. Horse lines	
"	3/9/17		Visited 114th Mob. Vet. Sec. Horses are umphatic 119th Met. Vet. Sec. Visited 114th New Zealand Div. 13 Bn. Mcht. Regt. Condition of animals fairly good with exception of horses recently issued to the squadron for details. 114th Machine Gun Co. Condition of animals fairly good, no of sick horses in isolation. Animals in excellent condition. 1 horse 17/3 evacuated suffering from Sandcrack Fest. 10. Bn. Mcht. Regt. Condition of animals fairly good. 15. Bn. Mcht. Regt. Condition of animals fairly good as the stbl. needs of this Bn. to Zealand Mcht. Regt. Form D.O. has been received, no replacement yet. Visited 130. Field Ambulance of this Bn. etc. good, Standings good, 129. Field Ambulance condition of animals excellent, Standings good, with exception of one. 1 horse very sick.	

WAR DIARY
or
INTELLIGENCE SUMMARY

Army Form C. 2118.

(Erase heading not required.)

Place	Date	Hour	Summary of Events and Information	Remarks and references to Appendices
DRAGON CAMP	3/9/17		Visit HQrs Mtd. W. See. B.A.G. Arab Lines Offrs Tents	
"	4/9/17		Visits Coup-Du-Bane, D.A.D.V.S. 57 Division, unfortunately he was at Hdqs bivouacked c/o, M.V.S. 57 Divn. and met	
			arrangements regarding to taken over L. meeting in by Hq.	
			Mtd. W. See.	
"	5/9/17		Accompanied by A.D.V.S. Mt. Corps + V.O./c. visited 38th Bde Ammn.	
			Column. Visits and inspected all Lines + A.P.	
			Visits Bttn. Rec. Animals getting very poor feet in condition	
"	6/9/17		Evacuated 2 for Deaths - 7 13 fat Debility. Visits Proven	
			with D.A.D. V.S. and inspected 23 newly arrived Remounts, for	
			Mule of this Brigade other than artillery 9 / HD. 10. 10	
			Mules 3 Police + 1 charged all in very good	
			condition. Visited Hqs Mt. W. See. Met Hd. Sec. +	
"	7/9/17		Conference HQs Africa Visits Hq. Mt. W. See.	
			B.A.G. Arab Lines.	

WAR DIARY or INTELLIGENCE SUMMARY

Army Form C. 2118.

(Erase heading not required.)

Place	Date	Hour	Summary of Events and Information	Remarks and references to Appendices
DAWSON CAMP	8/9/17		Attended conference at HQ. XIV Corps. A.D.S. visited A.D.M.S. 57 Division. Received and reported to XI. Corps HQ. for conference by A.D.S. Received Chief Horse Hazel Streeze visits etc. Particulars to follow and 2 Mt. C.C.H. shed 36, and visited camps. 1st Mot. Vet. Sec. and visited F.A.	
"	9/9/17		Visited 3rd N.Z. and 49th Mob. Vet. Sec., and Divisional H.Q.	
"	10/9/17		Visited 38th Div. of 6. fired lines Mt. Vet. Sec.	
"	11/9/17		Received mail from Army and to PROVEN. Visited Mob. Vet. Sec. visited F.A. casualty clearing station	
PROVEN	14/9/17		Received notification from visited 29/21 Res. 6th Mobilare 10/16 121 Res. R.F.A. for entrained Influenza. Alot Res. evacuated 1 case Influenza. Visited 9/132 Res. R.F.A. evacuated 1 case Influenza. Visited 20/122 Res. Influenza. 1 case Influenza. 1 Res. Influenza 6 cases Influenza. Bliss Res. evacuated 1 Res. Influenza. Visited A.P.O. A.S.C. echo v "Q" 38 Div. at outbreak of Mis. Received mail from PROVEN to ESTAIRES.	
"	13/9/17		Received mail from A.A.C.S. 57th Division at arrangements for Motor Vety. Section.	
ESTAIRES	14/9/17		Visited A.A.C.S. 57 Division	

WAR DIARY
or
INTELLIGENCE SUMMARY.

Army Form C. 2118.

Place	Date	Hour	Summary of Events and Information	Remarks and references to Appendices
ESTAIRES	14/9/17		To attend cple with 51 Div. M.S.	
"	15/9/17		Visite ADMS XI Corps. Visite Met. Vet. Sec. & F.M.B. horse lines.	
"	16/9/17		Visite HQ MVS DAD-VMP horse lines. Office routine.	
"	17/9/17		Received order from ESTAIRES to CROIX-DU-BAC. Visite HQS.	
			Met Vet Sec. and sites.	
CROIX DU BAC	18/9/17		Visite 38th Div. Signal Co. HQ Met Vet Sec.	
"	19/9/17		On tour of Artillery Units to England to 29/9/17	
"	30/9/17		As directed by A.D.C. Braxiver Visite & inspected 123 Co. R.E. animals in good condition except two, slightly sick, but are being informed. 151 Co. R.E. Animals in good condition standing on 124 Co. R.E. Animals in this Coy are not looking so well as the others. 3 horses to be examined at Dilley by Vet. Res. the others this animals in their lines R.E. are in good condition stabling. Remarks sent on inspection slip to C.R.E.	

MAJOR.
p. A.D.V.S. 38th (WELSH) DIVISION.

Confidential

War Diary

of

D.A.D.V.S. 38th (Welsh) Division.

From
1st October 1917
To
31st October 1917.

(Volume XXIII).

Vol 23

[signature]
Major. A.V.C.
D.A.D.V.S. 38th (Welsh) Division

1st November 1917.

WAR DIARY or INTELLIGENCE SUMMARY

Army Form C. 2118.

Place	Date	Hour	Summary of Events and Information	Remarks and references to Appendices
CROIX DU BAC	1/10/17		Held inspection of 19th M.V.S. and also No 1 Sect. M.V.C. picked out 2 animals sickly and sent them to Vety Section. Inspection at Ferme du Bretagne, allotted 3 mares to be sent for examination by Board formed for selection of mares for Breeding purposes or termination of hostilities.	
	2/10/17		Received visit from A.D.V.S. First Army and A.D.V.S. XI Corps who inspected 10th Brigade of Artillery and many Infantry Battns. expressed themselves as satisfied.	
	3/10/17		Received visit from Selection Committee for Brood Mares and accompanied them on tour of inspection.	
	4/10/17		S.D.R. visits billets and examined horses for casting. Capt. Bullen proceeded on leave.	
	5/10/17		Conference of Veterinary Officers and preparing weekly return.	
	6/10/17		Visited A.D.V.S. XI Corps picking up Capt. Best M.C. on the way. Visited 2 number of Units in 2nd Division with A.D.V.S. and examined their return of making Hay Racks and Hay nets ? Lines. Attended Conference of DADS.V.S. at HINGES.	
	7/10/17		Visited Th. V.S. and 3td Qn Lines also Turn. P.	
	8/10/17		The Committee appointed to select mares for Breeding purposes again visited and completed the inspection. I accompanied and assisted.	
	9/10/17		Received visit from A.D.V.S. XI Corps who instructed me to conduct a sale of horses at MERVILLE on the 7th November 1917. He visited C.R.A. to explain the reason	

Army Form C. 2118.

WAR DIARY
or
INTELLIGENCE SUMMARY.
(Erase heading not required.)

Instructions regarding War Diaries and Intelligence Summaries are contained in F. S. Regs., Part II. and the Staff Manual respectively. Title pages will be prepared in manuscript.

Place	Date	Hour	Summary of Events and Information	Remarks and references to Appendices
CROIX DU BAC	9 cont.		for subending his charge in his absence interviewed staff Captain and explained to him	
			Visited M.V.S. and understudy. Later interviewed CRA and explained, he informed himself as satisfied.	
"	10-10-17		Visited B/122 Battery RFA re mud & Ophthalmia case to M.V.S. for treatment gave advice re constructing Hay Racks and Hay driers. Condition of animals only fair. Visited M.V.P. found straw not being fed to animals, gave instructions for staffing same	
"	11-10-17		Visited 15th RWF, very dissatisfied with condition of animals, too many poor cubs. Saw that going back in condition informed Captain Smith to see BVO and tell him so and of improvement was not effected would have to report the matter to CO and "Q".	
"	12-10-17		Conference of Veterinary Officers. Visited August Coy and disapproved use of Detainers.	
"	13-10-17		Visited M.V.S., Signal Coy, 2Rde CA and Div HQ lines and attended to cases requiring treatment.	
"	14-10-17		Visited Both Field Ambulances, 114 M & Coy. inspected animals stables etc. alterations to existing standings in progress gave demonstration in construction of Hay Racks and they were also fitting of nosebags. Animals in excellent condition. Visited M.V.S.	
			Visited 14th Welch and gave similar demonstration. Animals in good condition.	

WAR DIARY
or
INTELLIGENCE SUMMARY.
(Erase heading not required.)

Army Form C. 2118.

Place	Date	Hour	Summary of Events and Information	Remarks and references to Appendices
CROIX DU BAC	14th	cont	repairs and alterations to standings being effected.	
"	15th		Attended at HQRS to meet DDR and ADVS and inspected the horses effected by laminitis.	
			Visited 12th Welsh and inspected animals, condition good. Saw demonstration in construction of Hay Racks etc. and fitting of nosebags.	
"	16-10-17		Visited 2nd/5, 176 M.G.Coy advised construction of Hay Racks etc. Condition of animals excellent.	
			Captain Coulbourn AVC returned from leave.	
"	17-10-17		Visited 131 Field Ambulance and found repairs and alterations to existing Horse Standings and building in progress. Condition of animals very good. Visited 383 Coy ASC and found a similar condition of affairs there – one case of Sarcoptic mange discovered in this Coy on Sunday and the parasite demonstrated under the microscope in my presence.	
			Visited 38th Div. Train. Visited 113 Fd. A. Coy. Was diligent in Transport Officer's absence in charge of H/Q/rs. were being watered at the time of my visit. Watering place unsuitable for few firm lines, horses in to scramps in wet weather will be under water, told visit again and find a T.O. and explain this to him.	
			Visited 14th RWF took horsing in Horse Standings. Animals in excellent condition. T.O. away on 2 days bonus at ABBEVILLE. Explained how to fix Hay Racks	

WAR DIARY
or
INTELLIGENCE SUMMARY.
(Erase heading not required.)

Army Form C. 2118.

Place	Date	Hour	Summary of Events and Information	Remarks and references to Appendices
CROIX DU BAC	17th cont.		with the men from Bales, also demonstrated how to fit on Nosebags and re-pointed shifting of Oats when feeding. No chaffing machine, told them to have oat	
	18-10-17		Accompanied ADVS. 31 Corps on tour of inspection of animals in this Division.	
	19-10-17		Proceeded with maps to ABBEVILLE and visited No 14 Vety Hospital and returned to Corps Headquarters the same night.	
	20-10-17		Attended conference of DADsVS at 31 Corps Headquarters. Lieut J Brabane applied for duty to relieve Captain Sinch AVC	
	21-10-17		Interviewed Lieut Brabane and Captain Sinch, gave instructions about handing over duties to Lieut Brabane. Condemned Bale of Hay at RA Hd Qrs.	
	22-10-17		Visited Divl Signal Coy Transport Lines and examined Horses with Lieut James Cruse during will progress formate. Visited Hd.Qrs R.A. and examined Capts mare's charge - gave instructions to take it to No V S for isolation and to await confirmation of diagnosis. Condemned bag of Oats at R.A. Hd. Qrs. Capt. Sinch left for 14 Vety Hospital	
	23-10-17		Visited Hd. Qrs. R.A. and Signal Coys Waggon Lines and attended to cases. Visited 15th R.W.F. and inspected the animals and Horse Standings. Horses shoe	

Army Form C. 2118.

WAR DIARY
or
INTELLIGENCE SUMMARY.
(Erase heading not required.)

Instructions regarding War Diaries and Intelligence Summaries are contained in F. S. Regs., Part II. and the Staff Manual respectively. Title pages will be prepared in manuscript.

Place	Date	Hour	Summary of Events and Information	Remarks and references to Appendices
CROIX DU BAC	23rd Oct		a little improvement evinced rather from the inside to be evacuated for debility also one horse. Forage was being chaffed at 123 Coy RE also Oats being crushed at the same unit. No attempt at making Hay Racks as they never got Grease given that the stables are going to be pulled down and rebuilt. Underneath one bale of Hay. Visited 124 Fld Coy RE and inspected animals also considerable improvement Hay Racks being made, they have already made but too small. This Unit is improving but one horse in very poor condition also duty although the horse is clipped. Drew the Sergeant's attention to it and instructed him to keep a sharp eye on the Driver.	
"	24-10-17		Visited Divl Signal Coy and examined horses with Veterinary Style improvement. Inspected 123 Fld Coy RE animals have fallen away in condition. No attempt at making Hay Racks yet on Hay drive in Barn Straw not being chaffed twelve horses clipped unable to proceed on account of clippers (blades) being out of order have spoken to D.A.D.O.S. about the matter. Gave instructions that Straw should be chaffed at 151 Coy RE. Inspected 151 Coy RE. Horses not quite so good as when I last visited. Straw being chaffed and clipping proceeding Hay Racks being made	

Army Form C. 2118.

WAR DIARY
or
INTELLIGENCE SUMMARY.
(Erase heading not required.)

Instructions regarding War Diaries and Intelligence Summaries are contained in F. S. Regs., Part II. and the Staff Manual respectively. Title pages will be prepared in manuscript.

Place	Date	Hour	Summary of Events and Information	Remarks and references to Appendices
CROIX DU BAC	24th cont		Visited 146 M.G Coy and find nothing has been done to make Hay Racks or get complete stabling. L.O still away on leave	
"	25-10-17		Visited 2nd Ques Rla and sent L.O Horse with double Ophtalmia to N.V.S. for injection with Lysol solution. Visited Signal Coy and attended to case of Scabies. Visited and inspected M.V.S. work of reconstruction of stables proceeding satisfactorily. Examined horses awaiting evacuation by barge tomorrow morning	
"	26-10-17		Conference of Veterinary Officers. Office Routine.	
"	27-10-17		Visited 13th Welsh Regt Transport Lines at feeding time found my instructions with regard to watering and horsage was not being carried out. Called the Transport Sergeant's attention to this and made him turn out his mess tin and properly try attempt his to get them made to make Hay Racks. Condition of animals good. New stabling nearly complete. Inspected 114th Tr. M. B. Coy Transport animals condition very good the staff Sergeant and NCOs were present visiting them to put up Hay Racks. Nosebags were fitted properly	

WAR DIARY or INTELLIGENCE SUMMARY

Army Form C. 2118.

Place	Date	Hour	Summary of Events and Information	Remarks and references to Appendices
CROIX DU BAC	28-10-17		Visited M.V. Section and inspected animals, one sent in from No. 1 D.A.C. and to be suffering from Ringbone. Gave instructions for shoe to be removed as I was of opinion the lameness was in foot. Left Inspector to shoe shoe and found bruised sole. Returned the horse to No. 1 Section M.T.C. Whilst there the animals were brought in from 6th Australian D.A.C. for inoculation this being the nearest to V section of cases of cellulitis.	
"	29-10-17		Visited M.V.S. and inspected animals for evacuation by barge. Received information from ADVS through DDVS that the time of departure of barge was in future to be at 3 p.m. and not as heretofore. Notified O.C. M.V.S. Captain Howard returned from leave.	
"	30-10-17		Visited and inspected No. 1 Sect 38th MVS accompanied by Captain Vernon Jones 8th Ret. Twenty eight teams of four mules out at ARMENTIÈRES for bricks, rest of animals in good condition. They looke had been inoculated but were uneethwise. No stay down in Barn. Construction of new stabling in progress. Sergt. Mayor & MVC Sergt running to Hd Qrs. Forge Lines for instruction in making stay Racks and Sieves. One horse very lame, gave instructions to remove shoe and examine foot.	

Army Form C. 2118.

WAR DIARY
or
INTELLIGENCE SUMMARY.
(Erase heading not required.)

Instructions regarding War Diaries and Intelligence Summaries are contained in F. S. Regs., Part II. and the Staff Manual respectively. Title pages will be prepared in manuscript.

Place	Date	Hour	Summary of Events and Information	Remarks and references to Appendices
CROIX DU BAC	30th cont.		Visited No.2 Sub. 38th Bde. Saw teams of six out on fatigue conditions of men & horses both starting and surroundings miserable. Men men in course of construction. Hay Racks similar to those on No.1 sect. Iron mangers and leg broken and much too small. Received wire from A.D.V.S. X Corps notifying he would call tomorrow.	
"	31-10-17		Visited Hd Qrs Lines and Signal Coy. Horse with Tetanus progressing favourably. Received visit from A.D.V.S. X Corps in sale of Horses	

Sgd. Major
38 (Welsh) Divn.

CONFIDENTIAL

WAR DIARY

OF

D. A. D. V. S.   38th. (Welsh) DIVISION.

FROM

1st.   NOVEMBER   1917.

TO

30th.   NOVEMBER   1917.

(Volume   XXIV.)

[signature]
Major. A.V.C.

1st. December 1917   D. A. D. V. S., 38th. (Welsh) Division

Army Form C. 2118.

WAR DIARY
or
INTELLIGENCE SUMMARY.
(Erase heading not required.)

Place	Date	Hour	Summary of Events and Information	Remarks and references to Appendices
CROIX DU BAC.	1/11/17		Office Routine during morning. Received visit from ADVS XI Corps re sale of horses to take place at MERVILLE on 7th inst. Arrangements to be made for horse standings and billets for men on day of sale. Visited MVS in afternoon.	
	2/11/17		Conference of Veterinary Officers in morning and preparation of weekly Returns. In afternoon visited Signal Company and reduced horse with Tetanus to be shot.	
	3/11/17		Visited 38th Divl Std Qrs Lines during morning and in afternoon attended Corps Conference at HINGES.	
	4/11/17		Visited 38th Divl Std Qrs Lines and 38th RA Hd Qrs in morning. Visited 19th MVS in afternoon. Received further particulars from ADVS XI Corps re sale of Cast Horses also notification that ADVS would visit 19th MVS at 2.30 p.m. tomorrow.	
	5/11/17		Visited MERVILLE and interviewed Town Major re sale of Cast Horses to be held on 7th inst. Arranged for horse standings and billets for men of 19th MVS. Also arranged conveyance of men to MERVILLE	

WAR DIARY
or
INTELLIGENCE SUMMARY.

Army Form C. 2118.

(Erase heading not required.)

Place	Date	Hour	Summary of Events and Information	Remarks and references to Appendices
CROIX DU BAC	5/11/17		Took and stock with 38th Division "Q".	
			Called at Auctioneer's Local office and found he had gone away.	
			Visited 49th M.V.S and met A.D.V.S by appointment to examine 2 Remounts which were sent up with last batch and returned to No V.S as unfit for work. One had to be evacuated at once with Ulcerative Cellulitis and the other suffering from Abscess on Heel.	
"	6/11/17		Interpreter Aufemain to collect horse at ARREWAGE. D.D.V.S. instructions.	
			Visited 49th M.V.S. and inspected horses for Evacuation.	
"	7/11/17		Attended Sale of Cast Horses at MERVILLE. Average price 500 francs. 13 unsold and returned to Section.	
			Visited 14th R.H.F and inspected Transport Lines. May Sacks had been constructed, but Hay dues too small. Recommended making another one. Condition of Animals very good.	
			Inspected 38th Mounted Military Police horses, Stable management indifferent, straw not being chaffed and not fed to the animals.	

WAR DIARY
or
INTELLIGENCE SUMMARY.
(Erase heading not required.)

Army Form C. 2118.

Place	Date	Hour	Summary of Events and Information	Remarks and references to Appendices
CROIX DU BAC	7/11/17	contd	Linseed Cake does not appear to be given as food either. One horse lame, strain muscle shoulder. A.D.n was out so also Traffic Control Officer, will pay another visit and see if there is any improvement.	
" "	8/11/17		Visited 76th G.Coy and inspected animals, condition fair. Transport Sergeant not there. Two Transport Officers just arrived, nothing has been done in erection of Hay Racks. Pointed out improvements to Transport Officers who promised to take matter in hand. Arranged for him to be at office at 3-30 p.m. to see Hay Racks and Sieves at Div Hd Qrs Lines and receive instruction as to method of building same. Visited 16th R.W.F., conditions of animals excellent. Hay Racks constructed but no Hay Sieve, gave instructions as to construction of latter. Visited 131. Fld Ambulance. Hay Racks being constructed, no chaffing machine and straw not being chuffed. Sergeant began out, revisited and found him in. The arrangements for storing	

War Diary or Intelligence Summary

Army Form C. 2118.

Place	Date	Hour	Summary of Events and Information	Remarks and references to Appendices
CROIX DU BAC	8/11/17 contd		Forage is very poor, but a new barn is being erected. Gave advice as to chaffing and feeding cake and construction of Sheds to prevent smell of Hay. Ordered one horse to go to 119th M.V.S. with punctured wound in shoulder. I inspected 113th & G Coy. Transport lines. Animals conditions good. Hay Racks being constructed. Station of Watering Place changed to place suggested by me on last visit.	
"	9/11/17		Met D.D.S. and A.D.V.S. at 119th M.V.S. for Remounts. Looking. Repaired Returns in afternoon. Informed A.D.V.S. 59th Brigade. Army Field Artillery had left area.	
"	10/11/17		147th Bde Army Field Artillery arrived in this Divisional Area to replace 169th Bde Army Field Artillery which left. A.D.V.S. notified and location of horse on Area. Received intimation from "A", 38th Division that Capt. R. Hobbs was sent from no. 3 Veterinary Hospital to relieve Capt. F. Chalk, V.O. i/c 147 Bde Army Field Artillery to no. 23 Veterinary Hospital	

Army Form C. 2118.

WAR DIARY
or
INTELLIGENCE SUMMARY.
(Erase heading not required.)

Instructions regarding War Diaries and Intelligence Summaries are contained in F. S. Regs., Part II. and the Staff Manual respectively. Title pages will be prepared in manuscript.

Place	Date	Hour	Summary of Events and Information	Remarks and references to Appendices
CROIX DU BAC	10/10/17 contd		Captain Macfarlane and Lieut Graham called and interviewed me, the former with regard to places to present picked up hail and latter with regard to 176 Th. G. Coy Horse Lines.	
"	11/10/17		With A/D.A.Q.M.G, Capt. J. H. Davies, visited 119th M.V.S to meet Committee from War Office at final Selection of Burot horses. Eleven selected	
"	12/10/17		Visited 129 Field Ambulance and inspected animals, stabling etc. Condition of Animals excellent, stabling good. Hay Racks not constructed but Hay tubs made from waste wire from Bales of Hay. Visited 119th M.V.S and inspected animals for evacuation tomorrow. Visited 38th Div. Hd Qrs and 38th R.A. Hd Qrs. Horse Lines.	
"	13/10/17		Inspected C/121 Bde R.F.A. Transport Lines. Condition of animals good, one horse I ordered to be evacuated for debility, no arrangements in Barn for serving Hay. No Hay Racks. No Dragon line. Sergt. or Officer in charge of these lines.	

WAR DIARY
or
INTELLIGENCE SUMMARY
(Erase heading not required.)

Army Form C. 2118.

Place	Date	Hour	Summary of Events and Information	Remarks and references to Appendices
CROIX DU BAC	12/11/17 contd.		Inspected D/121 Bde. R.F.A. Horses in fair condition with the exception of 1 Sub. Section which is poor. Ordered 2 Horses to be evacuated for Debility and one for special diet in lines for sick Horses. Visited 123rd Fld. Coy. R.E. Sick Horses in very poor condition. Ordered two to be evacuated for Debility. About 10 foot of Hay Racks made. they have made a small Hay Sieve in the Barn not large enough. Visited 151 Co. R.E. who have made a new Barn in which a sieve has been made but not large enough to hold all the Hay. Condition of animals in this Company better than in the 123rd Fld. Coy. R.E. Advised removal of all old manurings that was here as it only proved a means of wasting food and gave demonstration how to fit on nosebags. Captain Macfarlane accompanied me round these Units. Capt. R. Hopps. A.V.C. V.O. to 147th Army Field Arty. Bde. called at the Office during my absence.	

WAR DIARY
or
INTELLIGENCE SUMMARY.

(Erase heading not required.)

Army Form C. 2118.

Place	Date	Hour	Summary of Events and Information	Remarks and references to Appendices
CROIX DU BAC	14/4/17	—	Visited H.Q. 119th M.V.S. and 176 M.G.Coy. Drainage being carried out here and animals being clipped. A.D.V.S. called whilst I was on inspection of Units. 38th Div. R.A. Hd. Qrs. One horse lame in foot, gave instructions to take to Forge and take shoe off. Visited 38th Signal Coy and examined a horse salivating at the mouth, no apparent cause.	
"	15/4/17	—	Had foot of Rider from R.A. Hd. Qrs. examined and found it was a suppurating Corn. Visited H.Q. M.V.S. and examined horses to be evacuated tomorrow. A.D.V.S. X. Corps and Capt. R. Hopps called. Received circular from D.V.S. re Destruction of Horses.	
"	16/4/17	—	Conference of Veterinary Officers in morning and preparing Returns in afternoon.	
"	17/4/17	—	Visited Head Quarter Units. Received visit from A.D.V.S. to introduce Capt. R. Hopps R.V.C. V.O. i/c 107th Bde Army Field Artillery	

WAR DIARY
or
INTELLIGENCE SUMMARY.
(Erase heading not required.)

Army Form C. 2118.

Place	Date	Hour	Summary of Events and Information	Remarks and references to Appendices
CROIX DU BAC	17/11/17 Contd		who have relieved 169th Army Field Artillery Brigade in this area.	
	18/11/17		Visited 49th N.Y.S., 38th Div. Hd Qrs. 38th R.A. Hd Qrs & Dig.al Coy Lines. In afternoon C.R.V.S. called in reference to drawing of Forge Ambulance for sick horses. Received information that XI Corps were being relieved in the 22nd instant by the XV Corps.	
"	19/11/17		Received intimation from Lieut. Buchanan that horse was shot dead in the 15th R.W.F. Lines accident. Received visit from Capt. Macfarlane who brought his report in connection with Ophthalmia, also received similar reports from Capt. Howard and Capt. Cullaine.	
"	20/11/17		Visited 15th R.W.F. in consequence of horse accidentally killed and found that five shots were fired by some unknown person from a S.W. direction. One of the bullets struck a horse in the Off. Quarter and passed through his left kidney and lodged in the Animal died in a few minutes from intense hemorrhage. A party was dispatched to investigate the source of the firing and failed to discover anything.	

Place	Date	Hour	Summary of Events and Information	Remarks and references to Appendices
CROIX DU BAC	20/11/17	contd.	Inspected the animals in this Unit and found a great improvement in the animals and stable management. Sanitary condition good. Stabling also Hay Racks being erected, a new barn is in course of construction.	
"	21/11/17		Forwarded reports with my remarks to ADVS XI Corps in connection with. Visited 11th Bn which condition of animals excellent, also stables have been erected and a new design of Hay Rack Forage Barn, stable management excellent. Visited 38th Divl Train Hd Qrs. Received instructions from ADVS XI Corps with regard to taking over Corps Units pending arrival of Veterinary Officers of Corps Troops and Corps Heavy Artillery XV Corps. Clerk returned to duty today from sick leave	
"	22/11/17		Visited and inspected 151 Co. F.E. and examined Mangel issue - 1 cow remains from this Co. Examine animals on the farm condition good. Marshalls Huts being constructed, All Mangels still in pickle. Although a much age they were little injured and new resistance.	

WAR DIARY
or
INTELLIGENCE SUMMARY.
(Erase heading not required.)

Army Form C. 2118.

Place	Date	Hour	Summary of Events and Information	Remarks and references to Appendices
CROIX DU BAC	17/11/17		Ack in. Received instructions from A.D.V.S. XI corps to take over charge of the sick horse lines temporarily as a temporary measure until the arrival of 15 cobs.	
"	23/11/17		Inspected Veterinary Stores. Inspected sick filled in consignment of ambulant of 147th Bde A.F.A. that they have not been broke in at H.Q. Sick lines f sick are here which are latter at H.Q. Sick lines Examined 13 animals now inspected up to mk. Cpl. Laine and sick are not than Marines Horses are in good condition and there evacuated by Rly cases in A.V.C. so more than of shoe releted to B.A.&M.S. Civil Vetry. The Hastings on an election and animals the march when sick completed. Saw relation to B.A.&M.S. His mother Meetings are an excellent any annoyed and amusing on the lines ptgs very annihilated and hive ed no fuews to delting to thee from the arrival Cha. Bill. Vay has taken all the mullet with Veterinary Officer. Another of horses - very good.	

Army Form C. 2118.

WAR DIARY
or
INTELLIGENCE SUMMARY.
(Erase heading not required.)

Instructions regarding War Diaries and Intelligence Summaries are contained in F. S. Regs., Part II. and the Staff Manual respectively. Title pages will be prepared in manuscript.

Place	Date	Hour	Summary of Events and Information	Remarks and references to Appendices
CROIX DU BAC	25/10/17		Truck 398 MT let for continuance of filling in many shellholes and ruts in road to finish	
"	26/10/17		Received visit from A.D.V.S. XV Corps, and accompanied him to Mobile Veterinary Section and confield by him - returned through Nieppe with No such which had been done. Truck 13 Rev Mech Staff employment - animals in fair condition. Shoeings must be considered. Hay racks nearly completed and also sat trough have been used in situation and stabling machine Machine gun to be continued to be completed. Hay racks suitably enclosed in same, so as to be continued to be completed. Hay racks enclosed	
"	27/10/17		Visit is being clothed. Stables of animals PA H.Q. good. Truck 38th H.Q. Horse lines Mess Rooms Cooks	
"	28/10/17		Truck No. 3 Section, 38th D.A.C. - animals all in such a good condition and this inspection Stables require instruments - hay racks not ready and Horses are only staring - Hay racks limited - Shoeing not quite finish Truck 49/22 Div R.F.A. - Horse lines and Sat	

WAR DIARY or INTELLIGENCE SUMMARY

Army Form C. 2118.

Place	Date	Hour	Summary of Events and Information	Remarks and references to Appendices
CROIX DU BAC.	28/11/17		Condition of mules & horses on mules & horses & stables not excellent as all by Indians Battery. Horses require training, not require reconditioning. Condition of animals fair.	
"	29/11/17		Condition of animals fair. Linings good. Build 35th M.M.P. Horse Lines Sanitation of animals fair. Linings good. Build Ahr. Bde. R.F.A. Linings sufficient, require shoes in short supply. Condition of animals good, lameness require moving. Animals hard to just lameness. Horses to get Mule Class. Horses in part of lameness when cured. About shoes M.S. animal. The animal condition of the R.F.A. Linings sufficient. Animals according to Build 176th Machine Gun Co, 1 animal hoof in Animals good. The rest in fair condition. Incomplete amount of good nature. The rest in fair condition. Condition of Mules and asses. With temp making and condition of Mules greatly improved. Mules condition. 115 Am. Prk. Mules greatly improved and Mules remainder. Any such lines from escaped. Horses of animals. Two are good. Constantly saluted but not observed. Build 12th Am. Park. Harness and Animals the M.S. Part 13 in not excellent condition. The rest. Lines and	

Army Form C. 2118.

WAR DIARY
or
INTELLIGENCE SUMMARY.
(Erase heading not required.)

Instructions regarding War Diaries and Intelligence Summaries are contained in F. S. Regs., Part II. and the Staff Manual respectively. Title pages will be prepared in manuscript.

Place	Date	Hour	Summary of Events and Information	Remarks and references to Appendices
CROIX DU BAC	30/11/17		Veterinary Affairs Audit of Mobile Veterinary Section.	
			Returned Serums	

Xull Gam
MAJOR,
D.A.D.V.S. 38th (WELSH) DIVISION.

C O N F I D E N T I A L

WAR DIARY

OF

D. A. D. V. S.   38th. (Welsh) DIVISION.

FROM

1st.   DECEMBER   1917.

TO

31st.   DECEMBER   1917.

(Volume XXV.)

Major. A.V.C.

1st. January 1918.   D.A.D.V.S., 38th. (Welsh) DIVISION.

Army Form C. 2118.

WAR DIARY
or
INTELLIGENCE SUMMARY.
(Erase heading not required.)

Place	Date	Hour	Summary of Events and Information	Remarks and references to Appendices
CROIX DU BAC	1/10/17		[illegible handwritten entries]	
"	2/10/17			
"	3/10/17			

Army Form C. 2118.

WAR DIARY
or
INTELLIGENCE SUMMARY.
(Erase heading not required.)

Instructions regarding War Diaries and Intelligence Summaries are contained in F. S. Regs., Part II. and the Staff Manual respectively. Title pages will be prepared in manuscript.

Place	Date	Hour	Summary of Events and Information	Remarks and references to Appendices
CROIX DU BAC	4/12/17		Visit 49th Mot. Vet. Sec. and ambulance lines. Alkatinised horses to mainchery.	
"	5/12/17		Visit 49th MMS. Inspected Alkatinised cases. 30 animals left for to mainchery.	
"	6/12/17		Visit ?? Alkatinised animals to be remained.	
"			Ambulance to A.O.V.S 15th Corps. Alkatinised xv Corps & AM Athene R.A. XV Corps. Inspected 121. Bde R.F.A. and 123 & 151 7th Bde R.E.	
"	7/12/17		Conference VDS. Both Armies. Visited A.H.G. 2nd Army Cmd.	
"	8/12/17		Visit 49th Mot Vet. Sec. Visited & inspected Col Lionel Co.	
			Army Lines.	
"	9/12/17		Office Routine. Visited A.H.G. 2nd Army lines.	
"	10/12/17		Visit 49th Mot Vet. Sec. Animals in good condition for Alkatmium treatment - condition of Hastings Bde R.F.A. animals in good condition -- reported to MVS.	
"			Fail to require ?? met C.A.R. Fr. ?. Army & AVS XV Corps at H.Q. the Alkatmium animals and Alkatinised horses for active. Any one horse met 49th Mot Vet Sec and Alkatinised. Recovery which was sent off to ?.O.R. Animals from this Recovery which was sent off to ?.	

WAR DIARY
or
INTELLIGENCE SUMMARY.
(Erase heading not required.)

Army Form C. 2118.

Place	Date	Hour	Summary of Events and Information	Remarks and references to Appendices
CROIX-DU-BAC.	13/10/17		Visit Bde Headquarters 7 R.A. Hargreaves how lines	
"	13/10/17		Visit H.Q. Mt. Cil. for intel. Animals hard to exercise	22/
			days. Afternoon 6 cows. Mange H/ evacuated.	
"	14/10/17		Ambulance A.D. Visited No. 3 B² B.A.C. Animals in good	
			condition hill with management & villenage. All horsings bring	
			hearlooks in cond'n. Received instructions from D. A.N.	
			ADVS at feh. was calling to exhibit comments 1.20 p.m.	
			alert to the emergency had the ADVS was not present - mobile	
			Met many injured towards anight. Condition satisfactory. 1 case	
			Night Ringworm.	
"	15/10/17		Visited New Bde RFA. Afterwards of horses, Hoslings, very mucky	
			Horsings showing on ALM of what mud attaches new lines made	
			3 lines Whitehouse ques. instructions for them to be cut to	
			Met Vet Sec Sgt met. Sent Animals. arrival in mud - insufficient	
			Vet command management to be looking carried out. Visited HQ 2nd Bn	
			R.W.F. Condition of animals very good - not roomy. Harm. Rich.	

Army Form C. 2118.

WAR DIARY
or
INTELLIGENCE SUMMARY.
(Erase heading not required.)

Instructions regarding War Diaries and Intelligence Summaries are contained in F. S. Regs., Part II. and the Staff Manual respectively. Title pages will be prepared in manuscript.

Place	Date	Hour	Summary of Events and Information	Remarks and references to Appendices
CROIX DU BAC	15/10/17		Arrival of Advance Party. Great attention to this Unit by 89th M.S. and visiting Animals number of cases noted. Attended to by M.S. Knowin.	
"	16/10/17		Visit 180th Field Ambulance. Inspected lines. Met Lt. GORGUE. Animals excellent. Vehicle marks for vehicles feeling purposes. Lines numbered. Affair "Q" Branch. Standing of forage.	
"	17/10/17		Visit & inspected D.H.Q. Horse lines C.A.V.R.	
"	18/10/17		Visit 49th Met Vet Sec. Inspected all Michelin Lines. 53 Army	
			Marched for Veterinary. 5 cases for evacuation. Visit Nr. 1 Section 38th D.A.C. attended and heard to be sent to M.S. for mange and any case Michelin.	
"	19/10/17		Visit 17/5 M. Gun Co. most of the animals very out. Animals or Southern Entrenchment in very standings, visit 15th Bn. R.W.F. Animals condition excellent Horse Standings clean as good as can possibly be, with the material that is being supplied.	
			Met to being enlarged. Men have been engaged — men	

Army Form C. 2118.

WAR DIARY
or
INTELLIGENCE SUMMARY.
(Erase heading not required.)

Instructions regarding War Diaries and Intelligence Summaries are contained in F. S. Regs., Part II. and the Staff Manual respectively. Title pages will be prepared in manuscript.

Place	Date	Hour	Summary of Events and Information	Remarks and references to Appendices
CROIX DU BAC.	19/12/17		Arrgd. harn. exerd. hay and ankle Movements. Horses & Hantings in good order. Interments in the Lines not Remarkable.	
			Visited 12th. Co. R.E. - Most of the animals are working. Shoe-	
			ing on Hantings in good condition. Arm Hantings fair.	
			The mating of the Hantings are not much improved. Forage	
			Barn hay carts & foot & Lines.	
"	20/12/17		Visited ESTAIRES with Veterinary Adviser and conducted Lane which	
			by A.P.M. An Arrangement of M. Bouben Pricenphions to not	
			Concur with Instructions given.	
"	21/12/17		Ambulance K.O. Visited 49. M.F.S. Inspected animals sent to	
			evacuation. Received word from R.M.S. Zick Anny A. 16/17 red	
			Most of R.M.S. offrs. XV. Cahs xv. Rats is not short.	
"	22/12/17		Visited R.M.S. L.H.R. Arm. Linis.	
"	23/12/17		Visited 112th. Bn. M.Mch. Regt. Arratham of animals excellent. Hantings excellent.	
"	24/12/17		Meeting. Any. seed. Interment and displayed of animals by Veterinary Notes...	

Army Form C. 2118.

WAR DIARY
or
INTELLIGENCE SUMMARY.
(Erase heading not required.)

Place	Date	Hour	Summary of Events and Information	Remarks and references to Appendices
CROIX DU BAC	24/10/17		Visit to the various Field Regt. Section of animals excellent Standard of stabling good, must weight of hay racks excellent, hay used substituted, substituted by Portuguese fields.	
"	25/10/17		Visit D.H.Q. 30 S.W Amb. Visit Hq2 M.V. Vet Sec	
"	26/10/17		Visit R.A. R.C - D.H.Q. Horse Lines.	
"	27/10/17		Visit - ambulance D.H.Q. horse lines	
"	28/10/17		Conference V.O. Visit No.3 Section 38th D.A.C. and ambulance Remounts which were sent by road – one day stand, horses assigned no hard legs. I was informed by a Field that they have obtained from a mutual stocking smith, sufficient April I cogs to do the shoeing. My idea is that have horses have been shod. Visit sick horse Remounts Visit 151 No. R.C, and Standing in line Horses attached to the Portuguese Fields. I saw N.C. Wainwright. V amatelist to be sent to Metz Veterinary Section	

Army Form C. 2118.

WAR DIARY
or
INTELLIGENCE SUMMARY.
(Erase heading not required.)

Place	Date	Hour	Summary of Events and Information	Remarks and references to Appendices
CROIX DU BAC	29/12/17		Visited ADMS XV Corps and arranged for New Zealand Field Amb.	
			and ADMS Army and Corps the Canal Barge Ambulance sent down	
			line as at MERVILLE. Arranged with the 2/1 WMS to disembark the	
			sick horse and infects to NEUFCHATEL by rail.	
"	30/12/17		Visited R.M.S Army H. was that there were no New Zeal. Ambulance	
			Barges here being dismantled and railed to Montreuil.	
"	31/12/17		Visited DDG & CA 2G New Lines	

[signature]
MAJOR,
D.A.D.V.S. 38th (WELSH) DIVISION

CONFIDENTIAL.

WAR DIARY.

OF

D. A. D. V. S.   38th. (Welsh) DIVISION.

FROM

1st.   JANUARY   1918.

TO

31st.   JANUARY   1918.

(VOLUME XXVI.)

[signature]
Major. A.V.C.

1st. February 1918.   D.A.D.V.S., 38th. (Welsh) DIVISION.

Army Form C. 2118.

WAR DIARY
or
INTELLIGENCE SUMMARY.
(Erase heading not required.)

Instructions regarding War Diaries and Intelligence Summaries are contained in F. S. Regs., Part II. and the Staff Manual respectively. Title pages will be prepared in manuscript.

Place	Date	Hour	Summary of Events and Information	Remarks and references to Appendices
Croix du Bac.	1/1/18		Units O.H.Q. New Lines. C.R.R.G. Rail lines.	
"	2/1/18		Units No 1 38th C.R.G. found 76 animals sick and returned ready to	
			nothing. 1 mule at Merge sick at Meta Very below making starvation	
			forward to the R.A. a third in the induction sick and gave	
			recommendations to prevent starving of Merge lost also & which to	
			C. 38th Am. Ptn.S. XV Corps & 7 V.L. C.R.G.	
"	3/1/18		Units No 3 Sec 38th C.R.G. inspected animals. Visiting Vet Station.	
			of shown & mules very arch. 3 sick Williams lieut to Meta	
			Vets visits Units Vet No 1 Sec 38th C.R.G. 76 hours inspect visitation	
			of up within an allowance inch pa MC let see horses mentd. No that	
			any the events given. The the any inspector with animals	
			of ears of Abbathmar. Mt Col the any inspector with animals	
			recorder.	
"	4/1/18		Arrival at library terms with B.G. Inill lins.	
"	5/1/18		Units R.V.S. XV Corps. Ill and attends to Lists Prima &	
			resistance during the absence of ADVS at Calais or leave	

Army Form C. 2118.

WAR DIARY
or
INTELLIGENCE SUMMARY.
(Erase heading not required.)

Instructions regarding War Diaries and Intelligence Summaries are contained in F. S. Regs., Part II. and the Staff Manual respectively. Title pages will be prepared in manuscript.

Place	Date	Hour	Summary of Events and Information	Remarks and references to Appendices
CROIX DU BAC	6/1/18		Received instructions from Auths to meet A.F.A. 1000 for horses and mules initially in accordance with A.L.S. to 15/1/17 dated 9/12/17. No mules as only issued from Army from on all A.L.S. to others and also Advance motley return Posted B.H.Q. Lines Amies	
"	7/1/18		Field XV Coys A.D.S. Offd and stated to motorlorried are Field ng Lub H.E. Ae and indicate Manye and Wikems Field XV Coys A.D.S.	
"	8/1/18		Abdominal cases to ambulances with instructions received from A.D.S. Camp and is being A.D.S. XV Coys & reported 16 horses at the Large to Vogue for Mare by the Primaries for evacuation to No. 23 Aldrenny 10/1/16 All sick on advance days at dusk with animals Large Mare. 5 dead in the large mules of him, father by animals have no men in the vicinity he me, Met the C.C.P. they are about to travel of C.C.P. and advanced party PL at 9:00 he the M.T.S.	

Army Form C. 2118.

WAR DIARY
or
INTELLIGENCE SUMMARY.
(Erase heading not required.)

Instructions regarding War Diaries and Intelligence Summaries are contained in F. S. Regs., Part II. and the Staff Manual respectively. Title pages will be prepared in manuscript.

Place	Date	Hour	Summary of Events and Information	Remarks and references to Appendices
CROIX DU BAC	8/1/18		A.D.V.S. and explained to them the feeding animals of little value in their advanced stage of disease, as they seem not to much good for treatment and if dry. Insisted any horses to continue. more back in future.	
"	9/1/18		Visited 1st Feeding of D.A.C. and inspected the animals. All in good condition. 1st D of them which are carried on a horse's neck for holding mange. Some have lost their hair and require dipping. Fly no injection for fresh Matis all mes doubtful. Birk, Hugh Bingfield, each my men were also are less and horses. Arm required his horn suppulis for food man of Mange, which when returned to be issued. be clamped and are more than on in tail for the record. Note which told Matin and indicated 1 was McChesney and reduced 6 to be discharged.	
"	10/1/18		Multi MENZIES with Lamb Commonant indicated to fill out hills & cits for Mr McCrea file not made. Mr GAMES M.C. arrived. Interviewed. "A" Arriel marked to Season to be to M.L.S.	

WAR DIARY
or
INTELLIGENCE SUMMARY.

Army Form C. 2118.

Place	Date	Hour	Summary of Events and Information	Remarks and references to Appendices
CROIX-DU-BAC	12/1/18		Units No 3 Pe. R.R. Annual sports and standings 1 mule cracked shaft in stables. Officers received ambition. One case attempt 1 friend, 3 kicks. Intake 45 Recruits which arrived for this Brigade. All not healthy and about to be a party sent to Brent including the remainder of Recruits to make up the 70 promised. Received memo from RMS XV Corps re 1st Battalion Division memo to the effect that animals of the Bttn not suitable Mince are more incoming standings in the Douro area. Bus Standings have been examined by the Mrs. Officer since the last memo. Works by the Installation Officers shire to employing those matters 1 option "D" and ashes them to assist and enlist in standings. Q.M.I. on field standings that are about to be executed by not moving order. In use units this will should be inspected 1 General RMS some return 12th Colonel, who are about to RMS 12th Colonel, who are about to memo and sent to RMS standings forward enemy

WAR DIARY or INTELLIGENCE SUMMARY

Army Form C. 2118.

(Erase heading not required.)

Place	Date	Hour	Summary of Events and Information	Remarks and references to Appendices
CROIX-DU-BAC	13/1/18		Examined Grey Horse sent in by 38th M.M.P. suffering from Chillblains. This was a neglected case. Gave instructions for animal to be sent to M.C.S. for marking. Injected horse from P.P.P.B. sent to M.C.S. for marking. Injected horse from 38th M.M.G. and much obliged to be destroyed — from Park No. 2, and instructions for his animal to be returned to O.P.G. Lee and isolated. Visited 70% R.P.G.	
"	14/1/18		Visited 38th O.M.B. Horse lines. Visits to M.C.S. and inspects sick horses. Wind bad to rheumatism.	
"	15/1/18		Returned from Croix-du-Bac to MERVILLE.	
MERVILLE	16/1/18		Visited H.Q. M.V. Vet Sec at Merville and dis. Paid to a D.A.D. ground. I saw at Merges Trial in Stables Mules at Merville, released to M. FEARE, FRANCOIS, Rue d' Aire No. 11. Posted notes to A.P.M. to arrest animal summarily isolated.	
"	17/1/18		Visited H.Q. M.V. Vet Sec.	
"	18/1/18		Inspected Veterinary Units. Visited 38th O.M.B. horse lines.	
"	19/1/18		Inspected at A.V.L.S. XV Corps Office. Visits to M.C.S.	

WAR DIARY
or
INTELLIGENCE SUMMARY.
(Erase heading not required.)

Army Form C. 2118.

Place	Date	Hour	Summary of Events and Information	Remarks and references to Appendices
MERVILLE	20/1/18		Visits HQrs Mil Vet Sec, Mess Routine.	
	21/1/18		Visits No. 3 Section, 33th D.A.C. Animals and feed condition no first class. Visits & inspected No.1 Section, 35th D.A.C. fairly good. Hardings good. Visits & inspected hot Chlorhexol. Sterilizer of animals excellent. 1 cow to be evacuated. Sanitation excellent.	
			No.8 Section 97th D.A.C. v R.G. Animals fully rest covered. Hardings fairly good.	
	23/1/18		8 Heavy Anti. Corps. M.B. & Signal Co. Horse lines. Visits HQ Mil Vet Sec. & Signal Co. Horse lines.	
	23/1/18		D.A.C. & Signal Co. Horse lines. Mess Routine.	
	24/1/18		Conference Veterinary Officers. Visits HQ Mil Vet Sec.	
	25/1/18		Visits 131 Field Ambulance. Completed report of work & audit of vet.	
	26/1/18		Attend specially kind attention to this matter & to keep in charge horse lines. Visits HQ Mil Vet Sec.	
			Visits & inspected animals of 131 Bde. R.F.A. as also Mess of 127 Bde.	
	27/1/18		R.F.A. Also Bl. v C/ Btt. who had sent down to the training area. Sanitation of animals very good. Sanitation at G. of M. 127 Bde.	

Army Form C. 2118.

WAR DIARY
or
INTELLIGENCE SUMMARY.
(Erase heading not required.)

Instructions regarding War Diaries and Intelligence Summaries are contained in F. S. Regs., Part II. and the Staff Manual respectively. Title pages will be prepared in manuscript.

Place	Date	Hour	Summary of Events and Information	Remarks and references to Appendices
MERVILLE	27/1/18		am in my tent (cardelier) – The floors are broken & are perishing & am in a danger to the animals. The drains are too deep & too wide. Recommended to the Adjutant R.E. that the floors should be taken up and shall have drawn on all standings where this condition exists.	
"	28/1/18		Visited 38th Brit. Signal Co. Good medicines for our horses with Bucket. To Nr. Nortinghen. D.A.R. horse lines. An sick now evacuation. saw two medical (Spacey) mules 49th Mt. Vet. See. and to examined sick animals. Went to evacuation but horsed ambulance to FONTAINE to fetch charges suffering from Mange – belonging to Col. Pushen R.A.	
"	29/1/18		Visited HQ. Mt. Vet. Sec. Office Routine.	
"	30/1/18		Attended inspection of horses by the Capt. for that Mar Veterinary commys by D.A.D. Saw army at 49th Mt. Vet. Sec. 4 horses cast & 2 mules for Vet. & 1 mt. incurable on account of age for killing. Visited 38th R.A.B. horse line. Examined Mules Suffering charged suffering from contusion in chest. Mt. very ill.	

WAR DIARY
or
INTELLIGENCE SUMMARY.

Army Form C. 2118.

Place	Date	Hour	Summary of Events and Information	Remarks and references to Appendices
MERVILLE	30/1/18		Visited 38th Divl. Signal Co. Horse lines. Examined and horses and Cysl.	
			oronational—	
	31/1/18		Visited 113 Bn. R.W.F. Animals in excellent condition. Headings very	
			good. Animals well groomed. No sick cases.	

[signature]

MAJOR,
D.A.D.V.S. 38th (WELSH) DIVISION.

CONFIDENTIAL.

WAR DIARY.

OF

D.A.D.V.S. 38th. (Welsh) DIVISION.

FROM

1st. FEBRUARY 1918.

TO

28th. FEBRUARY 1918.

(VOLUME XXVII.)

[signature]
Major. A.V.C.

1st. March 1918.   D.A.D.V.S., 38th. (Welsh) DIVISION.

Army Form C. 2118.

WAR DIARY
or
INTELLIGENCE SUMMARY.
(Erase heading not required.)

Instructions regarding War Diaries and Intelligence Summaries are contained in F. S. Regs., Part II. and the Staff Manual respectively. Title pages will be prepared in manuscript.

Place	Date	Hour	Summary of Events and Information	Remarks and references to Appendices
MERVILLE	1/5/18		Assistant Veterinary Officer.	
"	2/5/18		Office routine. Visits HQ's MVS	
"	3/5/18		Visits DMS + Brit. Signal Co. Horse lines. Blamed our horse with Astigmatism. Arrange for feeding harness after the mod. This animal is with 130 field Amb.	
"	4/5/18		Visits DMS, Horse lines & Signal Co.	
"	5/5/18		Visits HQ's MVS - Inspected No. 3 Sec 38 AAC. Animals in good condition. Entailed remounts which arrived for Mrs Britannia. 20 horses fairly good, but 16 rather heel heel affection. Visits Brit Signal Co. Horse lines & horse vets	
"	6/5/18		Mangles. DMS. 1 cow Chronic Fairly total remours case suffering	
"	7/5/18		Visits HQ Met Sec and shopld + shopld sick animals sent to Mont lines.	
"	8/5/18		Visits DMS and Signal Co. Horse lines.	
"	9/5/18		Assistant Veterinary Officer Visits STEENWERCK - Stevens SAMS 59th Division in wait of not relieved. Animals etc for Mobile Veterinary Section and 2/3 Divn.	
"	10/5/18		Visits Brit Signal Co. 1 prob case MD. Mange case & fight cases doing well.	

Army Form C. 2118.

WAR DIARY
or
INTELLIGENCE SUMMARY.
(Erase heading not required.)

Instructions regarding War Diaries and Intelligence Summaries are contained in F. S. Regs., Part II. and the Staff Manual respectively. Title pages will be prepared in manuscript.

Place	Date	Hour	Summary of Events and Information	Remarks and references to Appendices
MERVILLE	11/3/18		3 cases Harness galls. An inquiry was informed and made has been sent in charge of these horses. Visited O.R.S. + F.A. H.Q. horse lines. 1 case of	
	12/3/18		Opthalmia removed from 38th M.V.C.	
			Visited O.R.S. + Signal Co. horse lines.	
	13/3/18		Visited + inspected 149th M.V. Vet. Sec.	
	15/3/18		Misc. Routine	
	14/3/18		F.A. H.Q. Signal Co. + O.R.S. horse lines.	
	15/3/18		On leave of absence to England from 15/3/18 to 1/3/18.	

signature
MAJOR.
A.D.V.S. 38th (WELSH) DIVISION.

CONFIDENTIAL.

WAR DIARY

OF

D. A. D. V. S., 38th. (Welsh) DIVISION.

FROM

1st. MARCH 1918.

TO

31st. MARCH 1918.

(V O L U M E XXVIII)

[signature]
Major. A.V.C.

3rd. April 1918.   D.A.D.V.S., 38th. (Welsh) DIVISION.

WAR DIARY
or
INTELLIGENCE SUMMARY
(Erase heading not required.)

Army Form C. 2118.

Place	Date	Hour	Summary of Events and Information	Remarks and references to Appendices
STEENWERCK	1/3/18		Returned to duty from leave. Mjr. Fordine.	
"	2/3/18		Capt. A. Young A.V.C. arrived & reported for duty and assumed command of Hq. 2nd M.V. Sec. from Capt. P. Howard. A.V.C. attached to XV Corps M.V.S. in accordance with A.V.S. instructions date 24/2/18. Units Hq. 2nd MVS – animals & buildings & men's quarters. I saw Mongolia patient case Ophthalmia. Leave Manor Farm No.1 Sec 39th D.A.C. Units No.3 Co. A.S.C. Col Tmd. and animals all animals that were on lines. Looking very fat, large quantity of manure remaining. All by Shettree Entered condition. Units D.A.C. MDU lines animals are in excellent condition.	
"	3/3/18		Units 139th Field Ambulance horse lines Animals in very good condition, stander good – horses well cared. Units R.A.M.C. 1 animals exhibiting skin Stanturgis as 139 Field Amb Stables very good. Units Hq. 2 Mdl. Bde. Div. Ofr. out being shewn round units. Hung taken out from Col. N.P. HOWARD. 3 horses came in during my inspection from 64th Bde. A.F.A. BJ & R.A.C. 1 case Ophthalmia and 1 case doubtful mange 1 horse mta Gunter and debility at the Station from 6H A.A.C. 1 gent	

WAR DIARY or INTELLIGENCE SUMMARY

Army Form C. 2118.

Place	Date	Hour	Summary of Events and Information	Remarks and references to Appendices
STEENWERCK	3/3/18		Instructions for the animal to be destroyed + sent to M.V.S. 1 mule from R.A.C. Cpl. Bec. N.Y.D. - suffering from drought trouble. Full instructions for the animal to be sent to the A.V.S.D. also Mule 330 Co. A.S.C. Animals in excellent condition. 6 Remounts arrived today with no any from Mule as MDS. 1 sore neck, 1 bobling behind - my best selection Quantity of manure left by Artillery Officers not being carried away to suit costs Mule 331 Co. A.S.C. findings in an outpost but appears to very low. a good Mule management animals in good condition. 1 care PUN. sent Instructions for N.O. 16 to be sent for by command. Mule 333 Co. A.S.C. Accumulation of manure. Animals in very good condition, no lift care. Interment in field manure left by Artillery Officers being removed. Management	
"	4/3/18		Mules S.H.Q. and command horse lines 7.W.M. Mules M.I. Sec 38th AVC. and infected animals Mules, good animals in excellent condition, with groomed and infected animals. Mules, good animals fed watered. Mules Res. Sec. IV AVC. Mules No hay tears, animals fed watered. Animals in excellent condition, to be good. Watering requires school.	

WAR DIARY or INTELLIGENCE SUMMARY

Army Form C. 2118.

(Erase heading not required.)

Instructions regarding War Diaries and Intelligence Summaries are contained in F. S. Regs., Part II. and the Staff Manual respectively. Title pages will be prepared in manuscript.

Place	Date	Hour	Summary of Events and Information	Remarks and references to Appendices
STEENWERCK	4/3/18		2 cases Ophthalmia arrived 6/3/18 sent to M.V. Hos. for treatment.	
"	5/3/18		Visited 408 Bde R.F.A. for inspection. Whole unit animals need to [inoculation?] only. And 11 cases for ambulance large. Visited B/152 Bde R.F.A. holdings good - Altcars good - animals in excellent condition. Management in this battery has shown great improvement.	
"	6/3/18		Visited 130th Field Ambulance. Holdings good - new managed and condition of animals excellent. This is an excellent & new managed unit. Visited A/152 Bde R.F.A. Holdings good, Picketing requires repairs, condition of animals good. No [hay?]. Lines muddy to chain material. D/152 Bde R.F.A. holdings good Picketing requires chains, condition of animals medium. Winter 10th Bn. L.N.L.R. Animals in this unit excellent. Holdings excellent, condition of animals excellent. Picketing and standings good.	
"	7/3/18		Visited b/152 Bde R.F.A. Animals in excellent condition, holdings good. 10% Animals seemed rather thin. Ration sheet correct. Chilling stand [clearing?] stand. A [general?] Cold, air line of cart. 1 animal to be branded all seen seemed inclined - Convalescent. Holdings - Ranges 3 [cent?] [green?] & [unmanageable?]	

D. D. & L., London, E.C.
(A5833) Wt. W67/M1671 350,000 4/17 Sch. 52a. Forms C/2118/14

WAR DIARY or INTELLIGENCE SUMMARY

Army Form C. 2118.

Place	Date	Hour	Summary of Events and Information	Remarks and references to Appendices
STEENWERCK	8/3/18		Visits 49th MT Coy. Inspected animals sent to slaughter. Labelled N.O.S. Visits 1st N. Staffordshire Bn. (15th Div. RHF) Stabling good, animals in good condition. Forage barn very clean. Clothing is done by Lewis Gun staffing machines. Visits 19th Bn. Princess Victoria's. Stabling fairly old – and of school – no field forage barn – mens heatied, everything in excellent standard. Most in fair yard. Instructions to heat it to put that a forage barn is erected. Visits 112th Bn. North Staffs. Stabling good, all animals now being wrote for this purpose, excellent Lewis, all animals in excellent condition.	
"	9/3/18		Visits 14th Bn. RHF. Stabling and condition of animals very good, grooming passing good. Hand clothed & mixed milk fair. Forage barn stocked with hay sacks. Fire is in order. Visits 176th M.Gun Co. Horses fair, condition of animals good. 1 of 7 animals feet requires taking down. Visits No.3 Sec. 98th Rnd attention to standard officer to be the matter. OAR. Stables good, condition of animals good, not all so good as other battery. Visits 61st Bn. RFA. Stabling good, condition particularly noticable.	

Army Form C. 2118.

WAR DIARY
or
INTELLIGENCE SUMMARY.
(Erase heading not required.)

Instructions regarding War Diaries and Intelligence Summaries are contained in F. S. Regs., Part II. and the Staff Manual respectively. Title pages will be prepared in manuscript.

Place	Date	Hour	Summary of Events and Information	Remarks and references to Appendices
STEENWERCK	9/3/18		of animals excellent. arrival ground & arrival stat. Visits Bly. Bde. RFA Battery grd. condition of animals very good. Shoeing requires more attention. Feet attention to good too long. Visits A/O. Bde. RFA. Condition of animals very good. Shoeing requires a little more attention. Same want of uniformity in Med. Vet. Lettering. Stantings grd. Picketed on hard standing to 47th Battery. D/O Bde. A.F.A. Animal suffering from Mange. Picketed on hard from 150 feet, which has been kept from M.F.A.E.S. of NIEPPE.	
			ap. M.I.S. hospital Abs.	
"	10/3/18		Visits HQ. M.V. Vet. Sec.	
"	11/3/18		Visits HQ. MV Vet Sec. Visits DAQ. I saw been educate on	
"	12/3/18		Visits D.A.G. Horse lines. Visit HQ 2nd MV Vet Sec. Informed of MVS that in on desirability of a 2nd Divisional arrangements will have to be made to move horse lines & and other forward to post for another site suitable for a Mob Vet Sec. Records will form ANDS XV Corps & B.A.N.S. 13th Division	
"	13/3/18		re arrangements to be made of the malingerers and convalescent camps. Visit 13 Bn. Mobile Lambard Lines Animals looking stout on different states	

WAR DIARY
or
INTELLIGENCE SUMMARY.
(Erase heading not required.)

Army Form C. 2118.

Instructions regarding War Diaries and Intelligence Summaries are contained in F.S. Regs., Part II. and the Staff Manual respectively. Title pages will be prepared in manuscript.

Place	Date	Hour	Summary of Events and Information	Remarks and references to Appendices
STEENWERCK	13/3/18		Condition of animals very good, with excellent and shoe. Stables clean, no sick cases. 3 mules had had too long and attention to hind right to be have this seen to at once. Visit 15 Bn. Welsh Reg. Inspect lines. Condition of animals and shoeings good, no sick. Bn. 38th N. Ind. Condition of animals excellent. Shoeing very good. Visit 16 Bn RWF. Bn. condition of animals very good. Shoeing in order. Visit 10 Bn. Stables good. Animals in good condition. Shoeing much and ... cold. Visit Regt. Hastings hair condition of animals very good. Condition of animals good.	
"	14/3/18		Visit HQrs ... R.E. Hastings good, condition of animals first to execution inspected girth, behind. A.B.C. Horse lines. Veterinary officer Pocklin.	
"	15/3/18		Veterinary Meins.	
"	16/3/18		Visit HQrs M. Vet Sec. D/153 Bde RFA. OC was out inspecting units. Visit D/153 Bde RFA. Hastings good, condition of animals good recall 3 - 3 horses + 1 mule. Making arrangements not good, attention on main not - animals picketed by rope. Halter without drinking bucket. Suggested to soft animals at the placard just placing. And troughs to be created. The event of the	

WAR DIARY
or
INTELLIGENCE SUMMARY.

(Erase heading not required.)

Army Form C. 2118.

Place	Date	Hour	Summary of Events and Information	Remarks and references to Appendices
STEENWERCK	16/3/18		Farm dept. to the fields to use this place although the mud is not mud by snow.	
"	17/3/18		5 most cases of Chilblains reported.	
"	18/3/18		Visits HQ M.V. Pol. Sec. Visits HQ M.V.S. Ambulance command at H.Q. to Colonel Fraser which took Lieut Knox to Kits. Visits of Entrenching Battn. Y and Laws, whereby and to Kits.	
			Received by Kitch Y and that R.O.R. was mobilising on Movements on account of Italia.	
			Am and around town that R.O.R. was mobilising on account of Italia. Visits 134 to R.E. who has to make Mail Stations. Visits 10 Res Hosp Stanford since and nothing. 1 mule - Stanford horses. Condition excellent and state management visits 131 Inf Fd Ambulance who also had to make Mail Stations on account of Italia.	
			Shelling Animals out in the sun at present and slowing out - and slowing are being erected for shelter of animals. Visits 131 Bde M.G. in excellent condition.	
"	19/3/18		Visits D.M.S. Med hors. Visits Hq M.V.S. & ambulance. Sick animals went to veterinary.	
"	20/3/18		Recommenced by A.D.V.S. 2nd Army, 7 A.Q.M.G., ambulance trained animals etc.	

WAR DIARY or INTELLIGENCE SUMMARY

Army Form C. 2118.

Place	Date	Hour	Summary of Events and Information	Remarks and references to Appendices
STEENWERCK	20/3/18		15th Am. P.M.F. and 1st Battalion Res, 11th Bn, I.R.B transport animals + 10th Motor transport animals. A.D.R. collected himself my kind & the condition and quality of the animals. He said these were the best animals of all the units of the First Army. Visit with the 119 Field Ambulances - Douzon inspected Res. in kind Army Med. for our two Sections. The animals to are alive in artificial exercise having to be removed from STEENWERCK on account of mobile stalling. Visited Hq MTS	
"	21/3/18		Visited D.M.S. a M.M.P. Area lines. 119 Field Ambulance. H9 M.T.S. L.H.J. Inspecting the standing from lines. A.M.T. F. Ashton AMS attached in lines. Set 10 days	
"	22/3/18		Conference H.Q. First Army H.Q. at Mixed Infirmary at LUMIERS, by the ADS. 9.16.	
"	23/3/18		Visited 5th Am D.M.F. Standings fairly good - stabling new case - general Mares changes excellent - fixed of lining transport conditions of animals Mares clean and in chains. Stalls clean and hay nets hoisted. Animals feet in condition. Stand in at stalls. Hay rack not reset. Horse areas good at hay lines at clothes.	

WAR DIARY or INTELLIGENCE SUMMARY

Army Form C. 2118.

Place	Date	Hour	Summary of Events and Information	Remarks and references to Appendices
STEENWERCK.	23/3/16		Anthrax found. Manure moved to a pit and by arrangements not satisfactory. No Morgols. Moll got Malime animals fired upon which from course smells. On enquiring into the feeding arrangements I found that the animals were being fed 3 times daily - quantity of feeding seems uncertain. Being fed to troops in many animals. Action taken - Recommended field to be place. 4 times daily. Now a measure of Manure cabecido. Recommended horses to be cleaned of new bed making Numbers and more Subsurface be given by the Forest, and with to mount up out but only at times as such as there is arrival. Wants B. Bn. R.W.F. Mountings taken down. Nail condition of animals good. Having fairly good. Full too long. Recommended feeding at least twice daily, watering arrangements & Morgols taken d.	
"	24/3/16		Visit Hq 2 M.M. M.G. hm. B.M.Q. horse lines.	
"	25/3/16		Visit reg.l M.T. Hot Fee and inspected. All animals shot to Inoculation Visit 130. Field Ambulance. Condition of animals very good. Mountings good. Across new gut. 1 horse with P.U.M. + 1 Horse with fire. ordered to the reph.M.	

Army Form C. 2118.

WAR DIARY
or
INTELLIGENCE SUMMARY.
(Erase heading not required.)

Instructions regarding War Diaries and Intelligence Summaries are contained in F. S. Regs., Part II. and the Staff Manual respectively. Title pages will be prepared in manuscript.

Place	Date	Hour	Summary of Events and Information	Remarks and references to Appendices
STEENWERCK	30/3/18		Visited A/Coy. 38th M. Gun Corps. Horses, general condition of animals good. Many animals had much too long. Give attention to standard. Whips to be used off. The condition + amount of a limited condition which could be gone into but to not out told him off. Giving forage these instructions for the feet to be taken care of need on nailing forage out. Found that 200 horses had been shown during the past week. allright feeling is low and unhappiness is all during carried out. Former owner of standard officer had been taken away from standard time to be away and unhappiness given. United Obs. 28th M.Gun Corps. Returned to easy and confusions good. condition good. I have feet much too Visited March Horses good — I feel rather not in condition. Insp. strong of the three horses had. An attending forage now small man in charge including feeds most attached to this small horses much with. mens meat cake hard to cut on thin much — subbean subbar most to have much clothes recommended with tithe les milk + hard to Visited the March and horses more meeting might of Mens Coy to	

Army Form C. 2118.

WAR DIARY
or
INTELLIGENCE SUMMARY.
(Erase heading not required.)

Instructions regarding War Diaries and Intelligence Summaries are contained in F. S. Regs., Part II. and the Staff Manual respectively. Title pages will be prepared in manuscript.

Place	Date	Hour	Summary of Events and Information	Remarks and references to Appendices
STEENWERCK	26/3/18		Lorries Cars & Mats moved early. Also 38th Div M Fred C/B Transport Officers arrived to carry out Bus Accommodation also N.C.O. & C/Co.	
			Water 19th Divnl Amn. Parties any fuel - found my Watering arrangements has been constantly very satisfactory. Any Mules are now in an unfit state no forage obtainable to M.T. Supply Coll on 12 by Lorry.	
			March on the mornings M M Workshops Also instructions to transport	
			Went to attack Mr J of our 2 horses unfit retired to	
			Mobile Section of animals southern	
	27/3/18		HQ AVC Sect per HQ D.A.C.	
"	28/3/18		HQ D.A.C. M.M.P. & F.A. HQ horse lines.	
"	29/3/18		Enlisted Veterinary Officers the horse lines	
"	30/3/18		HQ HQ M.T.S. 38 Div Sencl. Co 1 emb ambulance, good instructions	
			Sick animal to be evacuated	
"	31/3/18		Advance M.T.C. from STEENWERCK to MERVILLE.	

J.R.A.V.S. 38th WELSH DIVISION.
MAJOR.

CONFIDENTIAL.

WAR DIARY.

OF

D.A.D.V.S., 38th. (Welsh) DIVISION.

FROM

1st. APRIL 1918.

TO

30th. APRIL 1918.

(Volume XXIX.)

1st. May 1918.

Major. A.V.C.
D.A.D.V.S., 38th. (Welsh) DIVISION.

WAR DIARY
or
INTELLIGENCE SUMMARY.
(Erase heading not required.)

Army Form C. 2118.

Instructions regarding War Diaries and Intelligence Summaries are contained in F. S. Regs., Part II. and the Staff Manual respectively. Title pages will be prepared in manuscript.

Place	Date	Hour	Summary of Events and Information	Remarks and references to Appendices
MERVILLE	1/4/18		Returned men from MERVILLE — to the SOMME Area	
"	2/4/18		Move completed. A.H.Q. and Office at TOUTENCOURT. Units up Mr.Vet.Svc. + D.D.C.	
			New Lines	
TOUTENCOURT	3/4/18		Visits HQ Mr.Vet.Svc. Visits Office of A.V.S. & Units	
"	4/4/18		Visit HQ Mr.Vet.Svc. Third Army, who was out at the time of my call. Met	
			Mr.Svc. men from HQ. New Lines to find longer TOUTENCOURT.	
"	5/4/18		Inference by Officers. Visits Vet. Svc. and indicated that animals forced	
			great condition. Visits up Mr.Vet.Svc. Animals are looking in	
			to observation.	
"	6/4/18		Visits No. 3. Vec 28 VAC. Condition of animals very good. Met Commanding Officer	
			Vet. Sections. Animals in the whites have had no exercise. An card	
			Mortalis, Scabies, Mange to knock Personnel, Stabling facilities not good	
			animals being nature. Horse foot and ankles. Visits 15. Moto Box.	
			Transport Lines. Animals looking very good. Visits HQ. Mr.Vet.Svc.	
"	7/4/18		Visits 131 Field Ambulance and condition. All animals Sont instructions for	
			all M.C.S. to test all Ambulances. The signs of Strumitis Not unwell	

Army Form C. 2118.

WAR DIARY
or
INTELLIGENCE SUMMARY.
(Erase heading not required.)

Instructions regarding War Diaries and Intelligence Summaries are contained in F. S. Regs., Part II. and the Staff Manual respectively. Title pages will be prepared in manuscript.

Place	Date	Hour	Summary of Events and Information	Remarks and references to Appendices
TOUTENCOURT	7/4/18		Had already been attached to F Coys M.T. as an Auxiliary saw horses med from A.S.V.S v Coys for Ascension to V. Foken. Visited Z's + A.D.M.S.	
"	8/4/18		Visits hq. M.T. Vet. Sec. B.M.G. + M.M.P. horse lines and inspected sick animals prior to evacuation	
"	9/4/18		Visits hq. M.T.S. - A.H.Q. horse lines 49 M.T. Vet. Sec.	
"	10/4/18		Visits but signal to A.D.M.S. V Corps who branch on the animal side.	
"	11/4/18		Received my form A.D.V.S. V Corps who branch on the animal side. Retired to 131 F.A. Ambulance was not at Hermies care report	
"	12/4/18		Returned over from TOUTENCOURT to CONTAY. Reference with Veterinary Officers in evacuating units eg M.T. Vet Sec. and inspected all sick animals prior to evacuation	
CONTAY	13/4/18		Visits 26 Bn. Machine Gun Corps. Animals of this Bn. are trained in one pack and also trained bunches of pony teams. Bn. Transport officer was not present during my inspection. I informed lees' transport officer to inspect sick animals. Also Animals in fairly good condition. led Y Mules are missing tails - action taken - Drew attention to transport officer	

WAR DIARY
or
INTELLIGENCE SUMMARY.

(Erase heading not required.)

Army Form C. 2118.

Place	Date	Hour	Summary of Events and Information	Remarks and references to Appendices
CONTAY	13/4/16		The 1st General Survey and Arrival out fault. B/Co. Condition of animals good, with condition of one mule, which was suffering of stament was given. Not the return was given by our A.V.C field. Making inquiries into this C/Co. Animals in good condition, shoeing medium, B/Co. Condition of animals very good, shoeing good. 6st Cavalry of the Munster Bde. Muster 15 Bn Welch Transport lines, Saddlery good, shoeing good. 14 Bde. Welch. Condition of animals excellent. Material issued to three of B. Welch Muster 13 Bn Welch condition good, one sting horse came into the lines during the night. Sick installations tot animals 16 Bd sent to Mob. Vet. Sec.	
"	15/4/16		Muster 13 Bn. R.W.F. Had all animals turned out in faith good, will groomed. Shoeing fairly good. Had new shoes before me + turned out fault, shoeing Animals in correct standings. Muster 14 Bn R.W.F This unit is not so good as 14 Bn. Animals turned out faults, showing indifferent condition of animals good, turned out faults in shoeing. 16 Bn R.W.F. Animals in good condition, but not so good as on previous inspections, shoeing in good condition.	

WAR DIARY or INTELLIGENCE SUMMARY

Army Form C. 2118.

Place	Date	Hour	Summary of Events and Information	Remarks and references to Appendices
CONTAY	15/4/18		Many instances very bad forage on the ground, as attention given to men, haps, & fitted on daily - made taken place. Animals all now groomed at time of inspection (11.15 a.m.) had to see any tarried officer in any of these Bns. All on lib having been on duty until H.Q. a.m. action taken - present tarrier diligent of attention to all faults & now intimated a few minor instances again at an early date. Visits No.3 hs. CAC Nos 1 & men in excellent condition well groomed. Plantings in the shirt. Animals in excellent condition well groomed, not too divided.	
"	16/4/18		Visit 19th Divins Rv. condition of animals and shoeing good. Animals plantings in the shirt. I make sufferings from Enteric [?] though high. Visit HQ. Mt. Tel. Sec built "B" shed in pattern arrangements in CONTAY. AD & QMG is going to arrange the erection of men troughs and arranged for men that but watering animals.	
"	17/4/18		Visit H.Q. Mt. Vet. Sec and inspected sick animals sent to evacuation. Visit Vet. Signal Co. behind the animals, evacuation gone out over Visit Vets gone to Mt. Vet. Sec for evacuation. Visit 3rd Bn RNF.	

WAR DIARY
or
INTELLIGENCE SUMMARY.
(Erase heading not required.)

Army Form C. 2118.

Place	Date	Hour	Summary of Events and Information	Remarks and references to Appendices
CONTAY	17/4/18		Horsings in the open. All animals except H. are in good condition. Have of animals are in hard condition and growing special treatment, showing fait. Visit 10th Bn L.N.B. Lines. Condition of animals excellent. Shoeing good. — Horsings in the open, will correct, & will refer all. Visit 17th Bn RWF. Horsings also in the open. Condition of animals very good. Condemned one bag of oats - gave certificate. Visit HQ 113 Bde R.E. Horsings in the open. Condition of animals excellent.	
"	18/4/18		Visit Advanced Post 31 M.M.P. & attended to injured horse. Gave instructions for the animal to be sent to D.V.H. for treatment. Visit D.H.Q. took lunch.	
"	19/4/18		Conferred Veterinary Officers. Visit Amb. Vet. Sec. Co. Lines Remontes. Visit 151 Co. R.E. Horsings in the open. Animals condition on the whole good. 5 horses seriously hard in condition which I ordered to Mob Vet. Sec. for feeding up. No clothing being done in the unit. Issued order — no clothing machine. Visit 113 Co. R.E. Horsings in	

WAR DIARY or INTELLIGENCE SUMMARY

Army Form C. 2118.

Place	Date	Hour	Summary of Events and Information	Remarks and references to Appendices
CONTAY	20/4/18		The chief visit 151. G.F.C. Condition of animals good – chaffing plant built. Visit 124. G.F.C. Pickets in the open, in some field in shed. Pickets line arranged for those two Cos. to have chaffing machine to 151. G.F.C. Visit required. Visit 129th Field Ambulance. Condition of animals good. Pickets in the open. 1 new horse exhaustion case. Visit 149th Mot. M.T. Sec – examined sick animals now opened. Visit 140th Mot. M.T. Sec – examined sick animals now opened. Strong arrival playing out front line arm. Lorry horse sent in by A.P.M. arrived front line arm. Lorry horse sent in by A.P.M. arrived front line arm. Spent sometime [?] effects with Manor, and 10 sick horses arrived.	Visit
"	21/4/18		The animal to the Interim. Visit 6th Brit. Field Co. 1 new few cases Visit 130. Auth Ambulance in the open. Animals in excellent condition. 1 new Bethlehem. Visit. Visit Alc. 27th Machine Gun Bn. Section of animals at the time of my inspection good. Present 15 in a very bad way all feet allowed to grow into too long. arranged about to arrive in two months time. Had all being chaffed.	
"	22/4/18		Visit 175 and Maxim case Bttn finished units and rugged M.T. Reg.	

WAR DIARY or INTELLIGENCE SUMMARY

Army Form C. 2118.

Place	Date	Hour	Summary of Events and Information	Remarks and references to Appendices
CONTAY	23/4/18		Handed out the rest of Mrs machine. Making arrangements hastily slaughter the weak & sick. Visits O/Co B. M[ounted] Vet. Hosp. Condition of animals good. Horses sufficient & animals fit enough too long. Too much H[?] animals to the forge and priests out to shoeing smith's Lame's and condition to be shod. Horses shown & would without again in a few days. Lime to many plate to have a shoeing smith in each sub. Visits Mass plate to have a shoeing smith in each sub. 78 M[ounted] Vet. Hosp. Condition of animals very good. Shoeing smiths held hand. No other NS. Shed being shifted. No animals of this to do in itinerary location. None of the standard officers in the aforesaid as unit present during my inspection — no probit arrangements on made for feeding cake. Visits O/Co. 35? M[ounted] Vet. Hosp. Jo14 animals in the lo. and in fact condition, he rest fairly good. Horses naturally good. 1 mule had been drowned. Explained the handy to standard officers. He did not understand explained of "drowned". Must not lump shipped rate not lung Arthritic Mule. Here is no returns for the horses recipe of oats on the 22nd. I. Mules including Mrs Mules. New standard officer arrived	

WAR DIARY
or
INTELLIGENCE SUMMARY.

(Erase heading not required.)

Place	Date	Hour	Summary of Events and Information	Remarks and references to Appendices
CONTAY	22/4/18		A collarred to hand the horses, which I had found in all the Cos. he admits that the shoeing was all good. Reference to shifting steel, he states he could not give instructions that the shifting matters was to be altered by all COs forwarded to Section germ. sheets from Limber cases to assist the transport to each coy. Explained to him that instead of having limber cases, 1 mule and cart on an overhead trying, the mule got into lather cases, exerted around. Our Intelligence by the animal to inaccessible.	
"	23/4/18		Visit DHQ & Brit. [igard] Co. Horse lines.	
"	24/4/18		Visit HQ 2 Mb/4 Sec. and inspected sick animals that to evacuation. Visit NHQ Horse lines. Two [Armen] Asses come out to our lines with harness, found by 1/4th Bn. RWF - sent to HQ MVS.	
			Metived	
	25/4/18		Visit 13th Bn. Welsh. Inspection of animals good. Like lines thirsty. Visit HQ MVS. Visit HQ 1 CAV? 342. Reasons attributed from H.Q. 1 CAVS 342.	
			Review [ANC] No. 1280x Lieut ELLIS & AVC now killed in action on the	

WAR DIARY or INTELLIGENCE SUMMARY

Army Form C. 2118.

Place	Date	Hour	Summary of Events and Information	Remarks and references to Appendices
CONTAY	25/4/18		msgs 30/1/11 & Msgs 1918. Arrived A.V.C. and Records	
"	26/4/18		Returned H.Q. Visited H.Q. M.V. V. Bde.	
"	27/4/18		Visited H.Q. M.V. Bde. Examined German Horse A.M.V. Marlow Pit. Visited Sick Horse Co. 1 sent Horse gas infected sm case slit remains. M nerved	
			H.V.V. F.V. 63rd (Naval) Division assumed C.R.A. charges. Slight Colic. Received 66 horses.	
"	28/4/18		Visited 63rd Div Art H.Q. Horse lines C.R.A. Horse slightly improving.	
"	29/4/18		Visited 63rd Div Arty H.Q. Visited D.N.Q. Visited Gas Signal Co. 1 new Horse gas 1 new O.N. Received ordered to be observed. no current case. 10th Bn Slot B.	
			lines case gas at Beauzincourt. Went to PMS v Cates in accordance with instructions. Visited 17 Bn R.W.F. & Horses. Hospital moved.	
			Visited H.Q. M.B.	
"	30/4/18		Visited D.N.Q. Horse lines. H.Q. 63rd Div Arty H.Q. One Signal Co. Transferred lines. 10th Bn Slot B & H.Q. Horses. Rode there horse 7 gas cases dying	
			very well. Visited H.Q. M.B.	

J. Williams MAJOR,
A.D.V.S. 63rd (WELSH) DIVISION.

C O N F I D E N T I A L.

WAR DIARY.

OF

D. A. D. V. S., 38th. (Welsh) DIVISION.

FROM

1st. M A Y 1918.

TO

31st. M A Y 1918.

(Volume XXX.)

John Macfarlane
Captain. A.V.C.

1st. June 1918.   A/D.A.D.V.S., 38th. (Welsh) DIVISION.

Army Form C. 2118.

WAR DIARY
or
INTELLIGENCE SUMMARY.
(Erase heading not required.)

Instructions regarding War Diaries and Intelligence Summaries are contained in F. S. Regs., Part II. and the Staff Manual respectively. Title pages will be prepared in manuscript.

Place	Date	Hour	Summary of Events and Information	Remarks and references to Appendices
CONTAY	1/5/18		Visited 13th Bn Middx Regt. Hackneys in a week. Inspection of animals [etc.] [illegible] [illegible]. Lines [illegible] by [illegible] [illegible] [illegible] at [illegible] of my inspection. [illegible] AVC [illegible] and [illegible] [illegible] of the others that exists against having animals [illegible] to trees [illegible] [illegible] for [illegible] to be [illegible] away from [illegible] of the lines with [illegible] for [illegible] [illegible] [illegible] [illegible] Wilts Regt MTS. [illegible] [illegible] lines. I saw him to [illegible] [illegible] [illegible] [illegible] [illegible] [illegible] [illegible] [illegible] [illegible] as [illegible].	
"	2/5/18		Visited [illegible] [illegible] [illegible] [illegible] No. 10 [illegible] [illegible] he had [illegible] [illegible] [illegible] with [illegible] [illegible] [illegible] [illegible] [illegible] [illegible] [illegible]. No lame [illegible] by [illegible] [illegible] [illegible] [illegible] at HERBISART. He [illegible] [illegible] [illegible] [illegible] of Mrs [illegible] at HERBISART. He [illegible] my instructions [illegible] [illegible] to the clean [illegible] at HERBISART. the [illegible] was out of the lines. [illegible] [illegible] my [illegible] third HERBISART [illegible] [illegible] [illegible] [illegible] [illegible] [illegible] [illegible] [illegible] [illegible] [illegible] [illegible] [illegible] [illegible] [illegible] [illegible] [illegible] [illegible] [illegible] MT.S. [illegible] [illegible] [illegible] [illegible] [illegible] [illegible] [illegible] farm [illegible]. Wilts up. MTS [illegible] [illegible] [illegible].	
		am	Moved ambulance to [illegible] BSQ. [illegible] to Mobile No. R595. Pte Elliot A MoMillan to AVC [illegible] Remt Co. Artll Aring. [illegible] for transit. 2/5/18.	

WAR DIARY or INTELLIGENCE SUMMARY

Army Form C. 2118.

Place	Date	Hour	Summary of Events and Information	Remarks and references to Appendices
CONTAY	3/5/18		Advance Veterinary Officers. Visits 331 to ASC and inspected 35 animals which arrived for the Divisn. with Cohorts 3 horses with strangles discovered. Have instructions for the Cohort cases to be segregated. Distribution of Remounts: 10 to VARENNES and 10 to O.R.C. M.G. assisted in distribution of Remounts. Attended to horse casualties attached to — 38. M.M.P.	
"	4/5/18		Visits AVO. Battn Lines. Animals in fair condition. Visited ed horse — post-mortem. R.C. Conditions good. Ane cow examinations.	Visits 151. Co.
"	5/5/18		Visits AVO. Horse Lines. Ane cow examinations. Visits 82 M.V.S. 10th Bn. AVB and animals. Visit 10th Bn AVB and completed received and now examinations.	
			Y Lines with Horse Lines — Al animals not quite recovered.	
"	6/5/18		Returned army from CONTAY to TOUTENCOURT	Visits HQ. MVS
TOUTENCOURT	7/5/18		Visits AMG Horse Lines HQ MVS. Visits 131. Field Ambulance. Animals in very good condition. Mules in excellent strength. y 20 + 10 Mul in establishment. And mule and driver of HQ MVS visited HQ. AC Horse lines 1 cow ambulatoire returned to No. 5. V.E.S. for duty	No S.E. 15075 Pte. Pottingend B 19. MVS 7/5/18

Army Form C. 2118.

WAR DIARY or INTELLIGENCE SUMMARY

Place	Date	Hour	Summary of Events and Information	Remarks and references to Appendices
TOUTENCOURT	8/5/18		Visited 331 Co A.S.C. and inspected the animals and lines. The standing are in too much and mud, owing to the recent heavy rains. Condition of animals with exception of two - good. Drew attention to O.C. Coy. Most injured horses feet were too long. Two horses referred to and very hard in condition, and are in command with M.I.S. Most. Drew O.C. Coy's attention to the fact that these are the only two thin horses in the Coy, and such I was called singular that as they are the only horses shod and clothed and which had they were all doing more work than there were. Saw smithereens, these two animals to have off not altogether. These two animals to have off not altogether. Found animals grazing and games, which is about to be used as a sleep trunk. Animals are in excellent condition. Visited 333 Co A.S.C. - animals out in the sheds, horses are in very good condition. D.M.O. But Agreed to hard lines up. M.S. Visited 151 Co R.E. Discovered that they were 4 horses short of strength. I.R. + 130 found. Was from d attached to ARMENTIERES Area, and a statement was made	

WAR DIARY or INTELLIGENCE SUMMARY

Army Form C. 2118.

(Erase heading not required.)

Place	Date	Hour	Summary of Events and Information	Remarks and references to Appendices
TOUTENCOURT	8/5/18		Ly Coy commanded that the road referred to in the market to A.P.M. Ami L.O. horse was steven the other day.	
"	9/5/18		Visited D.A.Q. M.M.P. horse lines. Visited the Infantry Brigades areas with used to selecting Marks from grazing purposes.	
"	10/5/18		Conference A.D.S. Visited D.A.Q. horse lines. Visited Hg MMS and anghede.	
"	11/5/18		Visited D.A.Q. Sick animals sent to evacuation. Visited Coy Signal Co. horse lines. Hg Mil. Pol. Sec.	
"	12/5/18		Visited D.A.Q. Hg MMS. Inspected sick animals sent to evacuation.	
"	13/5/18		Visited Coy Signal Co. & Inspected sirand which had arrived from Base. condition good. Visited 14th Fd. Ambulance. Inspection of animals good. Visited 129. Field Ambulance. Animals in very good condition. Sick case isolated. Visited D.A.Q. + M.M.P. horse lines. Hg MMS. Instructions for two animals to be evacuated left lame. Remark	
"	14/5/18		Attended Conference at A.D.V.S. v. baths. Visited No. 3 Sec. A.Vet. Animals in excellent condition, 1 mule lame & 1 horse affined. To R.+S.B. Staff Dept. referee re Hg MMS. horses out and month's here - re engagement for dinner.	

Army Form C. 2118.

WAR DIARY
or
INTELLIGENCE SUMMARY.
(Erase heading not required.)

Instructions regarding War Diaries and Intelligence Summaries are contained in F. S. Regs., Part II. and the Staff Manual respectively. Title pages will be prepared in manuscript.

Place	Date	Hour	Summary of Events and Information	Remarks and references to Appendices
VAUDENCOURT	14/5/18		Instrns ADMS Issued (see Appx 13) from HQ MLS were to-day duplicated	
"	15/5/18		Visited HERISSART. Rear Bdgh. HAYNE. Came of O.A.D.M.S. Area 35 Divisions to make arrangements at Selens and Lane Boilo in relief D.M.Q. here. Jones. Visits HQ MLS	
"	16/5/18		Visits O.B. hosps lines & 38th M.M.P. & signal Coy RE. Visits HERISSART and assisted in finding quarters of 35th. Divisional Staff. Accompanies by M.A.D.M.G. enquiries arrangements arrived at this. Division.	
"	17/5/18		Conference 1.0.S. Visits D.M.Q. horsp lines HQ MLS D.M.Q. horsp lines HQ MLS. Received information from A.D.M.S. No 1 dec Major Hunnett re his horsp having rabies.	
"	18/5/18		Accompanied by A.D.M.S. visit No. 13 Mob. Bact. Laby. Bacilli's and was Telegram re rabies written. The bacteriologist informed me M.T. and two of three cults. negro status were found in M.T. and two of three cults. negro status were found in M.T. sites were forwarded by him to the Chief Bacteriologist etc.	

WAR DIARY or INTELLIGENCE SUMMARY

Army Form C. 2118.

Place	Date	Hour	Summary of Events and Information	Remarks and references to Appendices
TOUTENCOURT	19/5/18		His excy. A.D.M.S. came at my office today. He informed & reheated the fact concerning the late Military his company C.A.D.M.S. met us and informed me that the D.M.S. Third Army had sent instructions that myself and this who have intimate dealings with the H.Q. were to be evacuated to PARIS for Patent Treatment. A.D.M.S. V. Corps informed me that he would accept my order which he also informed me that Lt Coll S. MacFarlane A.D.C. should be recalled from the artillery and act for me, pending further arrangements which...	
"	30/5/18		Major F.G.GAVIN A.V.C. & Capt A. YOUNG RAC. V.C. M.B. signed the day to PARIS Lt Coll A... England. Arrived over from TOUTENCOURT by HERISSART.	
HERISSART	31/5/18		Capt J. MacFarlane A.C. arrived & assumed duties as A.D.M.S. once Major F.G.Gavin to Bethune	
"	1/5/18		Capt F.M.Cromb A.S. arrived and assumed duties	

Army Form C. 2118.

WAR DIARY
or
INTELLIGENCE SUMMARY.
(Erase heading not required.)

Instructions regarding War Diaries and Intelligence Summaries are contained in F. S. Regs., Part II. and the Staff Manual respectively. Title pages will be prepared in manuscript.

Place	Date	Hour	Summary of Events and Information	Remarks and references to Appendices
HERISSART	22/5/18		as Sunday. Office. Sun morning Hg. Mil. Vet. Sec.	
"	23/5/18		Visited Hq. M.V.S. and inspected sick animals. Went to vaccination lines of Norway Coy R.E. & 316 road construction Coy R.E. animals in good condition. D.M.Q. horse lines.	
"	24/5/18		Ordinary Veterinary Affairs. Office Routine.	
"	25/5/18		Visited D.M.Q. horse lines. Sidewood Signal Coy, horse lines. Motor Transit mulsiers horses. 1 Rifled tank, 1 mounted by enemy Shell fire.	
"	26/5/18		Visited VAL DE MAISON. Motor horses not abnormal, as showing smoke of 333 Coy A.S.C. Indicate horses of 333 Coy A.S.C. Visited Hq M.V.S. Inspected arrt. of new hot shoeing fotg?.	
"	27/5/18		Visited VAL DE MAISON. Visited 7 men het shoeing fotgr. Visited 316 Road Construction Coy R.E. Coll. a young A.V.C. returns from Solittal. PARIS	
"	28/5/18		Visited Hq M.V.S. and inspected sick animals about to vaccination. AVC F.M. Scouts A.V.C. returns to Divisions.	

Army Form C. 2118.

WAR DIARY
or
INTELLIGENCE SUMMARY.
(Erase heading not required.)

Place	Date	Hour	Summary of Events and Information	Remarks and references to Appendices
HERISSART	29/5/18		Visited 333 Coy ASC. Shearing Board. Visited HQ MCS. Attended 16	
"	30/5/18		French military Att. examined for Rabies. Visited DMS. Signal Coy RE. HQ MCS. Shearing Board. Inspected. Animals of 115th Inf Bde. at Malie Troughs.	
"	31/5/18		Visited 17 Bn RWF. Inspected 2 horses sick & 5 attended, 17 Army. Conference 105.	

John Macfarlane

Arthur MB
MAJOR
A.D.V.S. 38th (WELSH) DIVISION

CONFIDENTIAL.

WAR DIARY.

OF

D. A. D. V. S., 38th. (Welsh) DIVISION.

FROM

1st.   J U N E   1918.

TO

30th.   J U N E   1918.

(Volume XXXl.)

John Macfarlane
Captain. A.V.C.

1st. July 1918.   A/D.A.D.V.S., 38th. (Welsh) DIVISION.

WAR DIARY
or
INTELLIGENCE SUMMARY.
(Erase heading not required.)

Army Form C. 2118.

Place	Date	Hour	Summary of Events and Information	Remarks and references to Appendices
HEBUTERNE	1/6/15		Visited 333 Coy RSE. HQ. Mot. Mcl. Sec. 316 Field Ambulance Coy R.E. & 1st Vermar Coy R.E. Animals in good condition	
"	2/6/15		Visited 333 Coy R.E. Sick men of Section would not permit Rectal exam of rate injected rabbits. Animal in isolation	
"	3/6/15		Visited 38 Sig Signal Coy R.E. OMR 333 Coy Able. Having heard rumbling of 113 Bde.	
"	4/6/15		Visited to Brem Macomb sicilian horses wounded by enemy shell fire. Visited 288 ADC Aerto Lunis 316 Field Construction Coy. Sent to laboratory Examined four horses and exchanged sick animals sent them to A.D.M.S. for	
"			dog inhaled rabies. Animal autopsed Visited 13 & 14 Bns. R.W.F. animals Visited to Bacteriologist laboratory Visited 13 & 14 Bns. R.W.F. in good condition	
"	5/6/15		Received men from General S. Leonvilliers	
LEONVILLERS	6/6/15		Marshall Luis - Animals in good condition. Visited 15 Rd A.A. R.W.F. Visited 85rd Field Artillery HQ & 121 Brigade R.F.A. Animals are in fair condition and He had conditions. Making arrangements are very difficult	

WAR DIARY
or
INTELLIGENCE SUMMARY.
(Erase heading not required.)

Army Form C. 2118.

Place	Date	Hour	Summary of Events and Information	Remarks and references to Appendices
LEAL-VILLERS	1/10/18		Embraced Veterinary Officers 32nd D.A.C. Audit and inspected No 3 section 32nd D.A.C. Animals are in good condition	
"	3/6/18		Audit D.A.C. - Vet Signal Co. North lines up MM Vet Sec inspected sick animals prior to evacuation DADVS returned from leave	
			Hospital PARIS and ordered Audit Milked AOLS of cobs	
"	9/10/18		Audit B.A.P. - Vet Signal Co Cavs. No sick cases	
"	10/10/18		Accompanied by AOLS of Cavs Greenwald & Cobbs Horsemaster & Hall Mastersland RVC inspected animals of 362 Bn attillery 121 & 133 Bdes, Section of animals excellent A- Cl 133 Bde. require more attention to grooming. It was observed seems to no cold issue by the locks commander, no chains for picketing are in use & no RVS harness chains are impaired not used in section harness presumably by our brigadier and RVS in harness seem	
"	11/10/18		Audit D.M.S. - Signal Coy horse lines Audit up M.M.S.	
"	12/10/18		Audit Vet Signal Co. All animals are looking in good condition. Received visit from Col Williams ADVS. A.A.G. DAG.	
"	13/10/18		Audit 14 Bn INF Condition of animals very good, no feet cases 15 Bn INF.	

WAR DIARY or INTELLIGENCE SUMMARY

Army Form C. 2118.

Place	Date	Hour	Summary of Events and Information	Remarks and references to Appendices
LEAVILLERS	13/6/18		Animals in good condition. Visited O.M., Horse Lines.	
"	14/6/18		Conferred Veterinary Officers. Visited O.M. & Signal Cop. Horse Lines.	
"	15/6/18		Maj. F.C. Yearn A.D.V.S. proceeded on leave to England. 2/Lt F. McFarlane attd. and assumed duties as A.D.V.S. Visited D/131 & Signal Cop.	
"			10 Bn S.W.B. Animals in good condition.	
"	16/6/18		Visited No 3 Section R.A.C. Condition of animals very good. Horses very ?	
			Met M. Lee. and instructed him to concentrate effort on evacuation – sick animals.	
"	17/6/18		Visited D/131 Bde. R.F.A. Horse Lines. Evacuated one horse recent removed	
			Lt. Lussemodel's 3 animals caused by kicks, instructing I think greats are not	
			of nature to extend to be destroyed. Bent carefully into the matter	
			with the Major Line Officer who has only been with the unit for a	
			fortnight and learnt that they were suffering mainly of Muso discomforts.	
			inquiries and kept very strict about the destruction of a unit.	
			Visited H.Q. 131 Bde. R.F.A. & B/131 Bde R.F.A. Visited Bde. Signal Cop. Esarnnels	
			and Horse Alarm Square. All animals in very good condition and	
			Moving in good order. Making 3 times daily, no chaff until ful	

WAR DIARY
or
INTELLIGENCE SUMMARY.

(Erase heading not required.)

Army Form C. 2118.

Place	Date	Hour	Summary of Events and Information	Remarks and references to Appendices
LEALVILLERS	17/6/18		Staff is out at D.M.S. and mixed with bats. Staff is [?] 3 times daily. Visits 331 & 332 Coys A.S.C. Animals in excellent condition and Mule management leaves little to be desired. No timetable enquiries.	
"	18/6/18		Visits 328 Machine Gun Bn. Condition of animals on the whole good, with a few exceptions. Recommend and made to M.O. horse for evacuation. No hand clippers in Bn. and animals cond. clothing machine at present broken. Visits 17th Bn & 3rd Bn R.G.A. Animals on the whole in good condition. No cattle mud hire greasy unkempt. Bid Sig. Coy & D.M.O. Visited 139th Field Ambulance. Condition of animals very good. Recommend to harness i. & O. horse almost blind. Visits 130 Field Ambulance. Visits 151 Coy R.E. horses. Animals are in good condition. Visits 144 Coy R.E. Animals are in satisfactory condition. Visits 133 Coy R.E. Animals are in [?]	
"	19/6/18			
			A horse for evacuation. with one or two exceptions. Recommend 1 horse for evacuation.	

Army Form C. 2118.

WAR DIARY
or
INTELLIGENCE SUMMARY.
(Erase heading not required.)

Instructions regarding War Diaries and Intelligence Summaries are contained in F. S. Regs., Part II. and the Staff Manual respectively. Title pages will be prepared in manuscript.

Place	Date	Hour	Summary of Events and Information	Remarks and references to Appendices
LEALVILLERS	19/4/18		good condition, with H coupling. Recommended Y Noses for evacuation. Hind.	
	20/4/18		Visited 131 Bde RFA. 3rd Bde Sig. Coy. No 3 Sec 38 DAC & DAC.	
			Horse Lines.	
	21/4/18		Inspected 7.OS. BHQ & Signed Coy Horse lines.	
	22/4/18		Visited Nos 1 - 3 Sections 38 DAC. Animals in good condition.	
			Visited HQ 38th RA. Inspected stabling sheds to be established to	
			Remount Depot at Biettes.	
	23/4/18		Visited 131 Bde RFA. No 3 Sec 38 DAC.	
	24/4/18		Visited 149'6 Mt Al Bre and inspected sick animals. Freed to evacuation.	
	25/4/18		Visited HQ 3rd Bde Train & 330 Coy ASC. Animals in good condition.	
			Div Signal Coy DHQ. No 3 Sec DAC.	
	26/4/18		Visited MT Bde. 13 Bn MGC. Animals in good condition. 1st Bn Bedfs.	
			Condition of Animals very good. Visited 134 Coy RE. Animals in	
			good condition. 113 Bde. Animals in all the Battalions are in	
			very good condition.	

WAR DIARY
or
INTELLIGENCE SUMMARY.

(Erase heading not required.)

Army Form C. 2118.

Place	Date	Hour	Summary of Events and Information	Remarks and references to Appendices
LEAUVILLERS	29/6/18		Visits B/151. Bde. R.F.A. and attended to wounded horses	Visits No. 3 Sec.
"	30/6/18		38th A.B.G. DAQ most lame.	
"			Evidence Veterinary Officers. Visits Bde Signal Co. v QMs. Horse limbs
"	30/6/18		Visits 151. Bde. R.F.A. 2 horses injured by Bombs & wounds for	Visits No. 3 Sec. 38 A.B.G.
"			Road and one wounded in rich.	
"			Visits Bde. Signal Coy. Animals in very good condition.	
"	30/6/18		Visits Mixed Routine	DAQ vg Mpd Vet Sec

John McIntyre
for Capt. A.V.C.
for MAJOR.
D.A.D.V.S. 38th (WELSH) DIVISION.

CONFIDENTIAL.

WAR DIARY.

OF

D. A. D. V. S., 38th. (Welsh) DIVISION.

FROM

1st. JULY 1918.

TO

31st. JULY 1918.

(Volume XXXII.)

[signature]
Major. A.V.C.

1st. August 1918.   D.A.D.V.S., 38th. (Welsh) DIVISION.

WAR DIARY
or
INTELLIGENCE SUMMARY.
(Erase heading not required.)

Army Form C. 2118.

Place	Date	Hour	Summary of Events and Information	Remarks and references to Appendices
LEALVILLERS	1/1/18		Visit 131 Bn. R.F.A. Ord. signed to. No.3 Lt. 36. O.R.C. Visit Rifles M. Co.	
"	3/1/18		and attend to a fresh sickam horse with Mange	
"	3/1/18		Visit 131 Bn. R.F.A.	
"			In company with O.D.L. Hood Army inspected horses for casting.	
"			Cast 3 animals C/151 Bn. R.F.A. 1 mule 19th Bn. welch none	
"			horse 133 Inf R.G. + 1 horse 134. Inf R.G. Issued 35 Ord. Pets A.B.	
"			horse lines. All animals are in good condition; report one	
"			horse A.S.C. attached Visit B Col. signed Cert + O.R.B. horse lines	
"	4/1/18		19th Mob. Vet. Sec. Inspected sick animals short to vaccination.	
"			Visit Veterinary and ambulance animals of 131. Field Ambulance	
"			Both harness required substituting. Animals are in good condition.	
"	5/1/18		Acromiowed R.O.M.S. v. Capt.B + Sets Horsemith inspected M.S.	
"			of Bn. Horse lines. Suggested that forage heaps to built of	
"			material's available. Visit 15th Bn. welsh regt. one mile left better,	
"			animals require imbedding. Took one sick mule for betterly,	
"			Shoeing requires more submission. Visit 13 Bn. welsh regt	

Army Form C. 2118.

WAR DIARY
or
INTELLIGENCE SUMMARY.
(Erase heading not required.)

Instructions regarding War Diaries and Intelligence Summaries are contained in F. S. Regs., Part II. and the Staff Manual respectively. Title pages will be prepared in manuscript.

Place	Date	Hour	Summary of Events and Information	Remarks and references to Appendices
LEALVILLERS	4/7/18		2nd MG. MK Inf. Res. Condition of animals excellent.	
"	5/7/18		Conference 1.0.3. Accompanied A.A.M.S & A.D.S. + 1st/1.S. Divisional Horsemaster and inspected 115. Inf. Bn. Mobile Vet. Section At + O.R. + R.S. 38th Res. Machine Gun Bn. Visited 1/k. Bn. Welsh Regt.	
"	6/7/18		Accompanied A.A.Q.M.G. and inspected remounts which had arrived for Div's Division. Fairly good Division	
"	7/7/18		Visited No. 3. Sec. 38 C.A.G. D.M.G + Signal Coy. Horse lines. Also + C/131. Bde. R.F.A. Animals all in good condition. Visited S.S.O. and reserved issue to M.V.S.	
"	8/7/18		Visited 131. Bde. R.F.A. Office Routine Major Jones arrived from leave and assumed duties.	
"	9/7/18		Visited 132. Bde. R.F.A. Office Routine.	
"	10/7/18		Visited D.M.G + Signal Coy Horse lines. Office Routine.	
"	11/7/18		Visited 38th M.M.P. Strength 37 Riders. Condition of animals good. Grooming + shoeing good. Markings - Some in stables, others in the open. Condition of lines good. Manure moved daily to Carrefaye	

Army Form C. 2118.

WAR DIARY
or
INTELLIGENCE SUMMARY.
(Erase heading not required.)

Instructions regarding War Diaries and Intelligence Summaries are contained in F. S. Regs., Part II. and the Staff Manual respectively. Title pages will be prepared in manuscript.

Place	Date	Hour	Summary of Events and Information	Remarks and references to Appendices
LEAVILLERS	11/7/18		Animals. Feeding and watering 3 times daily. Water very good. Baths every 10 days. 1 case injury to Eye. 1 saw saddle gall. 1 horse injury to fetlock. Adv: 10. Field Ambulance. 1 case abscess jaw to sick various. Visits 130. Field Ambulance. Animals in the above Markings good. Sanitation excellent. Means used to carriage Animals. Shoeing good. Feeding & watering 4 times daily. General care of mules same as 33. MM.R. Grooming & condition good. 1 case PUM. Visits 134 Coy RE. Strength 31 mules 53 horses 1 total underweight. Markings in the above sanitation Moderate. Lines shrill & well cleaned. condition of animals with exception of 5. moderately good. 4 horses 1 mule had in addition — scorgate- and receiving special attention. More attention to be paid to grooming. 1 horse wounded by bullet. Shoot cloth and hay nets in use. No hay such. Shoeing & watering 4 times a day — mules lame. Service at 130. Field Ambulance. 1 case PoJs. Jan & 1 slight wounds. Service was to feed. Shoeing good.	

WAR DIARY or INTELLIGENCE SUMMARY

Army Form C. 2118.

Place	Date	Hour	Summary of Events and Information	Remarks and references to Appendices
LEAVILLERS	11/7/18		Recommendations:— More attention to be paid to sanitation of Horse lines. Clean filling into netts on lines.	to keep Horses 133 Coy R.E. Sanitation
			Strength:— 3 mules 67 horses undertrength. S.R. & 20. Hard groomed and to be have to animals moderately good. More attention to be have to grooming. Hard stuffed. Feeding & watering 3 times a day. Recommended it times a day. Shoeing fairly good. Veterinary Equipment complete. No hay issued. 1 cwt. Oats gram and Giv	
			Recommendations:— Hay lines - feeding & watering 4 times daily. More attention to grooming and sanitation.	
			Strength:— Hitch & Longhirst 151 Coy R.E. Strength 18 mules & 54 horses. 3 R. Understrength Sanitation very good. 100% better. Man when & last inspected. Hardings in the shed. One line of hardings required repairs. Feeding & watering 3 times daily. Sanitation fair. Shoeing fairly good. Grooming requires a little more attention. Manes require trimming. Hay issued and Oat No chaff issued. Oat straw is chaffed amply in use.	

WAR DIARY or INTELLIGENCE SUMMARY

Army Form C. 2118.

Place	Date	Hour	Summary of Events and Information	Remarks and references to Appendices
LEALVILLERS	11/7/18		at 103 Coy R.E. Nose bags and hay nets also in use. Veterinary equipment in good order. Hay mixed in with limes of lambsfoots and bluebent. Recommendations: — to feed 4 times a day instead of 3 — to get Artis solid salt and mens 4 times day. I saw Artely - Officers 3 sthl. - Good conditions, 1st animal to N.S. Nothing working and second shoed attention. Enclosed Veterinary Officers visit D.R.O. horses tails. Visited 149th M.V.S.	
"	13/4/18		Visits 139 Field Ambulance Strength 16 N.B. - 17 I.B. - 76 motorbrough it. Hardness very good in the sun Sanitation very good. Munro marks 3 times a day — testing and watering 3 times a day, grazing in between Stew forage cub and full milk hay and bran. Grooming very good, Nosing good, no hay seeds. Visits 113 Rev L.A.B.	
"	13/4/18		R.W.F. Singh 9 N.B. 37.I.Ott. W.R. I.P.R. — I.B. North. Condition good except N.O. Grooming moderately good. Feeding and watering 3 times a day. Ashew forage testi [illegible] occasionally when reinstle	

Army Form C. 2118.

WAR DIARY
or
INTELLIGENCE SUMMARY.
(Erase heading not required.)

Instructions regarding War Diaries and Intelligence Summaries are contained in F. S. Regs., Part II. and the Staff Manual respectively. Title pages will be prepared in manuscript.

Place	Date	Hour	Summary of Events and Information	Remarks and references to Appendices
LEAUVILLERS	13/1/18		From Brigade. No clothing machine, no hay kind in use. Markings in the shoes. Sanitation moderately good. Manure moved to an official dump. Recommendations :- 1. More attention to the hoof and taking them out of work and give special attention. 1 horse lame - had sore wound found foot under run.	
			Field 10th Hrs. Bde. Strength 9 Off. 6 W.O. 31 NCOs N.R. 7 P.M. 11 R. 1 L.D. short. Sanitation good. result 7 horses in the case of one patient discussing the matter with the V.O. 16. Markings in the shoes. Sanitation good. Manure moved 3 times a day to Manure Dump. No clothing machine. Here is a hay kind. hoof not in use. 1 Off. taken hors de Bde. 1 horse somewhat strained - sick. Recommendations:- More attention to grooming and continued and hay level.	
			Shelfield 17th Bn. R.W.F. Strength 9 Off. 8 W.O. 19 A.M. 7 P.M. 11 R. - 1 L.D. short. Markings in the shoes excellent condition, Sanitation excellent. Lines well clean and tidy. Manure moved frequently to excellent dump. Grooming very good. Condition of animals excellent.	

WAR DIARY or INTELLIGENCE SUMMARY

Army Form C. 2118.

(Erase heading not required.)

Instructions regarding War Diaries and Intelligence Summaries are contained in F. S. Regs., Part II. and the Staff Manual respectively. Title pages will be prepared in manuscript.

Place	Date	Hour	Summary of Events and Information	Remarks and references to Appendices
LEALVILLERS	13/7/18		Shoeing good. 1 mule hind feet too long. Difficult to shoe. Cattle 1st Hay Line. Recommends Sanitation hay served out. Attention to mules feet previously referred to. Indulged 115 Rds. Strength 3 A.O. 1 2/Lt. 115. Attached 5 Shoeings in the Shoers Sanitation daily. Manure removed to dump 3 times daily. Institution of animals good. Grooming and Shoeing good. No dirt. No hay presses of staff entirely. Men is no staff until in this Bde. Issued on Aligned by R.10 that before leaving ERQUINGHEM I was Serving out to Lance Major they had not had one issued Feeding and Watering three times daily.	No chaff
				N.B.
"	14/7/18	Visited 38 Div. Signal Coy at 12h.45. 12h.7 F.13 Y.12 Shrt. Handings in No. Shrs. good. Sanitation good. Manure moved four times daily. Emptions of animals good. Grooming good. Shoeing good and watering 4 times daily. No hay lines but hay nets on picket on 1/3 of Rations. No lure of hay chaff in this Coy. two or 8 or 10 chaff. Sand and hay chopped.	

Army Form C. 2118.

WAR DIARY
or
INTELLIGENCE SUMMARY.
(Erase heading not required.)

Instructions regarding War Diaries and Intelligence Summaries are contained in F. S. Regs., Part II. and the Staff Manual respectively. Title pages will be prepared in manuscript.

Place	Date	Hour	Summary of Events and Information	Remarks and references to Appendices
LEAVILLERS	14/7/18		animals are remarkable as H.Q. and are being fed on 20 rations	
			D.M.Q. Horse Lines. I saw F.M.A. I saw tractor. Visited 38th M.M.	
			Sauala armed in eye. Progressing satisfactory. Saddle galls unimproving	
	15/7/18.		Visited D.M.Q. 1 case Abrasure. Visited 38th M.M.P. 1 horse destroyed	
			Abscess. Visited H.Q. M.M.S. Arrived one horse both destroyed Gunshot Wound.	
	16/7/18.		Visited B/36. M. Gun Bn. Strength 3 99 6 OR. C.F. 34. LOM	
			Mangings in the dung good Sanitation good. Manure taken to dump.	
			Feeding and watering 3 times a day. Sweing good. Condition good. always	
			Hay 12lbs + Day Green in feeds I meal difficult to three always	
			lbs 16 lbs Straw. Visited C/36. M. Gun Bn. Strength 3 99.	
			134. OR. C.S. 12M. 36. 3 LOM. Shirt Standings in the open.	
			good Sanitation good. Manure moved to officer dump. Condition	
			of animals satisfactory. Grooming requires much more attention.	
			Feeding and watering 3 times a day. No hay nets. No Nose	
			bags. Feeding arrangements very unsatisfactory.	

WAR DIARY or INTELLIGENCE SUMMARY

Army Form C. 2118.

Place	Date	Hour	Summary of Events and Information	Remarks and references to Appendices
LEALVILLERS	1/7/18		Visited B.H.Q. & 38th Div. Signal Coy. Horse lines. Received word from A.D.V.S. 1. No A.S.	
"	8/7/18		Visited & inspected D/Coy. 38 Div. M.Gun. Horse lines in the shirt. Manure moved to dumps twice daily. Fed 3 times & watering 3 times daily. Manure moved to dumps daily. Men seem keen. Grain forage given. Hay stood in use. Hay nets used in use. Condition of animals moderately good. Shoeing moderate. Horse lines in the Grooming unsatisfactory. Inspected A/35. M.Gun. Bn. Horse lines in the open. Manure fairly good. Manure moved away all day. Condition good. Shoeing fairly good. Watering 3 times daily. Shoeing short. Grazed little hay. Bivouacs in N.W. Grooming sufficient. Hay given. Inspected 114 & R.H. Arth. Horse lines in the open. Sanitation good. Manure moved to dumps any day. Shoeing good. Condition of animals excellent. Grooming good. Hay nets in use. Chaffing of straw. Hay given. Inspected 114 Bn. H.Q. Standings in the open. Chaffing of animals. Condition good. Sanitation good. Manure moved daily. Shoeing forage. Grooming good. Condition of animals excellent. Shoeing good.	

WAR DIARY
or
INTELLIGENCE SUMMARY.

Army Form C. 2118.

Place	Date	Hour	Summary of Events and Information	Remarks and references to Appendices
LEAVILLIERS	18/7/18		Inspected 13 Bn. Alerts. Mountings in the am. Sanitation good. Manure taken away twice daily. Watering 3 times daily.	
			Chaffing, Grain and Green forage. Also a little hay. Hay dust in nose.	
			Horses out at time of inspection. Inspected 15ᵗʰ Bn. Welsh.	
			Feeding 3 times daily. Hay nets work for horses & not mules. Ruff	
			cut up. Grain and green forage chaffed. Water 3 times daily.	
			Horses out and watering at time of inspection. Recommended	
			picketing to be given 4 hours daily. All Reg. Med's NCO.	
"	19/7/18		Conference with O.M.S. Signal Cy. & 38 M.M.P. Horse Lines.	
			Had interview with O.C. Ordnance in reference to the condition of animals in	
			122 Bde. R.F.A.	
"	20/7/18		Visited C/122 Bde R.F.A. Sanitation of animals very poor. Evacuated 13 for Debility.	
			Picked out 22 animals to go on Sicinus lines for Special treatment. Recommended no	
			feeding and watering 4 times daily. Sanitation good.	
			Rations to animals in Sicinus lines not to scale. Picketed	
			C/122. Bde. R.F.A. Sanitation of animals on the whole good. Evacuated 3.	

WAR DIARY or INTELLIGENCE SUMMARY

Army Form C. 2118.

(Erase heading not required.)

Place	Date	Hour	Summary of Events and Information	Remarks and references to Appendices
LEAVILLERS	30/7/18		Quality picked out 6 animals for Special treatment. Feeding & watering 3 times a day. Animals receive plenty of green stuff. Sanitation good. Inspected A/152 Bde. R.F.A. Condition good. Grooming very good. Flannelette Y animals for debility. Picked out 3 to 6 animals for Special attention. Feeding and watering 4 times a day. 4 leaks of roof sent down. Airy. Sanitation good. Hay nets in use. No hay bare. Inspected B/152 Bde. R.F.A. Condition of animals moderate. Flannelette Y animals for Debility. Picked out 3 animals for Special attention. Feeding 4 times a day in the open. Not too good, in course of alteration. Sanitation moderate. No manure in now. Day watering 3 times a day. Shifting all hind and portion of day. No making with feed. 1 animal evacuated for P.U.V. forage received every day. Interviewed J.O.C. 1 38th R.F.A. re condition of Hv. Bns. R.F.A.	
"	31.7.18		Inspected B/152 Bde. R.F.A. Condition of animals excellent. No show. Manure moved very day. Feeding and watering 4 times a day. Grooming good. Shoeing good. Everything excellent	

WAR DIARY or INTELLIGENCE SUMMARY

Army Form C. 2118.

Place	Date	Hour	Summary of Events and Information	Remarks and references to Appendices
LEALVILLERS	31-7-18		Inspected Hqrs. IVth Bde. RFA. Condition of animals good. Everything in good order. Inspected C/IVth Bde. RFA. Feeding and watering 4 times daily. Condition very good. Shoeing good. Sanitation good. Manure moved 3 times day. Chaffing hard — and ration of hay, and grain stuff, which is brought down from the Corps Incident. Arrivage Cord. Arg-mts in use. Forge also in use. Inspected 9/IV Bde RFA. Condition good. Sanitation good. Manure moved 3 times daily. Shoeing good. Feeding and watering 4 times a day. Supply of green stuff good. Hard + hay chaffed. Arg-mts + arrivages in use. Condition of mules not so good. Grooming fairly good. Inspected B/IVth Bde. RFA. Feeding + watering 4 times daily. Shoeing all hard and little hay. Sanitation good. Manure moved away once daily to dumps. Condition of animals moderate. Mules are getting better than Cyst. Bde RFA except mv — feed of oats Indian has been reduced for the past week. Recommended this should be lifted and proper ration given. Visited A.M.O. + Signal Coy ATW lines.	

WAR DIARY or INTELLIGENCE SUMMARY.

Army Form C. 2118.

(Erase heading not required.)

Instructions regarding War Diaries and Intelligence Summaries are contained in F. S. Regs., Part II. and the Staff Manual respectively. Title pages will be prepared in manuscript.

Place	Date	Hour	Summary of Events and Information	Remarks and references to Appendices
LEALVILLERS	22/7/18		Visited 49th MVS. DADVS & Signal Coy. horse lines. Visited & inspected animals of 155th Hov. RFA.	
"	23/7/18		Visited DADVS horse lines. Mixed Routine.	
"	24/7/18		Visited DADVS. Inspected No. 3 Sec. 38th AVC. Standings in the chev. my standing and to keep rains protecting. Advance standings good. Sanitation good. Condition of animals very good. Shoeing good. Watering 4 times a day feeding 3 times a day. Recommended feeding 4 times only instead of 3 times. Hay chopped. Recommended Hay served in new. All short and moved to reserve area. Condition of animals good. Shoeing good. Stay stable stables. Hay served in new standings under coort. in own lines. Visited 15th Am. Portch. who have now moved to new standings. Condition of animals good. Shoeing good. Sanitation good.	
"	25/7/18		Visited 113 Hov. RA. Standings in the chev. Sanitation good. Manure removed to dumps once a day. All short clothes and green stuff. Condition excellent. Shoeing good. Artillery and hay all in use. There is no hay issue.	

WAR DIARY or INTELLIGENCE SUMMARY

Army Form C. 2118.

Place	Date	Hour	Summary of Events and Information	Remarks and references to Appendices
LEALVILLERS	25/1/18		Bomb Mattresses report chaining feeding 4 times and watering 4 times daily. I saw Quilts boots in use. Relieved 1st Bn R.W.F.	
			Lines in the open. Sanitation good. Manure removed to dump twice	
			daily. Sanitation good. Excellent care of horses is certainly the force a	
			duty. Saw the 0/61 Horse. She seemed well. All straw chaffed, as	
			also green stuff feeding and watering 4 times daily. Arrangements	
			for feeding account of day sure in use. All too small	
			Inspected 16th Bn. R.W.F. Standings in the open. Sanitation good. Sanitation good.	
			Manure removed each day to dump. Day sure hay nets and	
			All straw chaffed, also green stuff. Watering 13 times a day	
			nosebags in use. Watering 13 times a day. Horses good	
			Recommend feeding to take place 4 times daily. Sanitation good.	
			Inspected 13 Bn. R.W.F. Standings in the open. Sanitation good. Manure	
			removed twice daily. Condition moderate. Horses good. Chaffing all	
			straw and a little hay. Feeding 3 times daily. Watering 4 times.	
			Day sure in use. Also hay nets and nosebags. 1 light Art. Limber	

WAR DIARY or INTELLIGENCE SUMMARY

Army Form C. 2118.

Place	Date	Hour	Summary of Events and Information	Remarks and references to Appendices
LEALVILLERS	25/7/18		This Unit is improving general animals for the Divisional Show & worked at the moderate condition of the truck of the animals is now by the one and strength, and giving extra forage to the animals in preparation for the show. Visited 38th D.H.Q. Horse Lines	
"	26.7.18		Conferred Veterinary Officers. Visited D.H.Q. & Signal Coy. Horse Lines	
"	27/7/18		Visited 38th D.H.Q. 38th M.M.P. & Signal Coy. Hqrs. 1 M.G.	
"	28.7/18		Visited No. 1. Section 38th D.A.C. Condition good & Public lines to be thoroughly washing & feeding 4 times daily. Shoeing good. Range bars making recommended and are to be constructed. Hay seed in unsatisfactory. Traces of construction inspected No. Y. Sec. 38. C.A.C. Making and feeding 4 times a day. Malt good. Shoeing good. Action of hay. Condition of animals good. Shoeing good. Sanitary in the open - Horse Manure moved 4 times daily. Forage store satisfactory and now in course of construction. Visited 330 Coy A.S.C. Sanitary excellent. Shoeing good. Sanitation good. Watering & feeding good - 4 times daily. Chaffing Plant. No hay issued. Unit forage 23 cwt each mixed Northwards. Arrangements satisfactory.	

WAR DIARY
or
INTELLIGENCE SUMMARY.

Army Form C. 2118.

Place	Date	Hour	Summary of Events and Information	Remarks and references to Appendices
LEAVILLERS	28/7/18		Visited Hqrs M.L.V. Sec. DHQ & Signal Coy horse lines.	
"	29/7/18		Visited 332. Coy A.S.C. Horse lines in the open. Condition of animals excellent. Sanitation good. Shoeing good. Visited 10th Provisers Bn. Hay & Straw and Ration of Hay & grain. Hay licer. Condition fairly good. Sanitation good. Shoeing indiff. Making & feeding 4 times daily. Hay wet. Animals & articles. Visited 333 Coy A.S.C. Feeding 3 times. Altering H lines. Condition good. Sanitation good. No hay lickr, otherwise arrangements good. Recommended H lines a day to feed, and new lanterns for mixing forage.	
"	30/7/18		Attended Ambulance of R.A.M.S. Entrance at AMS. office & Cath.S.	
"	"		Visited 331 Coy A.S.C. Feeding H times & watering H times. Animals in excellent condition. Shoeing good. No hay licer. Lanterns in use.	
"	31/7/18		Visited DHQ & Signal Coy horse lines. Visited Div. Hqrs R.F.A. 49th MDS fed Sec. Inspected sick animals at DHQ & Signal Coy. sent to Mamel.rr	

[signature]
D.A.D.V.S. MAJOR.
38th (WELSH) DIVISION.

CONFIDENTIAL.

WAR DIARY.

OF

D.A.D.V.S., 38th. (Welsh) DIVISION.

FROM

1st. AUGUST 1918.

TO

31st. AUGUST 1918.

(Volume XXXIII.)

[signature]
Major. A.V.C.

1st. September 1918.   D.A.D.V.S., 38th. (Welsh) DIVISION.

WAR DIARY or INTELLIGENCE SUMMARY

Army Form C. 2118.

Instructions regarding War Diaries and Intelligence Summaries are contained in F.S. Regs., Part II. and the Staff Manual respectively. Title pages will be prepared in manuscript.

(Erase heading not required.)

Place	Date	Hour	Summary of Events and Information	Remarks and references to Appendices
LEALVILLERS	1/8/18		Visit A/M Bde R.F.A. Condition good. All fed animals on the lines. Horses to reported fit. Visited framed horse which V.O. Jo. inspects as a case of Epizootic Lymphangitis. Visits 38th R.F.A. H.Q. and Horse Lines. Visits 38th D.H.Q. and Horse Lines from Res.	
"	2/8/18		Conference Veterinary Officers. Received intimation from 3rd Bde H.Q. that Colonel M.C. Quinnell, A/V.C. has been ordered to proceed from Base and take over command of H.Q. M.V.S. and will be going N.C. to Amd Estbtlishment.	
"	3/8/18		Accompanied O.D.V.S. Fourth Army, C.R.A. V.A.V.S. & Lieut Staff Capt. 38 R.F.A. and inspected 172nd & 175th Bdes R.F.A. Also 38 Bde Ammn Column.	
"	4/8/18		Veterinary horse shod and race meetings.	
"	5/8/18		Office routine.	
"	6/8/18		Visits Hq 3rd M.V.S. D.H.Q. Signed for horse lines.	
"	7/8/18		Accompanied by Colonel V. Lobb, inspected CIII Bde R.F.A. Condition of animals good. This Battery has gone down in condition since my last inspection. Inspects also New R.F.A. Condition of animals moderate. This Battery has improved since last inspection. Visits D/155 Bde R.F.A.	

WAR DIARY
or
INTELLIGENCE SUMMARY

Army Form C. 2118.

Place	Date	Hour	Summary of Events and Information	Remarks and references to Appendices
LEALVILLERS	7/8/16		Condition moderate. Blt. Bde. RFA. Condition fairly good.	31st. Bde. RFA
"	8/8/16		Condition good. 31st Bde. RFA. Condition moderately good. Very good condition. 31st. Bde. RFA. Condition good. Visit 38th D.A.Q. Signal Coy. Hq. M.T.S.	31st. Bde. RFA.
"	9/8/16		Conference Veterinary Officers. Visits D.H.Q. & Signal Coy. horse lines. 35th, R.A. H.Q. & Divisional Train H.Q.	
"	10/8/16		Visits Town Major, VARENNES. M.O. & reference to message received from Q. and ack. 31st Bde. to 93rd Bde. RFA. Same. Vaccinated animals to 49 MTS. Visit 38th D.A.Q. & M.M.P. horse lines.	
"	11/8/16		Visits 97th Bde. Signal Coy. & 35th D.H.Q. horse lines.	
"	12/8/16		Visits 113 Bde. H.Q. Condition of animals very good. Feeding and watering at times faulty. Sanitation only fair. Becoming fair. There is no forage farm. Chilling machine. No hay issued. No dum fracases. Visit 14th Div. R.M.F. Standings in the blew. Dum fracases in aid of detail sanitation good. Condition good. recently opened to an my brethris attack. Food Forage farm fail hardly big enough. Feeding and watering at times	

Army Form C.2118.

WAR DIARY
or
INTELLIGENCE SUMMARY.
(Erase heading not required.)

Place	Date	Hour	Summary of Events and Information	Remarks and references to Appendices
LEAVILLERS	12/8/16		A hay chaffing carried out at Bde. H.Q. y of 13 animals affected with mange and all with animals on horse lines - no dist. lines. Recommended dist. lines to be put out at once. With 16 Bn. R.W.F. Markings in the skin. Sanitation good. Condition my good, except two. Horse harness require building up. And forage stand to be made. With 13 Bn. R.W.F. Markings in the skin. Horses standing 1st day and night. Condition of animals good. Feeding and watering 4 times daily. Horse blankets require making up. Grooming good.	
"	13/8/16		With 6/353 An. M.Gun batt. Condition of animals and the rest of the horses good. 8 animals in good condition. Sanitation good. Feeding and watering 4 times daily. Grooming good. Shoeing good. Recommended to construct a place for storing forage. Improvement in cleanliness, feeding, and this low. With 13th An. M.Gun batt. Condition of grooming animals on the whole good. y of 13 animals in bad condition. Condition of animals. Markings in the skin. Sanitation my good. But marking special attention. Feeding & watering 4 times daily. Grooming	

WAR DIARY
or
INTELLIGENCE SUMMARY.

(Erase heading not required.)

Army Form C. 2118.

Place	Date	Hour	Summary of Events and Information	Remarks and references to Appendices
LEAVILLERS	13/8/18		rendered shoeing good. Sanitation inferment in animal management. Visited A/38. Bde. M. Gun Corps. Condition of animals on the whole good. 3 animals in poor condition requiring special attention. Sanitation good. Feeding & watering 4 times daily. Grooming good. Shoeing good. Foot harness excellent. Recommended to continue detail accommodation for shoeing forage. Visited & inspected B/38. An M Gun Corps. Condition moderately good. Several animals in poor condition. Sanitation good. Feeding & watering good. 4 times a day. Grooming good. Shoeing on the whole good. Foot harness excellent. Recommended shoeing shed to be given 16 animals in poor condition. Lieut W L CARON AVC assume and relieves for duty.	
"	14/8/18		Visited Col Signed Coy these lines.	
"	15/8/18		Visited 134. Coy R.E. lines in the open. Sanitation very good. Day lines & night bivouacs. Sanitation good. Grooming good. Condition very good. Shoeing v.v. horse shoeing good. Feeding & watering 4 times a day. Visited 151. Coy R.E. bivouacs in the open day by night lines delimited.	

WAR DIARY
or
INTELLIGENCE SUMMARY.

Army Form C. 2118.

Place	Date	Hour	Summary of Events and Information	Remarks and references to Appendices
LEAMILLERS	15/8/18		Sanitation good. Condition good. Shoeing moderate, grooming good. Feeding & watering 4 times a day. Hay fed at night. Line only. Chaffing machine good. Forage shed. Everything satisfactory. Recommended ant hives. Dagnets & meetings. Visited OC Pencil Fr. of American.	
			Horses & Mules. Hardings on the drive, front harness.	
			Sanitation good. Ant lines very good. Dagnets. Condition very good. Grooming good. Watering 4 times a day. Meetings in new Everything satisfactory. Captain H. Mulgatour AMC left and Command.	
"	16/8/18		Visited 133 Coy RE. Standings in the drive Condition good. Excell. V. Grooming good. Shoeing good. Sanitation good. Feeding & watering 4 times day. Visited C/III & D/III Bns RFA. Obs. Rec much improvement. Cliff Rec	
			still more room for improvement. Captain A. Young AVG proceeded to England for home duty. Interio- OAB Ar. AVM duty nil 2nd/Lt. OAB, horse lines. Visited HQ MVS.	
"	17/8/18		Visited HQ MVS & OAB.	
"	18/8/18		Visited HQ MVS AMR. Visited VARENNES and returned to French lines. Visit first at the request of the Corps Major.	

WAR DIARY or INTELLIGENCE SUMMARY

Army Form C. 2118.

Place	Date	Hour	Summary of Events and Information	Remarks and references to Appendices
LEALVILLERS	19/8/18		March 11th. Rev. N.D. Standings in the open. Becoming good. Feeding + watering 4 times daily. Shoeing not good. Chaffing machine in use. Feeding 3 times and hay twice daily. Sanitation good. March 4 times daily. Condition good, except two Minorca's Sanitation good. Recommended Feeding 4 limes daily. Hay used in the open, not satisfactory if mud blows as such is blown away. March 1st An R.W.F. Standings in the open. Hay + meal limes. Animals in use. Feeding + watering 4 times daily. Hot + 5 animals sick in condition moderate. Shoeing moderate. Sick rates feet lame too long. Chaffing now at the N.D. with 10th Bn. S.W.B. Standings in the open. Hay + meal lines. Feet except V. aggravatedly short. 1 mess cart horse, + the other leg very N.D. Seven 10th animals in deep lines, and not to be mobile. Standings in mud of what + in very unsatisfactory condition.	

T2134. Wt. W708—776. 500000. 4/15. Sir J. C. & S.

WAR DIARY or INTELLIGENCE SUMMARY

Army Form C. 2118.

Place	Date	Hour	Summary of Events and Information	Remarks and references to Appendices
LEALVILLERS	9/8/18		Lines hanging slack — suffering posts a few inches from the ground. No air lines. No chafing sores. Altogether very unsatisfactory. Visited HQrs. M/S B.S.D. Horse lines.	
"	30/8/18		Visited 14th Bn. Welsh Regt. Haidings on the drum, day & night lines, harness lines for night lines. Condition excellent. Grooming excellent. Picking arrangements very good. Making 4 times dry sanitation good. Manure removed daily. Shoeing very good. Visited 152 Fd. Amb. Haidings on the drum, day & night lines, horse harness. Grooming fairly condition fairly good. Except one mule. Feet in condition. Feeding arrangements unsatisfactory. His mort has existed a very good harness room and state for officers mounts, but has made a miserable attempt for a forage barn, which consists of a lite with bits of canvas and mutilated sheets. The shew is no more than 8' by 6' in size and is altogether inadequate to protect the forage from the weather. There is a small hay store about 3' in length, which consists of a mere pretence. The hard feeds is on the ground, there	

T2134. Wt. W708—776. 500000. 4/15. Sir J. C. & S.

WAR DIARY or INTELLIGENCE SUMMARY

Army Form C. 2118.

Instructions regarding War Diaries and Intelligence Summaries are contained in F. S. Regs., Part II. and the Staff Manual respectively. Title pages will be prepared in manuscript.

(Erase heading not required.)

Place	Date	Hour	Summary of Events and Information	Remarks and references to Appendices
LEALVILLERS	30/8/16		Has been no green forage for 7 days. Transport Mules & Horses the only exceptions. 7 issues of meat. And Horse Forage (half-strength) on 1/8/16. Not sent to HQ MUS. Have instructions for animals to be sent at once to MTS. Requested matter to O.A. & Q.M.G. Visited 13 Rn Welsh. Standings in open. Sanitation good. Day & night lines. Bent traverses erected. Mangers require repair to spears. 3 animals in bad condition. Have instructions for the sick animals to the Slaves on sick lines. Shoeing good. Grooming materially good. Feeding good. Forage turn in good but sick, not large enough. Visited 114 Bde. F.A. Artillery very good. Shoeing good. Grooming good. Sanitation good. Standings in the open. Day & night lines. Sanitation good. No. 2 Sec. D.A.C. Standings in the open. Day & night lines. Shoeing good. Grooming good. Using & watering at times daily. Everything satisfactory. No. 1 Sec. N.A.C. Standings in the open. Boy & night lines. Bent traverses erected. Sanitation good. Sanitation very good. Grooming good. And forage Excellent. Shoeing is only actual Forage turn in & Arrangements Excellent.	

WAR DIARY
or
INTELLIGENCE SUMMARY.

(Erase heading not required.)

Army Form C. 2118.

Instructions regarding War Diaries and Intelligence Summaries are contained in F.S. Regs., Part II. and the Staff Manual respectively. Title pages will be prepared in manuscript.

Place	Date	Hour	Summary of Events and Information	Remarks and references to Appendices
LEALVILLERS	20/8/16		Work and chief at times. Day's green forage twice daily.	Weighting
"	21/8/16		Satisfactory. Horses fit, improvement in shoeing. Visits D.H.Q. H.Q. M.V.S. C.LXV Bde. R.F.A. 105 Bn. L.I.B	
"	22/8/16		all D.M.V. Police. A.V.C. armed & inspected for duty, also Lieut. W. Carr	
"	23/8/16		A.V.C. to Base. Visits No. 3 Sec. D.A.C. H.Q. M.V.S.	
"	24/8/16		Visits "N" Special Coy. R.E. 178 Coy. Siege Bey R.E. Conference H.S.	
"	25/8/16		Visits D.H.Q. Signal Coy H.Q. M.V.S.	
"	26/8/16		Divisional move to Hedauville. Visits HQ M.V.S & gave instructions	
HEDAUVILLE	27/8/16		for section to move to Varennes. Divisional move from Hedauville to Bouzincourt	also HQ M.V.S.
"			march to same place.	
BOUZINCOURT	28/8/16		My office and HQ M.V.S. move from Bouzincourt to W.12. on outskirts of Aveluy ANGRE	
W.12.a.	29/8/16		Visits & inspects 115 114 115 Inf. Bde. M.I.Bs. mobile Sanitary animals. Visits D.H.Q	Battn. proceeding move into new lines.

Army Form C. 2118.

WAR DIARY
or
INTELLIGENCE SUMMARY.
(Erase heading not required.)

Instructions regarding War Diaries and Intelligence Summaries are contained in F. S. Regs., Part II. and the Staff Manual respectively. Title pages will be prepared in manuscript.

Place	Date	Hour	Summary of Events and Information	Remarks and references to Appendices
W 15 a central Sheet 57.D	29/8/18		Visited 132 Bde. R.F.A. No.1 & 2. Sections, 38th D.A.C. 38th D.H.Q.	
"	30/8/18		Visited No.3 Sec. 38th D.A.C. 38th D.H.Q.	
"	31/8/18		Visited 38th D.H.Q. 38th Div. Signal Coy. R.E.	

[signature]

MAJOR,
D.A.D.V.S. 38th (WELSH) DIVISION

CONFIDENTIAL.

WAR DIARY.

OF

D. A. D. V. S., 38th. (Welsh) DIVISION.

FROM

1st. SEPTEMBER 1918.

TO

30th. SEPTEMBER 1918.

(Volume XXXIV.)

1st. October 1918.

[signature]
Major. A.V.C.
D.A.D.V.S., 38th. (Welsh) DIVISION.

WAR DIARY
or
INTELLIGENCE SUMMARY.
(Erase heading not required.)

Army Form C. 2118.

Place	Date	Hour	Summary of Events and Information	Remarks and references to Appendices
ANCRE.	1/9/16		Visited 38th D.H.Q. & Col. Signal for Horse Lines. Visited "A" Batt. "B" Batt. & "C" Batt. 121 Brigade. R.F.A.	
"	2/9/16		A.D.O.I.S. Office and Hq. Mot. Vet. Sec. move to X.15.a.5.4. Sheet 57d. (map) Visited No.3 Sec. 38th. O.A.C. Macon Lines.	
X.15.a.5.4. Sheet 57d.	3/9/16		Visited and inspected 38th Bn. Machine Gun Corps. Animals are nothing in fairly good condition, in spite of the heavy mud during the present active operations.	
"	4/9/16		A.D.O.I.S. Office and Hq. Mot. Vet. Sec. move to S.14.c.3.7. Sheet 57.c. (Bray en tin le- Grand.) Visited 38th D.H.Q. & Signal Coy. Horse Lines.	
S.14.c.3.7. Sheet 57.c.	5/9/16		Visited C/121 Bde. R.F.A. In hard working condition. 5 animals understrength. B/121 Bde. Evacuate 5 horses for debility. 18 animals understrength. D/121 Bde. Evacuate 6 animals for debility. 13 animals understrength. A/121 Bde. Evacuated. 4 horses for debility. 11 animals understrength. Visite and inspected C/122. Bde. R.F.A. 6 animals for evacuation. 12 horses understrength. A/122. Bde. 5 horses for evacuation. 17 animals understrength. D/122. Bde. 1 horse for evacuation. 2 animals & Animals etc. B/122.	

Army Form C. 2118.

WAR DIARY
or
INTELLIGENCE SUMMARY.
(Erase heading not required.)

Instructions regarding War Diaries and Intelligence Summaries are contained in F. S. Regs., Part II. and the Staff Manual respectively. Title pages will be prepared in manuscript.

Place	Date	Hour	Summary of Events and Information	Remarks and references to Appendices
S.14.c.37 Sheet 57c	5/9/18		In good working condition.	
"	6/9/18		Visited D.H.Q. & 38th Bn. Signal Hq. 38th Bn. Machine Gun Coys.	
"	7/9/18		Visited D.H.Q. Inspected newly arrived Remounts, got Mrs Bohem.	
"	8/9/18		Visited Signal Coy Horse Lines.	
"			Visited 131. Field Ambulance. I saw pole gall. I saw Nomad. Heidi.	
"	9/9/18		D.H.Q. Horse Lines. I saw patient in a A.D.	
"			O.R.O.V.S. Office and HQ. Mot. Tpt. Sec. move to 0.35.c.3.4. Sheet 57c. (Le Transloy)	
LE TRANSLOY	10/9/18		Visited D.H.Q. and Signal Coy Horse Lines.	
"	11/9/18		Visited 113 Bau. M.H. Bn. & 115 Bn. Trench Coy & Pioneer Bn.	
"			and 139. Field Ambulance.	
"	12/9/18		Visited D.H.Q. O.R.O.V.S. Office and HQ. Mot Tpt. Sec. move to	
			ROCQUIGNY.	
ROCQUIGNY	13/9/18		Visited D.H.Q. Went out to select place for HQ. M.V.S. Killed	
"	14/9/18		O.R.O.V.S. and HQ. M.V.S. move to V.1.b.8.8. (near Epricourt.)	
V.1.b.88	15/9/18		Visited IVth Bn. 115. Bn. D.H.Q. Visited B O.R.O at night '17	

WAR DIARY or INTELLIGENCE SUMMARY

Army Form C. 2118.

Place	Date	Hour	Summary of Events and Information	Remarks and references to Appendices
V.1.b.8.8. Sheet 57c	15/9/18		Animals attacked by bombs from enemy aircraft, 1 mare killed outright, the balance were destroyed.	
"	16/9/18		Visits to D.H.Q. 38 D.A.C. H.Q. D.H.Q. Mt. Bde. 115 Bde. & 115 Bde.	
"	17/9/18		Visits D.H.Q. Inspected all sick animals at H.Q. M.M.S. Area No. 16. Vaccination.	
"	18/9/18		Visited 133. Bde. & 38 D.A.C. Visited Bde. H.Q. & Signal Coy. horse lines.	
"	19/9/18		Visited 114. Bde. Inspected two calls of poisoning in 15. Bn. Welsh Regt. Conference A.D.V.S. v. Lords, by motor giving location and treatment. Visited 10th Bn. No.8. Animals are in good condition. Visited 1st. Bde. R.F.A. – C Battery, condition of animals good, much entrenchment. B Battery, 1 section horse lines away on site, the other section conditions of animals is good. B Battery condition good all around. Accompanied by O.R.Q.M.S. inspected H.Q. Remounts which had just arrived for the Division, at No. 3 Section, O.R.C. Sent one horse to H.Q. M.M.S. the animal suffering from Police Paralysis. The rest of the Remounts were good.	

Army Form C. 2118.

WAR DIARY
or
INTELLIGENCE SUMMARY.
(Erase heading not required.)

Instructions regarding War Diaries and Intelligence Summaries are contained in F. S. Regs., Part II. and the Staff Manual respectively. Title pages will be prepared in manuscript.

Place	Date	Hour	Summary of Events and Information	Remarks and references to Appendices
N.b.8.8. Sheet 57c.	20/9/18		Infantry came out of line last night. American Artillery remains in gun positions. Conference Veterinary Officers.	
"	21/9/18		Visits R.H.Q. and Signal Coy. Horse lines. Accompanied by R.A.D.V.S. inspected Remounts which had arrived for the Division. Fairly good lot.	
"	22/9/18		Visits R.H.Q. Monte Louis Division BEAULENCOURT and inspected 13th Bn. Machine Gun Corps B/Coy. Condition of animals very good. Shoeing good. B/Coy Condition good. Shoeing good. C/Coy Condition of Animals moderately good. Shoeing moderately good. Made post-mortem examination on horse died Pleuro Pneumonia good. B/Coy Condition moderately good, two or three animals in poor condition.	
"	23/9/18		Visits 9/VIII Bde R.F.A. Condition of animals very poor, diagnosed 5 horses and 1 mule for Debility. Good forage, barn feeding is carried out satisfactorily. I do not think that the animals are put out to grazing enough. On Medicines too long. Any complaints not getting full ration of forage. Am taking the matter up with the A.D.S.O.	

Army Form C. 2118.

WAR DIARY
or
INTELLIGENCE SUMMARY.
(Erase heading not required.)

Instructions regarding War Diaries and Intelligence Summaries are contained in F. S. Regs., Part II. and the Staff Manual respectively. Title pages will be prepared in manuscript.

Place	Date	Hour	Summary of Events and Information	Remarks and references to Appendices
V.I & SS.	24/9/16		Visited B/132 Bde. R.F.A. Condition of animals good, evacuated one horse for debility.	
"	25/9/16		Visited and inspected D/132. Bde. R.F.A. Condition of animals moderate. C/132. Bde. R.F.A. Condition good. Feeding and grazing arrangements satisfactory.	
"	26/9/16		Visited 157 Bde. R.E. Condition of animals very good. Feeding and grazing fairly satisfactory. Visited 123. Bde. Coy. R.E. Condition of animals on the whole = good. Feeding and grazing arrangements fairly satisfactory. Visited & inspected 134. Field Coy. R.E. Condition of animals very good, not good. Visited (which Bn.?) Field coy R.E. Feeding and grazing arrangements satisfactory both 19th Bn. Visited (which Bn.?) feet too long. Condition of animals method shoeing not good. More attention to be had to shoeing.	
"	27/9/16		Visited and inspected 129th + 130th + 131st Field Ambulances. All animals are in excellent condition. Shoeing good, grazing arrangements satisfactory.	
"	28/9/16		Attended conference of D.A.D.N.S. Divisions at A.D.V.S. Office. V. Corps.	
"	29/9/16		Visited D.H.Q. and Div. Signal Coy. Horse lines.	

T2134. Wt. W708—776. 500000. 4/15. Sir J. C. & H.

Army Form C. 2118.

WAR DIARY
or
INTELLIGENCE SUMMARY.
(Erase heading not required.)

Instructions regarding War Diaries and Intelligence Summaries are contained in F. S. Regs., Part II. and the Staff Manual respectively. Title pages will be prepared in manuscript.

Place	Date	Hour	Summary of Events and Information	Remarks and references to Appendices
V.1.b.88	30/9/15		Visits D.H.Q. and Supply Coy Horse Lines. My Officer and Staff rejoined our A.D. today.	

Ian E. Lyon
MAJOR.
D.A.D.V.S. 53th WELSH DIVISION

CONFIDENTIAL.

WAR DIARY.

OF

D. A. D. V. S., 38th. (Welsh) DIVISION.

FROM

1st. OCTOBER 1918.

TO

31st. OCTOBER 1918.

(Volume XXXV.)

1st. November 1918.

[signature]
Major. A.V.C.
D.A.D.V.S., 38th. (Welsh) DIVISION.

Army Form C. 2118.

WAR DIARY
or
INTELLIGENCE SUMMARY.
(Erase heading not required.)

Instructions regarding War Diaries and Intelligence Summaries are contained in F. S. Regs., Part II. and the Staff Manual respectively. Title pages will be prepared in manuscript.

Place	Date	Hour	Summary of Events and Information	Remarks and references to Appendices
V.1.b.8.8.	1/10/18		Visited A.D.Q. horse lines. Went out to select site for H.Q. Mot. Vet. Sec.	
Sh.57.c.	2/10/18		Divisional move to Sorel-Le-(Grand). Visited H.Q.S Mot. Vet. Sec. D.H.Q. and Rec. Signal Coy horse lines. Accompanied by A.D.Q.M.G. inspected any sick or injured animals at M.S. Division, at No. 3 Sec. S. C.H.C. Forty gun'd situation.	
Sorel-Le-Grand.	3/10/18		Visited 171 + 178 Bdes. R.F.A. animals are picking in moderate condition. Inspected animals of 33' Coy. R.S.C.	
"	4/10/18		Accompanied by A.M.S. v. Oaths visited and inspected animals of 171 Bde. R.F.A. Visited H.Q. Mot. Vet. Sec. No. 3 Section S. C.H.C.	
"	5/10/18		Visited Mot. A.D.Q. and evacuated sick horse from 35e M.M.P. visited H.Q. M.V.S.	
"	6/10/18		Visited B.H.Q. and Signal Coy horse lines. visited H.Q. Mot. Vet. Sec. and inspected sick animals prior to evacuation	
"	7/10/18		Visited and inspected animals of 172 Bde. R.F.A. Division Arty. and H.Q. and H.Q. Mot. Vet. Sec.	
"	8/10/18		J.A.D.V.S. Offices and H.Q. Mot. Vet. Sec. move to X.18.c.9.5. St. Quentin Canal.	

WAR DIARY
or
INTELLIGENCE SUMMARY
(Erase heading not required.)

Army Form C. 2118.

Place	Date	Hour	Summary of Events and Information	Remarks and references to Appendices
X.L.C.95.	9/10/18		Visited O.H.Q. and Div Signal Coy. No.3 Sec. 38th D.A.C. Received mail from A.D.S. & Vet.S.	
"	10/10/18		D.A.C.I.S. Office and HQ. Mot Vet Sec. moved to MALINCOURT.	
"	11/10/18		Visited O.H.Q. " M.M.P. horse lines. Div Signal Coy.	
"	12/10/18		D.A.C.I.S. Office and HQ. Mot Vet Sec. moved to BERTRY.	
BERTRY	13/10/18		Visited 3rd A.H.Q. Signal Coy M.M.P. horse lines	
"	14/10/18		Visited B/121 Bde. R.F.A. Animals in the majority are good about 15 other horses in condition.	
			B/155 Bde. R.F.A. Animals in very good condition	
			B/152 New R.F.A. Condition of animals very good, except one which has low mounted fat flesh.	
			Class Bde R.F.A. Condition of animals could not be judged as animals were not in condition.	
"	15/10/18		Visited HQ. M.V.S. and inspected sick animals. Horse to Marneting.	
"	16/10/18		Visited the Maire of BERTRY and arranged for them to have the meat of carcases destroyed, to feed the civilians remaining in the territory suffered from the enemy.	

WAR DIARY or INTELLIGENCE SUMMARY

Army Form C. 2118.

Place	Date	Hour	Summary of Events and Information	Remarks and references to Appendices
BERTRY	11/11/18		Captain Graham AVC. came to say that he had 5 cases of Mange in C/32? Bn. Machine Batt. & proceeded with him and examined the animals. I found 1 horse and 4 mules with slight tongues and twelve members much infected with cats and blisters. Animals were isolated at time of visit. History on enquiry these animals formed a section of No. 16 which came from "A" Section, in front of Troisvilles M.C.O.C. Sent down a message to say that 14 mules and the transport officer horse was sick sent out to link others to arrive. An animal attain Madame ANC was sent for. He immediately visited as inside Nov. 17th. the lines although simulating Mangelike were of the nature of the Peliving of I gave instructions during the process might prove further which were ganged and admitted to Bertrie. Instructions gave instructions for all animals to have temperatures taken, any further temperatures to be recorded and animals on isolation lines, and strict watch met to me. Visit C/32? Bn. Machine Gun Batt. D.Ves. and Line Bn. Horse Lines.	

Army Form C. 2118.

WAR DIARY
or
INTELLIGENCE SUMMARY.
(Erase heading not required.)

Instructions regarding War Diaries and Intelligence Summaries are contained in F.S. Regs., Part II. and the Staff Manual respectively. Title pages will be prepared in manuscript.

Place	Date	Hour	Summary of Events and Information	Remarks and references to Appendices
BERTRI	16/10/15		Visit C/138th Bn. M.Gun Coys. Visit Adv. B.F.A. B/158 Adv. B.F.A. H.Q'rs met Vet. Sec. Conference Veterinary Officers.	
"	19/10/15		Visit 13 Bn. R.W.F. and examined Mule infected by Capt T. Graham A.V.C. as a case of Infectious sore mouth. Confirmed same with Capt A.N. Lewis A.V.C. as a case of gas poisoning. Gave instructions Armed for necessary precautions to be taken. Visit HQ. M.V.S. and ambulants Sick animals sent to evacuation.	
"	20/10/15		Callin ? MacFarlane A.V.C. returned from leave. Visit 13 + 14 Bns. R.W.F. 33rd An M.Gun Coys. B.H.Q. 2.F.A. 1 horse wounded by shell fire. Civ. Signal Coy 6 animals killed owing to night by Enemy Shell fire.	
"	21/10/15		Visited Sick animals at H.Q. M.V.S. sent to evacuation. Calline A.N. Lewis A.V.C. proceeded on 4 days leave. Visited B.H.Q. and Divisional Signal Coy.	
"	22/10/15		Visited B.H.Q. 33rd Div. Signal Coy. 13 An. R.W.F. 2/38 An. Machine Gun Coys.	
"	23/10/15		Visited HQ. M.V.S. and ambulants Sick animals sent to evacuation. Visited No. 1 Sec. 33 D.A.C.	

Army Form C. 2118.

WAR DIARY
or
INTELLIGENCE SUMMARY.
(Erase heading not required.)

Instructions regarding War Diaries and Intelligence Summaries are contained in F. S. Regs., Part II. and the Staff Manual respectively. Title pages will be prepared in manuscript.

Place	Date	Hour	Summary of Events and Information	Remarks and references to Appendices
BERTRY	24/10/18		O.R.O./S. Officer and H.Q. M.V.S. move to TROISVILLES	
TROISVILLES	25/10/18		Visits 13th & 17th Bns R.W.F. H.Q. Nos 1 & 2 Sections 83rd O.P.C. D.H.Q. Signal Coy & R.A. H.Q. horse lines	
"	26/10/18		O.R.A.V.S. Officer and H.Q. M.V.S. move to K.17.c.11.	
K.17.c.11	27/10/18		Inspected sick animals sent to evacuation @ H.Q. Mobile Vet Sec. North O.H.Q. Div. Signal Coy. R.A. H.Q. No 115 Bn. Trench lines Visits 13th Bn. R.F.R. Section. Sub Joined Hy. Sec. much away	
"	28/10/18		Visits D.H.Q. Signal Coy R.A. H.Q. 15th Loy. R.E. Advance Section Visits O/39 Bn Machine Gun Corps. 19th Pioneer Bn. Condition of animals and grooming excellent	
"	29/10/18		D.H.Q. H.Q. M.V.S. No.3 Section 83rd O.P.C.	
"	30/10/18		D.H.Q. Signals Coy P.L. R.A. H.Q. H.Q. M.V.S.	
"	31/10/18		Visits D.H.Q. 330 Coy R.A.S.C. Animals in very good condition 9/133. Bn. R.E.A. condition of animals very moderate. H.Q. M.V.S.	

[signature]
MAJOR,
D.A.V.S. 38th (WELSH) DIVISION

CONFIDENTIAL.

WAR DIARY.

OF

D.A.D.V.S., 38th. (Welsh) DIVISION.

FROM

1st. NOVEMBER 1918.

TO

30th. NOVEMBER 1918.

(Volume XXXVI.)

1st. December 1918.

Major. A.V.C.
D.A.D.V.S., 38th. (Welsh) DIVISION.

WAR DIARY or INTELLIGENCE SUMMARY.

Army Form C. 2118.

(Erase heading not required.)

Instructions regarding War Diaries and Intelligence Summaries are contained in F. S. Regs., Part II, and the Staff Manual respectively. Title pages will be prepared in manuscript.

Place	Date	Hour	Summary of Events and Information	Remarks and references to Appendices
MONTAY	1/11/18		Conference Veterinary Officers. Visits D.M.Q., R.A. H.Q. and Signal Coy. Horse lines	
"	2/11/18		Visits H.Q. Mob. Vet. Sec.	
			Accompanied by D.A.Q.M.G. proceeded to ROMERIES and inspected Remounts which had arrived for the Division.	
"	3/11/18		D.M.Q. Signal Coy. Horse lines. Visits H.Q. M.T.S. and inspected sick animals.	
			Arrival Nº 26 evacuations	
"	4/11/18		Accompanied by D.A.Q.M.G. proceeded to RUMILLY and inspected a further batch of Remounts which had arrived for the Division.	
"	5/11/18		D.A.D.V.S. Office and H.Q. Mob. Vet. Sec. move to WAGONVILLE.	
WAGONVILLE	7/11/18		D.A.D.V.S. Office and H.Q. M.V.S. move to ENGLEFONTAINE	
ENGLEFONTAINE	8/11/18		D.A.D.V.S. Office and H.Q. M.V.S. move to LOCQUIGNOL	
LOCQUIGNOL	9/11/18		Conference of D.A.D's.V.S. Divisions by A.D.V.S. 4 Corps at my Office.	
"	10/11/18		D.A.D.V.S. Office and H.Q. M.V.S. moves to AULNOYE	
AULNOYE	11/11/18		H.Q. M.V.S. Armistice terms comes into force.	
			Hours from NCO Horse	
"	13/11/18		Visits D.M.Q., R.A. H.Q. & Aux. Signal Coy. Horse lines	

Army Form C. 2118.

WAR DIARY
or
INTELLIGENCE SUMMARY.
(Erase heading not required.)

Instructions regarding War Diaries and Intelligence Summaries are contained in F. S. Regs., Part II. and the Staff Manual respectively. Title pages will be prepared in manuscript.

Place	Date	Hour	Summary of Events and Information	Remarks and references to Appendices
AULNOYE	14/11/18		Captain James Deford M.R.C.V.S. arrived and reported for duty with 131. Bde R.F.A. Mo. Captain A.M.V. Rivers R.V.C. gazetted for Home Service by Medical Board.	
"	17/11/18		Visited 131 Bde R.F.A. Condition of animals very good.	
"	18/11/18		Visited and inspected 132 Bde R.F.A. Condition of animals moderate, exclu- ding sick horses and on my own inspection.	
"	19/11/18		Captain L. Graham R.V.C. proceeded on 14 days leave.	
"	20/11/18		Visited D.H.Q. M.M.P. & Bde Signal Coy horse lines.	
"	22/11/18		Performed Veterinary Officer's duties. Visited sick animals at 119 M.V.S. prior to evacuation.	
"	23/11/18		Accompanied by D.A.D.V.S. visited No. 2 Sec D.A.C. and inspected Animals which had arrived for 32nd Divisional Artillery. 1 horse sent to 119 M.V.S. for destruction and 148 for issue as a remount.	
"	24/11/18		Visited D.H.Q. 38 M.M.P. Signal Coy & R.A.H.Q. horse lines. No. S.E. 13933 Sergt. E. Allgood R.V.C. sent for duty with Bliss Bde R.F.A.	
"	25/11/18		No. S.E. 5384 Sergt. Parris L. R.V.C. sent for duty with 131 Bde R.F.A.	

WAR DIARY
or
INTELLIGENCE SUMMARY

Army Form C. 2118.

Place	Date	Hour	Summary of Events and Information	Remarks and references to Appendices
Aut-No/E	24/11/18		No. S.C. 13973 Sergt. Chorley. M.C. A.V.C. arrived for duty with 38th Bn. Machine Gun Corps on 21/11/18. To relieve No. 1690 Sergt. Martin C.D.C. to Army Horse lines.	
"	25/11/18		Visit No. 3 Sec. D.A.C. H.Q. M.V.S. D.H.Q. horse lines.	
"	26/11/18		Visit 38th Bn. Machine Gun Corps. Animals are in moderate condition.	
			Vehicle sick animals of H.Q. M.V.S. sent to evacuation.	
"	27/11/18		Visit Clyst. Maj. R.F.A. and investigate 3 mares sick horses which occurred within the last few days — with a view to observing of — No.	
			same. There was no evidence of contagious disease.	
"	28/11/18		Accompanied by D.A.Q.M.G. visited and inspected Remounts for distribution.	
			Ponies units at No. 3 Sec. D.A.C. Critique and Charges at D.H.Q.	
			Machine Guns. 2 Remounts from inspection made at No. 3 the D.A.C. were sent back. 1 Artillery and 1 Camel Train confirmation.	
"	29/11/18		D.H.Q., H.Q. M.V.S. Signal Regt, R.F.A. H.Q. horse lines.	
"	30/11/18		Visit horses at D.H.Q. and inspected all animals.	
			Visit H.Q. M.V.S.	

CONFIDENTIAL.

WAR DIARY.

OF

D. A. D. V. S., 38th. (Welsh) DIVISION.

FROM

1st. DECEMBER 1918.

TO

31st. DECEMBER 1918.

(Volume XXXVll)

John Macpherson
Capt R.A.V.C.
for
Major. R.A.V.C.
D.A.D.V.S., 38th. (Welsh) DIVISION.

1st. January 1919.

Army Form C. 2118.

WAR DIARY
or
INTELLIGENCE SUMMARY.
(Erase heading not required.)

Instructions regarding War Diaries and Intelligence Summaries are contained in F. S. Regs., Part II. and the Staff Manual respectively. Title pages will be prepared in manuscript.

Place	Date	Hour	Summary of Events and Information	Remarks and references to Appendices
AULNOYE	1/12/18		Visited D.H.Q. H.Qs Mot. Vet. Sec. Inspected sick animals prior to evacuation.	
"	2/12/18		A.D.R. Rail. Signal Coy. 82 M.M.P. H.Q. Mot. Vet. Sec.	
"	3/12/18		A.M. Mr King Hindle through AULNOYE at 1100 hours. Visited H.Q. M.T.	
"	4/12/18		Visited 133. Bde. R.F.A. B/133 Bde condition of animals for evacuation. B/133 Bde condition of animals good. Admit 7 horses 4 horses evacuated for debility. of animals good. 7 animals evacuated for debility. C/133 Bde. animals condition good. A/131 Bde. R.F.A. Condition of animals fairly good. 7 horses evacuated for debility. 1 case suspected Mange. 3 M.T. and 1 Frank. Bathing shed 4 mectages and hoynets. B/131 Bde. Condition of animals good. 3 evacuated for Debility. B/131 Bde. condition of animals 5 horses Bathing shed at hoynets. Very short on horse shoes. evacuated for debility.	
"	5/12/18		Visited C/131 Bde. R.F.A. Animals are in good condition & evacuated for	

WAR DIARY or INTELLIGENCE SUMMARY

Army Form C. 2118.

(Erase heading not required.)

Instructions regarding War Diaries and Intelligence Summaries are contained in F. S. Regs., Part II. and the Staff Manual respectively. Title pages will be prepared in manuscript.

Place	Date	Hour	Summary of Events and Information	Remarks and references to Appendices
AULNOYE.	5/12/18		Jot Details.	
"	6/12/18		Visited 1 and inspected HQ. Nos. 1, 2 & 3 Sections, 33rd D.A.C. All animals are in good condition.	
"	7/12/18		With AD.V.S. & Staffs. S.A.G. M/S and committee for selection of Brood Mares for breeding purposes, inspected all animals brought as per instructions.	
"	9/12/18		Visited HQ. M/S. D.H.Q. Signal Coy. R.A. HQ. horse lines.	
"	10/12/18		Went out with O/C HQ. M/S to arrange for mule site for the M/S.	XIII Corps.
"	11/12/18		A.D.V.S. Office and HQ. M/S move to ½ Beaumont per request.	
BEAUMONT.	12/12/18		D.H.Q. Signal Coy, R.A. HQ. horse lines.	
"	13/12/18		Conference Veterinary Officers. D.H.Q. & HQ. M/S	
"	14/12/18		Signal Coy. D.H.Q. and HQ. M/S.	
"	15/12/18		To Bruxelles	
"	16/12/18		D.H.Q. HQ. M/S horse lines. D.A.C. HQ. M/S.	
"	17/12/18		Visited 33rd Signal Coy. R.A. HQ.	

Army Form C. 2118.

WAR DIARY
or
INTELLIGENCE SUMMARY.
(Erase heading not required.)

Instructions regarding War Diaries and Intelligence Summaries are contained in F.S. Regs., Part II. and the Staff Manual respectively. Title pages will be prepared in manuscript.

Place	Date	Hour	Summary of Events and Information	Remarks and references to Appendices
BERLAIMONT	18/12/18		Visits 3rd M.M.P. D.A.C. Signal Coy. - Hq. M.I.S. Horse lines.	
"	19/12/18		Visits 115th Inf. Bde. Hq. Signal Coy. D.A.C. Hq. M.I.S.	
"	20/12/18		Performed Veterinary Officers D.A.C. Signal Coy. Hq. M.I.S.	
"	21/12/18		Proceed on leave to England for 14 days.	

John M [signature]
Lt. Colonel R.A.V.C.
A/D.A.D.V.S. 38th (Welsh) Division

CONFIDENTIAL.

WAR DIARY.

OF

D.A.D.V.S., 38th. (Welsh) DIVISION.

FROM

1st. JANUARY 1919.

TO

31st. JANUARY 1919.

(Volume XXXVIII.)

1st. February 1919.

Major, R.A.V.C.
D.A.D.V.S., 38th. (Welsh) DIVISION.

Army Form C. 2118.

WAR DIARY
or
INTELLIGENCE SUMMARY.

(Erase heading not required.)

Instructions regarding War Diaries and Intelligence Summaries are contained in F.S. Regs, Part II. and the Staff Manual respectively. Title pages will be prepared in manuscript.

Place	Date	Hour	Summary of Events and Information	Remarks and references to Appendices
NEUVILLY	1/1/19.		D.A.D.V.S., and 49th. Mobile Veterinary Section move to MASNIERES.	
MASNIERES	2/1/19.		D.A.D.V.S., and 49th. Mobile Veterinary Section move to MALANCOURT.	
MALANCOURT.	3/1/19.		D.A.D.V.S., and 49th. Mobile Vetetinary Section to MEAULTE.	
MEAULTE.	4/1/19.		D.A.D.V.S. and 49th. Mobile Veterinary Section move to LAHOUSSOYE.	
LAHOUSSOYE.	5/1/19.		Received visit from A.D.V.S. Vth. Corps.	
"	6/1/19.		Inspected sick animals prior to departure to Vth. V.E.S. at PICQUIGNY.	
"	12/1/19.		D.A.D.V.S. returned from leave and resumed duties on 14/1/19.	
"	14/1/19.		Inspected and visited animals of 38th. Divisional Signal Coy., 39th. D.H.Q. and 38th. M.M.P.	
"	15/1/19.		Visited 49th. Mobile Veterinary Section. D.H.Q., Signal Coy. D.A.D.V.S. office move to QUERRIEU.	
QUERRIEU.	16/1/19.		Visited Divisional Headquarters, Signal Coy. and 38th. M.M.P.	
"	17/1/19.		Conference Veterinary Officers. Visited Divisional Headquarters, Signal Co.	
"	18/1/19.		Visited Nos. 1 and 2 Sections, 38th. Divisional Ammunition Column, issued instructions to Veterinary Officer in charge for "Y" cases to be tested with Mallein at once.	
"	19/1/19.		Visited 148th. Labour Coy., at AVELUY WOOD. Accopmanied by Divisional Remount Classifying Officer, classified animals of 38th. Divisional Signal Coy.	
"	20/1/19.		Visited MONTIGNY CHATEAU Inspected "Y" animals prior to despatch to Base Remount Depot, DIEPPE. Visited 121st. and 122nd. Brigades R.F.A. Classified animals that was left undone.	

Army Form C. 2118.

WAR DIARY
or
INTELLIGENCE SUMMARY.
(Erase heading not required.)

Instructions regarding War Diaries and Intelligence Summaries are contained in F. S. Regs., Part II. and the Staff Manual respectively. Title pages will be prepared in manuscript.

Place	Date	Hour	Summary of Events and Information	Remarks and references to Appendices
QUERRIEU.	21/1/19.		Visited 121st. and 122nd. Brigades. Classified animals who were out working yesterday.	
"	22/1/19.		Visited 13th. and 15th. Bn. Welsh Regt., and 332nd. Coy. A.S.C. and classified animals, with Divisional Classifying Remount Officer. Visited 122nd. Brigade R.F.A. with Divl. Remount Officer and inspected "Y" animals for despatch to Base Remount Depot, DIEPPE. Classified remainder of Divl. Signal Coy. horses. Visited and inspected and classified animals of 114th. Infantry Brigade and 14th. Bn. Welsh Regt.	
"	23/1/19.		Classified animals of 124th. Field Coy. R.E. with Divisional Remount Classifying Officer. Visited Divisional Headquarters and Divl. Signal Coy. Horse lines. Tested one officer's Charger, 38th. D.H.Q., for despatch to ENGLAND.	
"	24/1/19.		Conference Veterinary Officers. Accompanied by Divisional Remount Classifying Officer, classified animals of 2nd. and 17th. Bns. R.W.F.	
"	25/1/19.		Accompanied by Divisional Classifying Officer, classified animals of 123rd. and 151st. Field Cos. R.E.	
"	26/1/19.		Visited 49th. Mobile Veterinary Section and inspected Sick animals. Visited Divisional Headquarters and Divisional Signal Coy. R.E.	
"	27/1/19.		Inspected 145 "Y" animals for despatch to BOURDON for Base Remount Depot, DIEPPE. Classified animals of 115th. Infantry Brigade and 10th. Bn. S.W.B.	
"	28/1/19.		Visited 211st. Prisoners of War Coy. at BRAY and attended to sick horses. Accompanied by Divisional Remount Classifying Officer, classified animals of 330th. Coy. A.S.C.	
"	29/1/19.		Accompanied by Divisional Remount Classifying Officer, classified animals of 331st. Coy. A.S.C. 14th. and 16th. Bns. R.W.F.	

Army Form C. 2118.

WAR DIARY
or
INTELLIGENCE SUMMARY.
(Erase heading not required.)

Instructions regarding War Diaries and Intelligence Summaries are contained in F. S. Regs., Part II. and the Staff Manual respectively. Title pages will be prepared in manuscript.

Place	Date	Hour	Summary of Events and Information	Remarks and references to Appendices
QUERRIEU.	30/1/19.		Accompanied by Divisional Remount Classifying Officer, classified animals of 13th. Bn. R.W.F. and 130th. Field Ambulance.	
"	31/1/19.		Conference Veterinary Officers. Visited Divisional Headquarters and Divisional Signal Coy. R.E. horse lines.	

[signature]

Major. R.A.V.C.
D. A. D. V. S., 38th. (Welsh) DIVISION.

CONFIDENTIAL.

WAR DIARY.

OF

D.A.D.V.S., 38th. (Welsh) DIVISION.

FROM

1st. FEBRUARY 1919.

TO

28th. FEBRUARY 1919.

(Volume XXXIX.)

1st. March 1919.

Major, R.A.V.C.
D.A.D.V.S., 38th. (Welsh) DIVISION.

Army Form C. 2118.

WAR DIARY
or
INTELLIGENCE SUMMARY.
(Erase heading not required.)

Instructions regarding War Diaries and Intelligence Summaries are contained in F. S. Regs. Part II. and the Staff Manual respectively. Title pages will be prepared in manuscript.

Place	Date	Hour	Summary of Events and Information	Remarks and references to Appendices
QUERRIEU.	1/2/19.		Accompanied by Divisional Remount Officer, visited 131st. Field Ambulance and classified all animals.	
"	2/2/19.		Visited Divisional Signal Coy. R.E. Nos. 1. and 2. Sections, 38th. D.A.C. and 124th. Coy. R.E. to select "Z" animals for despatch to PARIS.	
"	3/2/19.		Inpsected 51 "Z" animals prior to despatch to BOURDON, en route for PARIS. Accompanied by Divisional Remount Officer, visited 129th. Field Ambulance, 123rd. Coy. R.E. and 333rd. Coy. R.A.S.C. and classified all animals.	
"	4/2/19.		Classified animals of 38th. Divisional Headquarters and 49th. Mobile Veterinary Section at ALLONVILLE, with Divisional Remount Officer.	
"	5/2/19.		Inpsected 55 "Y" animals prior to despatch to BOURDON. Visited BEHENCOURT, inspected and classified remaining animals with Units, which had not already been classified.	
"	6/2/19.		Accompanied by Divisional Remount Officer, visited GLISSY and classified all remaining animals of this Division in that Area, which had not already been classified. In the afternoon, visited 253rd. P. O. W. Coy. Evacuated two horses for Debility.	
"	7/2/19.		Conference with Veterinary Officers, 38th. Division. Visited 38th. Divisional Headquarters and Divl. Signal Coy.	
"	8/2/19.		With Divisional Remount Officer, visited and selected a number of "Z" animals from 115th. Inf. Bde., 122nd. Brigade R.F.A. and 130th. Field Ambulance.	
"	9/2/19.		Accompanied by Divisional Remount Officer, visited and selected "Y" animals from 114th. Inf. Bde., 122nd. Brigade R.F.A. and 38th. Divisional Train.	
"	10/2/19.		Inspected 127 "Y" animals and 48 "Z" animals which were despatched to BOURDON, en route for Base Remount Depot, DIEPPE. Visited 49th. Mobile Veterinary Section.	

Army Form C. 2118.

WAR DIARY
or
INTELLIGENCE SUMMARY.
(*Erase heading not required.*)

Instructions regarding War Diaries and Intelligence Summaries are contained in F. S. Regs., Part II. and the Staff Manual respectively. Title pages will be prepared in manuscript.

Place	Date	Hour	Summary of Events and Information	Remarks and references to Appendices
QUERRIEU.	11/2/19.		Visited G.H.Q. Farms at CORBIE and branded 150 horses, to be ready for sale on 12/2/19. Met D.D.V.S., Third Army at CORBIE. Visited 49th. Mobile Veterinary Section.	
"	12/2/19.		Visited 13th. Bn. R.W.F. Divisional Headquarters. Signal Coy. R.E.	
"	13/2/19.		Visited 49th. Mobile Veterinary Section. Divisional Headquarters.	
"	14/2/19.		Conference with Veterinary Officers, 38th. Division. Visited CORBIE with Divisional Remount Officer and interviewed Area Commandant.	
"	15/2/19.		Visited 49th. Mobile Veterinary Section at ALLONVILLE. D.H.Q. M.M.P.	
"	16/2/19.		Inspected 102 "Y" animals prior to despatch to BOURDON, en route for Base Remount Depot, DIEPPE. Visited 49th. Mobile Veterinary Section.	
"	17/2/19.		Visited Divisional Headquarters, Signal Coy. horse lines.	
"	18/2/19.		Visited Divisional Headquarters, Signal Coy. horse lines.	
"	19/2/19.		Inspected 200 "Z" animals for despatch to 5th. Veterinary Evacuation Station at MONTIERE. Animals to be sold at AMIENS on Saturday, 22nd. inst.	

Army Form C. 2118.

WAR DIARY
or
INTELLIGENCE SUMMARY.
(Erase heading not required.)

Instructions regarding War Diaries and Intelligence Summaries are contained in F. S. Regs., Part II. and the Staff Manual respectively. Title pages will be prepared in manuscript.

Place	Date	Hour	Summary of Events and Information	Remarks and references to Appendices
QUERRIEU	20/2/19.		Visited Divisional Headquarters, Signal Coy. horse lines.	
"	21/2/19		Conference with Veterinary Officers, 38th Division.	
"	22/2/19.		Visited Divisional Headquarters. No. 22227, Pte. O.G.THOMAS, 6th Bn. South Wales Borderers, Clerk to D.A.D.V.S., 38th Division, left for demobolization. Instructions for demobolization of Major F.C.GAVIN, D.A.D.V.S., 38th Division, cancelled.	
"	23/2/19.		Visited Divisional Headquarters.	
"	24/2/19.		Inspected 200 "Z" Animals prior to despatch to FORGES-LES-EAUX. Visited No. 141 Chinese Labour Company and evacuated two horses to 49th M.V.S. Visited Divisional Headquarters in the evening re despatch of horses tomorrow.	
"	25/2/19		Inspected 202 "Z" Animals prior to despatch to No. 5 V.E.S. for sale. Visited 49th M.V.S. with A.D.V.S., V Corps. Visited Divisional Headquarters.	
"	26/2/19.		Visited 49th Mobile Veterinary Section. Inspected two mules required for Divisional Headquarters, but same not approved.	
"	27/2/19		Inspected two mules for Divisional Headquarters, sent to replace ones not approved of yesterday. Visited Divisional Headquarters re further sale of Animals. Visited 49th M.V.S. with Remount Officer to superintend branding, etc. of animals for sale tomorrow at AMIENS.	
"	28/2/19.		Attended Sale of Animals at AMIENS with Remount Officer, and sold 348 Animals, averaging 1072.12 francs.	

Major, R.A.V.C.,
D.A.D.V.S., 38th (Welsh) Division.

CONFIDENTIAL.

WAR DIARY

OF

D. A. D. V. S., 38th (WELSH) DIVISION

FROM

1st MARCH, 1919

TO

31st MARCH, 1919.

(Volume XL).

John Macfarlane
Captain, R.A.V.C.,
A/D.A.D.V.S., 38th (Welsh) Division.

1st April, 1919.

Army Form C. 2118.

WAR DIARY
or
INTELLIGENCE SUMMARY.
(Erase heading not required.)

Instructions regarding War Diaries and Intelligence Summaries are contained in F.S. Regs., Part II. and the Staff Manual respectively. Title pages will be prepared in manuscript.

Place	Date	Hour	Summary of Events and Information	Remarks and references to Appendices
QUERRIEU	1/3/1919		Accompanied by Remount Officer, classified two horses belonging to 38th Div. M.M.P.	
"	2/3/1919		Received allotment for demobolization of No. 595 Pte. A. PITSON, 49th M.V.S.	
"	3/3/1919		Inspected 39 animals - 1 for re-purchase and 38 for purchase. To D.H.Q. with Remount Officer to inspect horse, purchase of which is desired by Lt. Col. J.E.MUNBY, G.S.O. 1, 38th Division. To 49th M.V.S. to arrange about "X" Animals to be sent to the Base on the 5th instant, and about "Z" Animals for sale at AMIENS on the 7th.	
"	4/3/1919		Received instructions for demobolization of No. 2815 Sergt. W.C.PUTNAM, attached No. 2 Section, 38th D.A.C. To Divisional Headquarters re sale of Horses. Despatched two Horses to No. 14 Veterinary Hospital, ABBEVILLE, for transfer to 4th Dragoon Guards for General CARTON DE WIART. Visited 49th M.V.S.	
"	5/3/1919		Inspected 200 "X" Horses and despatched same to BOURDON CAMP en route for ENGLAND. Visited D.H.Q.	
"	6/3/1919		Visited 49th M.V.S. both morning and afternoon superintending the branding and numbering, etc. of the animals for sale on the 7th instant. Interviewed "D" 38th Div. H.Q. with regard to Units sending in the full numbers as instructed.	
"	7/3/1919		Conference of Veterinary Officers. Visited Sale in AMIENS of 353 "Z" Animals. Average prices obtained:- Horses 931 francs; Mules 707.5 francs.	
"	8/3/1919		Inspected horse to be purchased by Lt. Col. MUNBY, G.S.O. 1, 38th Div. Attended sick horse at Horse Lines of 38th Div. Signal Coy. Visited AMIENS and inte rviewed D.D.V.S., 3rd Army. Preparation of report on equipment of Veterinary Services.	
"	9/3/1919		Received allotment for the demobolization of No. 7572, Pte. J.F.YALLOP, 49th M.V.S. Inspected 27 "Y" Animals before departure for BOURDON en route for ENGLAND; also 4 "X" Horses for BOURDON en route for COLOGNE. Sent in report on Veterinary Equipment to Major-General T.A.CUBITT, Commanding 38th Division.	

Army Form C. 2118.

WAR DIARY
or
INTELLIGENCE SUMMARY.
(Erase heading not required.)

Instructions regarding War Diaries and Intelligence Summaries are contained in F. S. Regs., Part II. and the Staff Manual respectively. Title pages will be prepared in manuscript.

Place	Date	Hour	Summary of Events and Information	Remarks and references to Appendices
QUERRIEU	10/3/1919		Inspected 45 "X" Horses - 44 before departure for BOURDON en route for DIEPPE, and 1 re-classified. Attended at Div. H.Q. and gave evidence before Comission on Equipment of the Veterinary Services. Made recommendations in accordance with my Report of yesterday, with the addition of a limbered wagon for M.V.S. and 200 web halters and equipment for M.V.S. and 300 web halters and equipment for V.E.S.	
"	11/3/1919		Inspected the animals of the 38th Bn. M.G.C. - condition good; shoeing bad; grooming moderate. Visited the 49th M.V.S. and inspected the animals for sale tomorrow.	
"	12/3/1919		Attended Sale at CORBIE of 49 "Z" Animals.	
"	13/3/1919		Visited 49th M.V.S. and superintended the branding, etc. of "Z" Animals from the 38th Div. R.A. for sale on the 15th instant.	
"	14/3/1919		Inspected and re-classified two mules from the 115th Brigade Headquarters. Attended 49th M.V.S. and superintended the branding, numbering, etc. of animals for sale tomorrow. Withdrew two Heavy Draught horses from the sale in accordance with D.D.R's wire.	
"	15/3/1919		Attended sale at AMIENS of 300 "Z" Animals. Average prices:- Horses 1248.6 francs; Mules 890.4 francs.	
"	16/3/1919		Attended rendezvous at MONTIGNY CHATEAU and inspected 16 "X" Horses and 51 "X" Mules transferred from the 38th Div. R.A. and 38th D.A.C. to the 38th Bn. M.G.C. Inspected 10 "X" Horses en route for BOURDON and COLOGNE. Received instructions for the demobilization of No. 445 Corpl. A.BOND, 49th M.V.S. and No. 12767 Sgt. A.GRAY, attached 122 Brigade, R.F.A.	
"	17/3/1919		Visited Div. H.Q. to bid good-bye to Major-General T.A.CUBITT on his leaving the Division.	

Army Form C. 2118.

WAR DIARY
or
INTELLIGENCE SUMMARY.
(Erase heading not required.)

Instructions regarding War Diaries and Intelligence Summaries are contained in F.S. Regs., Part II. and the Staff Manual respectively. Title pages will be prepared in manuscript.

Place	Date	Hour	Summary of Events and Information	Remarks and references to Appendices
QUERRIEU	18/3/1919		Visited No. 267 P.O.W. Coy. at MORLANCOURT - all animals in good condition; two mules very old; one blind, the other two old for work-- try to exchange. Visited No. 222 P.O.W. Coy., MEAULTE - one very old horse, very poor - try to exchange. Visited 120 P.O.W. Coy., MEAULTE - one horse with suppurating wound on the heel, ordered him to be sent to 49th M.V.S. tomorrow to try and get another in his place. Visited 289 P.O.W. Coy., MEAULTE - one very old horse in very poor condition - try to exchange. Visited No. 258 P.O.W. Coy., MEAULTE - all correct; animals in fairly good condition.	
"	19/3/1919		Inspected 12 "Z" Riders to be sent to No. 5 V.E.S., MONTIERES - passed 11 and evacuated one mare from the 122 Brigade R.F.A. to 49th M.V.S. for destruction. Re-classified one horse from the 38th Div. R.A. from "Y" to "Z". Received instructions for No. 5071, Pte. J.MARRIOTT and No. 16996, Pte. B.LUSH, 49th M.V.S., to be transferred to No. 5 V.E.S.	
"	20/3/1919		Inspected 5 "Z" Horses and 14 "Z" Mules before departure for BOURDON. Interviewed A.D.V.S., V Corps, at QUERRIEU re Capt. J.M.CULHANE, recommended for service with Indian R.A.V.C., and other matters Visited 49th M.V.S. in the afternoon and inspected "Z" Mules for sale tomorrow.	
"	21/3/1919		Inspected 7 "X" H.D. Horses before their departure for BOURDON CAMP. Inspected 5 "X" L.D. Horses for transfer from the 38th Div. Train to the 38th Bn. M.G.C. Conference of Veterinary Officers. Visited sale in AMIENS of 103 "Z" Mules and 3 "Z" Horses.	
"	22/3/1919		Visited Railhead at LA FLAQUE and examined linseed cake; gave certificate for same, with reservations. Received instructions for the demobilization of Major F.C.GAVIN, D.A.D.V.S., 38th Division.	
"	23/3/1919		Inspected 26 "X" Horses and 100 "X" Mules before their departure for BOURDON CAMP. Visited Divisional Headquarters.	
"	24/3/1919		Gave instructions for Captain J.M.CULHANE, in charge of 122nd Bde. R.F.A. to take over duties of O.C., 49th M.V.S. and Captain J.MACFARLANE, O.C., 49th M.V.S., to take over duties of D.A.D.V.S., 38th Division.	

Army Form C. 2118.

WAR DIARY
or
INTELLIGENCE SUMMARY.
(Erase heading not required.)

Instructions regarding War Diaries and Intelligence Summaries are contained in F. S. Regs., Part II. and the Staff Manual respectively. Title pages will be prepared in manuscript.

Place	Date	Hour	Summary of Events and Information	Remarks and references to Appendices
QUERRIEU	25/3/1919		Visited D.H.Q. Received allotments for the demobolization of No. 11002, Pte. W. LITTLE, 49th M.V.S.; and No. S.E. 13933, Sergeant J.L. APPLEYARD, attached B/122 Bde. R.F.A.	
"	26/3/1919		Inspected 4 "X" Mules before departure for BOURDON. Captain J.M. CULHANE, R.A.V.C. I/c 122 Bde. R.F.A. took over duties of O.C., 49th M.V.S., and Captain JOHN MACFARLANE, R.A.V.C., O.C. 49th M.V.S., came to Div. Headquarters to take over duties of D.A.D.V.S. Detailed No. S.E. 23850, Sgt. E.B. ABRAHAMS, attached 121 Bde. R.F.A. to proceed to Devastated Areas, GREVILLERS. Gave instructions for No. S.E. 12803, Sgt. J.J. BROWN, No. 1 Sec. D.A.C.; and No. S.E. 22505, Sgt. F.G. THORNTON, D/121 Bde. R.F.A. to proceed to 49th M.V.S. and there to await further orders.	
"	27/3/1919		Visited AMIENS and collected money for the Animals sold on the 21/3/1919.	
"	28/3/1919		Major F.C. GAVIN, D.A.D.V.S., proceeded to England for demobolization. Captain J.H. WATT, I/c 121 Bde. R.F.A., proceeded to England on Special Leave. Made arrangements for move of 49th M.V.S. from ALLONVILLE to QUERRIEU – arranged billets. Detailed No. S.E. 22976, Sergeant T. DEANE to proceed to Devastated Area, North, YPRES.	
"	29/3/1919		Inspected 38 "Z" Horses and 28 "X" Horses before departure for BOURDON CAMP. Gave instructions for Captain J.M. CULHANE, O.C., 49th M.V.S. and Captain T. GRAHAME, I/c Infantry Group to report to D.A.D.V.S., Lowland Division, tomorrow for duty. Received instructions for demobolization of No. S.E. 7803, Sgt. W.C. FRECKNALL, attached 115th Infantry Bde; No. S.E. 7536 Sgt. J.S. MYLES, attached C/121 Bde. R.F.A. and No. 21725 Pte. MILLINER, J., 49th M.V.S.	
"	30/3/1919		Captain J.M. CULHANE, O.C., 49th M.V.S. and Captain T. GRAHAME, I/c Infantry Group, proceeded to Lowland Division for duty. No. 23850 Sgt. E.B. ABRAHAMS, attached No. 121 Bde R.F.A. proceeded to Devastated Area, North, GREVILLERS. No. S.E. 22976, Sgt. T. DEANE, attached 38th Bn. M.G.C., proceeded to Devastated Area, North, YPRES. Visited sick animals at No. 202 Prisoners of War Company and "C" Coy., Tank Field Battalion, LA FLAQUE.	

Army Form C. 2118.

WAR DIARY
or
INTELLIGENCE SUMMARY.
(Erase heading not required.)

Place	Date	Hour	Summary of Events and Information	Remarks and references to Appendices
QUERRIEU	31/3/1919		Received instructions from A.D.V.S., V Corps, that 49th M.V.S. is to be reduced to Cadre strength at once, and surplus personnel sent to No. 5 V.E.S. Saw D.A.A.G., 38th Div. Headquarters on the matter. No. 23183, Pte. R. HOLT, 49th M.V.S., transferred to No. 5 V.E.S., and No. 29642 Pte. W. BARTHOLOMEW, 49th M.V.S., ordered to report at No. 5 V.E.S. on his return from leave to the United Kingdom. No. S.E. 22505, Sgt. THORNTON, F.G. proceeded to C/190 Bde. R.F.A., London Division, for duty.	

John Macfarlane
Captain, R.A.V.C.,
D.A.D.V.S., 38th (Welsh) Division.

CONFIDENTIAL.

WAR DIARY

OF

D. A. D. V. S., 38th (WELSH) DIVISION

FROM

1st APRIL, 1919

TO

5th APRIL, 1919.

(Volume XLI)

John Macfarlane
Captain, R.A.V.C.,
D.A.D.V.S., 38th (Welsh) Division.

5-4-1919.

Army Form C. 2118.

WAR DIARY
or
INTELLIGENCE SUMMARY.

(Erase heading not required.)

Instructions regarding War Diaries and Intelligence Summaries are contained in F. S. Regs., Part II. and the Staff Manual respectively. Title pages will be prepared in manuscript.

Place	Date	Hour	Summary of Events and Information	Remarks and references to Appendices
QUERRIEU	1/4/1919		Received instructions for the demobolization of Captain J. Macfarlane. Visited 49th M.V.S. and 38th Div. H.Q.	
"	2/4/1919		Inspected "X" Horse from the 2nd R.W.F. before despatch to BOURDON.	
"	3/4/1919		Received wire from A.D.V.S., V Corps, to re-constitute 49th M.V.S. Examined horses belonging to the Machine Gun Battalion. Arranging about surplus wallets of R.A.V.C. Sergeants. Interviewed A.D.V.S., V Corps, re re-constitution of M.V.S., etc.	
"	4/4/1919		A.D.V.S., V Corps, visited D.A.D.V.S., 49th M.V.S., and 38th Div. H.Q. Office Routine, Returns, etc. Arranged about packing records of D.A.D.V.S. for return to R.A.V.C. Records Office, WOOLWICH.	
"	5/4/1919		Office of D.A.D.V.S. closed. Captain J. Macfarlane proceeded to England for demobolization.	

John Macfarlane

Captain, P.A.V.C.,
D.A.D.V.S., 38th (Welsh) Division.

www.ingramcontent.com/pod-product-compliance
Lightning Source LLC
Chambersburg PA
CBHW080827010526
44112CB00015B/2470